A NEST
OF TIGERS

A NEST
OF TIGERS

The Sitwells in Their Times

by

JOHN LEHMANN

with illustrations

An Atlantic Monthly Press Book

LITTLE, BROWN AND COMPANY   BOSTON   TORONTO

LIBRARY OF CONGRESS CATALOG CARD NO. 68-24243
FIRST AMERICAN EDITION

ATLANTIC–LITTLE, BROWN BOOKS
ARE PUBLISHED BY
LITTLE, BROWN AND COMPANY
IN ASSOCIATION WITH
THE ATLANTIC MONTHLY PRESS

PRINTED IN THE UNITED STATES OF AMERICA

ACKNOWLEDGMENTS

My grateful thanks are due to Sir Osbert Sitwell and Mr Sacheverell Sitwell, Dame Edith Sitwell posthumously, Mr Reresby Sitwell, and Mr Francis Sitwell, Dame Edith's literary executor, for all the friendly assistance they have given me, and their unfailing co-operation in putting at my disposal, and allowing me to quote from, so much of the material that made this book possible. I would also like to thank, in this connection, the publishers of their works which are still in print: Messrs Macmillan, Hutchinson, Gerald Duckworth, and Cassell.

My particular thanks are due to Sir Osbert Sitwell, the present head of the family, for having listened to my reading of the typescript so patiently, and having objected only on points of accuracy, never on criticisms I may have expressed.

My thanks also go to the following recipients of letters from Dame Edith, who readily put them at my disposal: The Dowager Lady Aberconway, Mr Harold Acton, Mr Ronald Bottrall, Sir Maurice Bowra, Mr Rache Lovat Dickson, Mr Tom Driberg, M.P., Sir John Gielgud, Mrs Frank Gilliatt, and Mr Geoffrey Gorer on behalf of his mother, Mrs Rée Gorer.

For permission to use quotations, acknowledgments are further due to the following authors, publishers and copyright holders: Mr Harold Acton for *Memoirs of an Aesthete* (Methuen), Mr Sidney Coles (editor) for the *Municipal Review*, Mr Cyril Connolly for the *The Condemned Playground* (Routledge) and a review in the *Sunday*

Times, Mr David Garnett for *The Familiar Faces* (Chatto & Windus), Mr L. P. Hartley for *The Novelist's Responsibility* (Hamish Hamilton), Mr T. F. Higham, Dr F. R. Leavis for *New Bearings in English Poetry* (Chatto & Windus), Mrs Wyndham Lewis for the late P. Wyndham Lewis's *The Apes of God* (Arthur Press; Simpkin), Miss Dilys Powell for *Descent from Parnassus* (Cresset Press), Mr Peter Quennell for *The Sign of the Fish* (Collins), Mr Stephen Spender for an obituary notice in the *Observer*, Mr Frank Swinnerton for *The Georgian Literary Scene* (Hutchinson), the University of Texas for *The Denton Welch Journals* (Hamish Hamilton), the executors of Mr Evelyn Waugh and Messrs A. D. Peters for an article in the *Sunday Times*, and Mr Leonard Woolf for *Roger Fry* by Mrs Virginia Woolf. Also to the *Sunday Times* for quotations from the record of the party in honour of Dame Edith Sitwell's seventieth birthday, and to the B.B.C. for quotations from Dame Edith's two programmes in the series *Face to Face* and *This is Your Life*.

Finally I must express my debt to Mr Alan Maclean and Mr Richard Garnett of Messrs Macmillan (London) and Mr William Abrahams of the Atlantic Monthly Press (Boston) for their invaluable advice and assistance while this book was in preparation; and to Mr David Ferris for his technical assistance in deciphering my original manuscript for typing.

JOHN LEHMANN

LIST OF ILLUSTRATIONS

INTRODUCTION

THIS book was originally undertaken while Dame Edith Sitwell was still alive, and with her warm approval for the project, as well as the approval of her two brothers. Her death, so soon after I had started work, has made the task more complex, but not, I believe, changed its essential limitations. I did not think then, nor do I think now that the time has come to attempt a full evaluation of her work, nor of that of her brothers, who are after all still alive and still have work to publish. Again, I do not think it is possible yet to write a full biography of Dame Edith (let alone biographies of Sir Osbert and Sacheverell): the material is not yet assembled, the perspective is not yet deep enough.

What I have attempted, rather, is to describe and make a personal interim assessment of the impact of the three Sitwells on their times, that is on the last fifty years of literary, artistic and musical history in Britain (and to a certain extent also, of course, in America). This is obviously a two-way traffic: if they affected the opinions and intellectual actions of their contemporaries, their contemporaries also affected them. It is the tension between these two thrusts that makes the phenomenon of this extraordinarily gifted family, all three suddenly emerging from an aristocratic background to be in the forefront of an avant-garde revolution, so remarkable and so absorbing.

They are all three creative writers: I have therefore made a study at some length of what I consider to be their most important or most characteristic works of poetry, fiction, travel and autobiography. They have all three — Dame Edith and Sir Osbert in particular — been actively controversial intelligences: I have therefore given an account, as far as I could, of their most significant and lively critical engagements and disputes. They have been leaders of taste in their generation, and I have tried to explain where their most influential contributions lay, and how they encouraged and helped many young or little-known writers and artists at the outset of their careers. Finally, they have been social personalities who have acted as a fermenting yeast on the society of their time. This has involved a study of their social and historical background, as well as of their changing circle of friends and admirers.

The title is taken from a remark of Dame Edith's about herself and her brothers: 'We are as cosy as a nest of tigers on the Ganges.'

JOHN LEHMANN

July 1967

I

At three o'clock on the afternoon of 12 June 1923 a
performance was given of a new work at the Aeolian
Hall in London. The programme announced: 'Osbert
Sitwell presents Miss Edith Sitwell in *Façade*'. The music
had been composed by a young and almost unknown
musician called William Walton, and the work consisted of
twenty-one poems by Edith Sitwell with accompanying
music. The poems were read from behind a curtain through
a kind of megaphone called a 'sengerphone', which, according to Osbert Sitwell, 'triumphantly preserved the purity of
the tonal quality it magnified'.

This first public performance of a work which has since
become world famous caused a critical storm and created
the image of the two Sitwell brothers and their sister as
eccentric avant-garde iconoclasts who shouted nonsensical
verses at their audiences through loud-speakers. Though
there was considerable applause from certain quarters, the
house as a whole was infuriated, and the atmosphere was
by the end so hostile that Edith Sitwell was warned not to
leave the hall until the audience had dispersed. 'For several
weeks subsequently,' Osbert Sitwell has written, 'we were
obliged to go about London feeling as if we had committed
a murder. . . . In fact, we had created a first-class scandal in
literature and music.

'The morning after the entertainment,' he continues,
'brought indeed a black, bleak dawn for us in the press.

The fun, the wit, the tunefulness, the beauty, to which qualities, when three years later the performance was repeated at the Chenil Gallery, Mr Ernest Newman was to draw attention in the columns of the *Sunday Times* — he was not present at the first performance in the Aeolian Hall — on this occasion completely escaped the critics. All the papers except the *Daily Mail* combined in attack. The mask on the curtains (designed by Frank Dobson) was characterised as a "meaningless, crudely-painted moonface", the music as "collected from the works of the most eccentric of the ultra-moderns", while the words were dismissed as "drivel".' One critic wrote: 'If Beerbohm wanted to do a really funny drawing of the Sitwells, instead of the stupid one of them now on view at the Leicester Galleries, he should have gone to the ridiculous recital at the Aeolian Hall which I am surprised to see was taken seriously by some newspapers.' And again: 'Edwin Evans sat through a series of meaningless, rhythmless, childish words called "Ass-Face": but Noël Coward was strong enough to walk out, while the fireman, asked his opinion at the end, said that never in twenty years' experience of recitals at that hall had he known anything like it. Surely it is time this sort of thing were stopped.'

'Never, I should think, was a larger and more imposing shower of brickbats hurled at any new work,' Edith Sitwell has written. 'Certain newspaper critics, enraged and alarmed by the performance, rushed from the hall and, lassoing a passing postman, asked him what he thought. Dashing back to the hall they waylaid a fireman and anxiously asked his opinion. These modern substitutions for the Delphic oracle replied promptly, and in no uncertain terms. They opined that we were mad.'

It was, one must admit, a facer for the critics. The evening's entertainment demanded of them an exceptional effort of the imagination — and a sense of humour. Even those who could pardon the music had to cope with the words. And if the undemanding sentiments and moonlit phrases of the latest volume of *Georgian Poetry* were echoing — if anything was echoing — in their minds, what were they to make of a piece called *Trio for Two Cats and a Trombone*, which began:

> Long steel grass —
> The white soldiers pass —
> The light is braying like an ass.
> See
> The tall Spanish jade
> With hair black as nightshade
> Worn as a cockade!

Or the even more unconventional assault of *Fox Trot*:

> Old
>   Sir
>   Faulk,
> Tall as a stork,
> Before the honeyed fruits of dawn were ripe, would walk,
> And stalk with a gun
> The reynard-coloured sun,
> Among the pheasant-feathered corn the unicorn has torn,
>   forlorn the
> Smock-faced sheep
> Sit
>   And
>   Sleep;
> Periwigged as William and Mary, weep . . .

Nevertheless, there were a few critics who understood

that they were present at an exciting new artistic event. In *Vogue* (July 1923), Gerald Cumberland wrote: 'Miss Sitwell half spoke, half shouted, her poems, in strict monotone, emphasizing the metre rather than the rhythm. . . . Her voice, beautiful in tone, full, resonant and clear, could without effort be heard above the din of the music. . . . To this hour I am by no means certain what some of her poems mean, but if I do not understand their beauty, I divine it, and for that reason am all the more attracted, drawn, seduced.'

In his *Memoirs of an Aesthete*, Harold Acton, who had already acquired a reputation as a literary avant-gardiste while a schoolboy at Eton, and was then an undergraduate at Oxford, has given a vivid impression of this first night. 'The stage was hung with a back-cloth painted by Frank Dobson the sculptor: this consisted of two masks, the large one in the centre half pink and half white, and the small one on the right a blackamoor, with sengerphones protruding through their open mouths. Osbert Sitwell announced each poem through the blackamoor's mouth and Edith recited through the lips of the pink and white mask. Osbert had explained that the purpose of reciting behind a back-cloth through a sengerphone was to stop the reader's personality from invading the poems.

'Very distinctly, stressing the rhythms in a dispassionate voice, Edith read, to the accompaniment of a sextet by William Walton, a series of tunes which have since been orchestrated for ballet and popularized by frequent broadcasts. No dance can serve as a proxy for such flashing poems, and I preferred this first performance. Willie Walton interpreted Edith's colour-schemes with extraordinary precision. . . . In the evening there was a party at Osbert's house in Carlyle Square, a shrine of eighteenth-century shell furniture, sailing ships of spun glass, humming birds under globes, petit-point screens, porcelain spaniels, daguerrotype albums and musical boxes combined — one tinkled out "Home, sweet Home" — so many and so varied that at moments one felt one was in an aquarium (the walls had a subaqueous iridescence), at others in an aviary.'

Harold Acton's poetic image might give the impression that the house contained nothing but exotic *objets d'art*; but in fact the walls were a crowded picture-gallery of modern art, with paintings or drawings by Severini, Picasso, Gaudier-Brzeska, Modigliani and many English artists of the time, including Sickert, Wyndham Lewis, Paul and John Nash, Mark Gertler, Roger Fry and Nina Hamnett.

The 'Sphinx' (Ada Leverson) was there, in an ecstasy, exclaiming, 'Wasn't it wonderful?' Harold Acton had brought the young Evelyn Waugh, Desmond Harmsworth and Francis Palmer with him. Lytton Strachey, Clive Bell, St John Hutchinson and Eugene Goossens took part in the charades which concluded the evening, while Edith Sitwell herself relaxed, exhausted by the performance.

A certain bitterness, implanted in the breasts of the chief performers by the hostile philistinism of the press and general public, was, Osbert Sitwell relates, somewhat assuaged by an incident which occurred a little later in a slow Italian train, one hot spring afternoon when he, his brother Sacheverell and William Walton were returning from an expedition to Caserta. To while away the boredom of the journey, they started, quietly in their corner, to chant several numbers from *Façade*: the *Waltz*, *Rose Castles*, the *Fox Trot* and *Trio for Two Cats and a Trombone*. There was nobody else in the carriage except 'a dignified figure in one corner, in black gaiters, sky-blue breeches, tunic and shako.'

This person, as they had already found out in a brief conversation, understood no English: nor did he appear to have the marks of an intellectual, but rather of the typical cavalry officer of any country, bored and morose. As, however, they recited, 'his face began to glow with interest and then with pleasure, and half-way through *Two Cats and a Trombone* he leant forward and, with an air of discovery and delight, enunciated in his beautiful, clear Italian voice his verdict, "Ecco la vera poesia!"'

That evening at the Aeolian Hall can be said to have launched the three Sitwells as the *enfants terribles* of the arts in the immediate post-war years. It was not, however, the first performance of *Façade*, which had taken place in the house in Carlyle Square fifteen months earlier. Osbert Sitwell maintains that he finds it almost impossible to decide which of the four of them — Osbert, Sacheverell, Edith and William Walton — was responsible for particular points of the finished product, because they were all continually in one another's company discussing its shape and growth. The title itself had its origin in the remark of a disdainful artist who, when shown Edith's poems, had remarked 'Very clever, no doubt — but what is she but a façade?' Characteristically, the Sitwells seized on this sneer as a compliment, and gleefully adopted it as their hall-mark.

The origin of the idea, however, is clear: it came from technical experiments which Edith Sitwell had been conducting in her poetry. She has written in her autobiography: 'At the time I began to write, a change in the direction, imagery and rhythms in poetry had become necessary, owing to the rhythmical flaccidity, the verbal drabness, the dead and expected patterns, of some of the poetry immediately preceding us.' And for the sleeve of the last

*Edith Sitwell and
her mother*

*Osbert and Sacheverell
as boys*

Sacheverell, Edith, Osbert

Outside the Chenil Gallery (Façade 1926): Osbert, Edith, Sachever
William Walton, and friend

authentic* recording of *Façade* she wrote: 'They are *abstract* poems — that is, they are patterns in sound: they are, too, in many cases, virtuoso exercises in poetry (of extreme difficulty) — in the same sense as certain studies of Liszt are studies in transcendental techniques in music. My experiments in *Façade* are in the nature of enquiries into the effect on rhythm, and on speed, of the use of rhymes, assonances, dissonances, placed outwardly and inwardly (at different places in the line) and in most elaborate patterns.'

More revealingly, perhaps, she also wrote, referring to her early critics, 'It has now at last dawned on these people that *Façade* is a work for the most part of gaiety, although sometimes there is a veiled sadness. The audience is meant to laugh. It has dawned on them, too, that the work is utterly devoid of malice, and of the stupid and vulgar trick known as leg-pulling.'

This dawn broke, as a matter of fact, quite early on. Osbert records that at the second London performance of *Façade* on 27 April 1926, just before the General Strike, an enthusiastic audience tried to obtain encores of every number. Arnold Bennett, in his *Journals*, described this audience as consisting of 'Crowds of people, snobs, highbrows, low-brows, critics and artists and decent folk.' And the following Sunday, Ernest Newman, the most influential musical critic of his time, wrote in the *Sunday Times*: 'Here is obviously a humorous musical talent of the first order; nothing so good in the mock-serious line has been heard for a long time as the *Valse*, the *Polka*, the *Jodelling Song* and *I do Like to be Beside the Seaside*; the deft workmanship, especially in the orchestration, made the heart of the listening musician glad.

* Decca Mono. LXT. 2977

'The curious thing was the happiness of the correspondence between all the factors of the affair; the music, the words, the megaphone and the piquant phrasing of the lines by the reciter were as much bone of each other's bone and flesh of each other's flesh as the words and music are of each other in *Tristan*, or *Pelléas*. At its best, *Façade* was the jolliest entertainment of the season.'

Of the earliest, private performance in Carlyle Square little is recorded, except by Osbert Sitwell. 'The rehearsals for the first performance,' he has written, 'dwell with an ineradicable vividness in my memory, and there prosper with their own warmth, kindling even the bleak prospect outside.' Osbert's drawing-room on the first floor at No. 2 was of the characteristic London L-shaped type, three windows looking out westwards on to the square, and one, in the narrower part of the room at the back, looking on to a towering sycamore tree, which in this bitterly cold February weather loomed utterly black against the contrasting snow which lay on the ground and the tops of the horizontal branches. The sextet of players — flute, clarionet, saxophone, trumpet, 'cello and percussion — were grouped under the three windows, through which the snow-covered square garden outside seemed to radiate with an alpine intensity under the obscure, green-white sky. 'Inside, the room, with its tones of pink and blue and white and violet, seemed filled with polar lights from windows and tropic lights from fires: for all the glass objects, of which there were so many, and the doors lined with mirror, glittered with redoubled vehemence. As the strange new sounds shaped themselves under the hands of the rather angry players, the evening outside began to envelop the world in a grape-bloom blue, the lights had to be turned on, and the pictures glowed from the white walls. .... I had, of course, always comprehended the genius of the words, but as I heard the music I understood, too, its genius, the incomparable manner in which the composer, who was not yet twenty years of age, had played with every idea, and matched, under-lined and exhibited the words. This music was full of the feeling of the growth of animals and green things, of crude bird song, of breaths of a world of felicity forfeited, of a tender melancholy, and, in some numbers, of the jauntiest, most inexplicable gaiety.'

The performance took place the next evening at 9.30. The front part of the room was densely packed with concert chairs, on which were assembled an audience consisting in the main of painters, musicians and poets. In the com-paratively small proportions of the room, the volume of sound, through the sengerphone, was deafening, and many of the audience were confused and bewildered. With ironic foresight, Osbert had arranged a special hot rum punch to be served downstairs afterwards, which, he claims 'served to revive quickly those who had lost their bearings on a voyage of discovery'.

On this occasion, there appear to have been twenty pieces in the programme, and the list ended with a note to say that all the poems would shortly appear in 'a limited edition with a special frontispiece in colour by Gino Severini — at the Favil Press, Kensington'. *

* The bibliographical history of *Façade* is extremely complicated, even confusing. All the pieces set to music by William Walton did *not* appear in the Favil Press edition, which consisted of nine poems only under the heading *Façade*, and five under the heading 'Winter', one of which, 'En Famille', was then absorbed into *Façade*. The eventual musical text (if we go by the Decca recording) consisted of twenty-one poems, which do not include all the Favil Press con-

Edith and Osbert had already begun to publish their poems a few years earlier, during the war, though *Façade* was the first opportunity they had had of attracting wider public notice. Edith's *The Mother and Other Poems* appeared in 1915, a very small booklet of twenty pages containing five poems only. It seems on the whole to have been well received, *The Times* speaking of 'a glowing fancy', and 'a rare poetic ideal', and the *Daily Mail* of 'many lines of passion and tragic beauty', which might well be a description of some of the poetry she was writing thirty years later, during the course of the second World War. In a letter to the present author (August 1951) Edith wrote: '*The Mother* was afterwards rewritten as *The Hambone and the Heart*. The first poem I ever wrote was *Serenade*, beginning "The tremulous gold of stars within your hair".' The next book, *Twentieth Century Harlequinade*, came out in 1916 and was a collaboration between Edith and Osbert, the former contributing seven poems and the latter three.

By then *Wheels* had been launched, the first number appearing in late 1916. It was an annual collection of poems which lasted for six numbers until 1921. Edith was in fact the editor, though she did not appear as such on the title-page until 1918. All three Sitwells contributed to each number, Sacheverell being at the time of the first number only nineteen years old. The rest of the contributors, who were never more than ten in all, were a group of friends, the most constant of whom were Aldous Huxley, who was twenty-two in 1916, Arnold James, Sherard Vines and Iris

---

tents. In Dame Edith's *Collected Poems*, the last edition of her life, there are thirty-four poems under the heading *Façade*. Apart from this, several of the poems were given different titles in the course of the years.

Tree. Apart from the poems by the Sitwells themselves, undoubtedly the chief *coup* of *Wheels* was the publication in the fourth number of seven of Wilfred Owen's war poems; of which more later.

Thus the image of the Sitwells as an inseparable trio was established at the very outset of their careers. But *Wheels* did more than this; it drew on their heads for the first time, though admittedly only in the small circle of poetry readers, the contempt and rage of the Philistines. 'None of them sing!' cried one critic; and another denounced the poems as 'conceived in morbid eccentricity and executed in fierce factitious gloom'. A third decided, with a superior sneer, that 'they have apparently come to the conclusion that there is some mysterious virtue in originality'.

It is only fair to say that there were sympathetic voices as well. 'We have no doubt whatever that, fifty years hence, the publication of *Wheels* will be remembered as a notable event in the inner history of English literature,' wrote the *Morning Post*. And, according to the *Observer*, 'It is a love of truth that makes them shun romantic subjects. They are all practised verse writers. They are all clever and stimulating.' The same reviewer also claimed that 'every page shouts defiance of poetic conventions'. Though this judgment was made with friendly intention, and though it referred to the contributors as a whole, it was prophetic of the trouble that was soon to be brewing for the three Sitwells.

An extremely sympathetic and influential partisan in an older generation was Arnold Bennett, who already in 1919 had been invited to dinner by Osbert at Swan Walk, in a mixed, very Bloomsbury, company, and had enjoyed it very much, as he later enjoyed *Façade*. In 1922 he made a favourable mention of Edith's poetry in the *Outlook*, and in

November she asked him if she could dedicate her new volume of poems to him: 'I want to do it as an act of homage to your work, and in proof of my gratitude for your great kindness and encouragement.'

In his study of *The Georgian Literary Scene*, Frank Swinnerton writes of the young Sitwells: 'In the beginning, they were three *enfants terribles*. Being excluded, either by their own act or by the repulsion of the editorial canon from "Georgian Poetry", they established a counterblast to which they gave the name "Wheels"; and to this all three contributed greatly, adding jovial and insulting annotations with which they lambasted uncomplimentary reviewers.'*

Who were these young iconoclasts, who by the time of the production of *Façade* had already shown themselves to be so defiant, inventive and energetic? To examine the background from which they emerged, and the influence which formed them, one must go back a little in time, aided by their own copious writings on the subject.

* *Wheels* was followed by *Art and Letters*, in intention a quarterly but in fact published only intermittently, from July 1917 to 1920. Frank Rutter was the original editor, in association with Charles Ginner and Harold Gilman as art editors, but in the summer of 1919 Osbert Sitwell took over as poetry editor. It was produced in handsome quarto format, with original illustrations in woodcut and line by Walter Sickert and many of the outstanding younger artists of the time: in addition to Ginner and Gilman, Paul and John Nash, C. R. W. Nevinson, Frank Dobson, E. McKnight Kauffer, Nina Hamnett, Gaudier-Brzeska and others. Apart from the Sitwells, Herbert Read was a frequent contributor on a list that included Siegfried Sassoon, Ronald Firbank, Katherine Mansfield, Wyndham Lewis, Ezra Pound, Aldous Huxley, Dorothy Richardson and Ford Madox Ford. It was a stimulating venture, exciting to explore forty years after; perhaps a little too miscellaneous for continuing success.

2

THE scene: a large ancestral home set in the coal-mining district of Derbyshire, not far from the town of Chesterfield, with the towers of Elizabethan Hardwick and the 'lofty stone keep' of Bolsover visible on the horizon when the air is clear. The name: Renishaw Hall.

The house itself is, in the main, Jacobean with Regency modifications and additions. A long line of battlements and pinnacles crowning its many-windowed grey-stone mass, it stands on a plateau dominating the surrounding countryside, with chimneys far away that indicate the industrial riches on which the Sitwell fortunes were founded. Elaborately designed formal lawns stretch down, terrace by terrace, in front of the house to the lake at the furthest descent, and the valley of the Rother in the distance. But these terraces are not original with the house, though they may to a large extent follow the pattern of the vanished Jacobean garden: they were conceived and planted by Osbert Sitwell's father, Sir George, whose restless garden-planning genius and ample financial resources transformed a scene that had become partly derelict during the course of the nineteenth century. Every level, as you look southwards, has its water-feature, flanked by the obelisk shapes of yew and box, rectangular beds of flowers enclosing smoothly kept areas of green lawn, pedestals with plant-filled terracotta pots and white statues, Neptune, Diana and Hercules, looking into the noonday haze. On the left — to the east — lies the 'wilderness', a survival of the typically 'English garden' of the eighteenth century, with winding glades that are filled with bluebells in spring and in the summer with canterbury bells and other wild flowers 'no doubt descended from flowers escaped long ago from older enclosed gardens of monasteries and manors', that deeply impressed the imagination of the young Sitwell children. To the west, the more formal Avenue extends, with ancient elms and limes originally planted, so the story goes, at the end of the seventeenth century.

The Sitwell family appears to have been settled in this district since the early fourteenth century; but it was not until 1625 that an ancestor actually came to live at Renishaw. This ancestor, George Sitwell, built there the original stone house, three storeys high, crowned with gables, and surrounded it with formal garden courts characteristic of the period. By 1793, however, when Osbert's great-great-grandfather, Sitwell Sitwell, inherited the estate, the house had been enlarged, the gables had been removed and the present battlements imposed on the roof-line to give it a gothic appearance. Sitwell Sitwell, possessed of a large fortune and a craze for building, made many additions to the house itself as well as creating gates and triumphal arches. In particular, he built a large ballroom specially for a grand reception and rout given in honour of the Prince Regent in 1806. Though Sir George, Osbert's father, inherited his great-grandfather's craze for building, the general look of the house must have been very much the same during the childhood of Edith, Osbert and Sacheverell as it was in 1806.

This house made a lasting mark on the children, though in fact none of them was actually born there, and much of their early years was spent in other family homes, especially at Scarborough. It inspired idyllic prose descriptions from all three, and reappears again and again in their poetry. In *All Summer in a Day* Sacheverell describes an early September morning at Renishaw: 'It seems misty and cloud-bound all the year among the Derbyshire hills, and this actual month is the dimmest and most distance-hiding of the seasons. No statue can be seen, let alone a passing human figure — gardener or woodsman — at a further distance than ten yards before you. There are the few remaining trees of a lime and elm avenue, in front and to the right of the house; and their old and splintered masts still towered a dizzying height into the air, too far for the eye to follow them, these autumn mornings. . . . We came out from these trees soon enough on to the road or drive, and this led through a level meadow to the brink of a wide, sweeping slope leading to the country beyond and out of the park. This descent, as to the road, was closed in by a long, leafy tunnel of trees, that looked shimmering and rather ghostly in the half-light, until another gate was reached and we were out into the countryside, though not in fact, for there was one more gate to be passed through before the drive joined the highroad.

'As one opened this last gate, and then turned round to shut it so that none of the sheep wandering in the field could escape on to the public road, one looked invariably a little to the right down the slope, where the lake should have showed blue and shimmering beyond the fields. But it was not there to-day: or, at any rate, not yet. Instead, the hollow that those sparkling waters should have filled lay absolutely hidden under the fleeces of mist. It looked stark and despairing down the meadows, sopping wet to the feet, and cold as ice when one's hand touched the iron of a gate. And indeed the clanging and cold of the metal brought one quickly out of these reveries across the public road to another gate on the far side. Coming down the road there were a whole straggling convoy of miners, carrying their bundles, and showing faces of an intensified blackness against the hedges.'

'To me,' Osbert has written, 'my home always meant Renishaw; and the summer took me there, so that it meant the summer, too; summers that from this distance all merge into one. . . .' He remembers that as soon as he arrived every year he would hurry to a little painted door, rather taller than himself, in the pillared hall, over which, as he stood on tiptoe, the scent of the garden he loved so much would come to him through the open window, a scent subtly combined of stocks, clove carnations, tobacco plants and sun-warmed hedges of box. And he remembers what happiness it always gave him to come there and how sad he was to leave it every autumn, feeling as he did that he belonged there far more completely than at Scarborough or any of his grandparents' homes. 'I felt this with peculiar intensity, experiencing a curious attachment to the soil, a sympathy with the form of the country, with its trees and flowers, the frail blue spires of the bluebells in May, or the harebells and toad-flax of August, which has never left me and has made me wonder at times whether my ancestors, in the building-up of an estate through so many hundreds of years, and by the hunger and passion for this land which must have inspired them — for it was an estate gradually accumulated, not obtained by huge grants or the purchase of Church property — had not bequeathed to me something still very real and active in my nature; this love seemed to me so much older than myself and so much part of me.'

Edith had a particular reminiscence of her childhood associated with the ancestral house, which seems to have remained especially vivid to her to the end of her days: 'When we were at Renishaw, punctually at nine o'clock every morning (it is strange how birds and animals have an accurate sense of time) the peacock would stand on leads outside my mother's bedroom, waiting for me to come and say good morning to her. When he saw me, he would utter a harsh shriek of welcome (I do not, as a rule, appreciate ugly voices, but I loved him so much that nothing about him could be wrong in my opinion). He would wait for me until I left my mother's room, then, with another harsh shriek, would fly down into the large gardens. We walked round these, with my arm round his lovely neck, that shone like tears in a dark forest. If it had not been for his crown, which made him slightly taller than me, we should have been of the same height. Davis* said to me, "Why do you love Peaky so much?"

'I said, "Because he is beautiful and wears a Heavenly Crown." '

Her romance with Peaky lasted many months, until in fact he jilted her in favour of a bride her father had bought him. It was, she says, her first experience of faithlessness, and remained an indelible impression. She had to console herself with a puffin with a wooden leg and a baby owl that had fallen out of its nest, 'which used to sleep with its head on my shoulder, pretending to snore in order to attract mice'.

In this passage Edith reveals what was to remain a strong characteristic of her nature, as indeed of her two brothers, a

* Edith's nurse.

love of animals. It is impossible, I find, not to think, as she describes walking through the garden with Peaky, of Alice in the 'wood where things have no names' with her arm round the neck of the Fawn.

The three Sitwells have always been very conscious of their aristocratic lineage, stretching back as it does to the Plantagenet Kings. 'In the distance,' writes Osbert describing his ancestry, 'can just be discerned Robert Bruce, King of Scotland, Wallace the Patriot, the gleaming golden armour of Plantagenet Kings of England and of the Kings of France, their plumes flowing from helms that almost mask their strong profiles, the sturdy figures of numberless yeomen upon their farms, and beyond again, various squires of adventurous disposition, leaving their homes, acquired not so long before, in Normandy, to follow their Duke across the Channel, while on the horizon, on the border between history and legend, stand out the immortal figures of the Macbeths.' Osbert maintains, a little further on in the same passage, that beyond one's great-grandparents 'about whom their sons and daughters have told us, so that we know their manner of speech and dress, their peculiarities, and in their children have heard their voices reflected', one's relatives 'enter the realm of myth, their faces lose their identity and no longer connect with those round us'. And he proceeds to enumerate his own great-grandparents, who include the celebrated Lady Conyngham, favourite of George IV in the last ten years of his life, whose exceptional gift for extracting valuable presents from the King was one of the great jokes of the gossips and wits of the time, but who (as Edith reminds us) also managed to get flogging abolished in women's prisons; her husband Lord Albert Conyngham, who after her death became the

Earl of Londesborough; a Duke and Duchess of Beaufort; and Colonel Hely-Hutchinson, nephew of the Lord Donoughmore who as General Hutchinson turned Napoleon out of Egypt;* as well as the Sir George Sitwell whose financial misfortunes caused him to shut up Renishaw and sell many of its treasures, a situation that was only reversed by the skilful management of the widow of Sir George's son Reręsby, during the long minority of the second Sir George, Osbert's father.

The Londesborough house became extremely important in the early history of the three Sitwell children. Of his first visit to his grandparents at Londesborough, Osbert writes: 'This was a different world, given over to those pomps and vanities which, in their own day so overwhelming, notwithstanding, leave no shadow behind them . . . a world of horses, carriages and liveries, an immense machine, producing little, unless it were the love given for its own sake, scarcely, even, rewarding with smooth working, still less with any pleasure, those to whom it ministered. Here there were major-domos, grooms of the chamber, powdered footmen, wearing velvet knee-breeches on the right occasions, grooms, gamekeepers, the cool and ordered processes of the dairy, and stables full of haughty and glossy gods, well tended. In their fragile glass cases were caged the steamy fragments of Africa and Asia, orchids and rare, strong-smelling flowers, while, in their season, ripe peaches and grapes and nectarines and melons flourished within their crystal orchards.'

Edith confessed that the *mise-en-scène* of her long poem *The Sleeping Beauty* was Londesborough, the memories of

* A fine portrait of the General is in the living-room at Weston (see later, p. 259).

which stayed hauntingly with her after her childhood visits. Malinn, in the poem, was one of the Londesborough house-maids, as was ' "The gossiping naiad of the water" and the other country maids, with their butter-yellow satin hair.' She tells us that her grandmother, Lady Londes-borough, was one of the great hostesses of the age, and that 'the eighteenth-century luxury of Londesborough was remarkable in its opulence'. Her recollections take us back to the turn of the century, and nothing can more vividly point the difference between that world — only sixty years away — and our own, than when she writes: 'Lady Londes-borough's footmen (who constituted as large a regiment as that of my grandmother Sitwell's curates) were forbidden to look at each other in her presence, or to speak excepting in their professional capacity. They might speak to Martin, the butler, but on no account were they to look at him. Otherwise, their silence was only broken at their extreme peril.'

Edith's irreverent spirit of knock-about fun, which was so pronounced throughout her life, and which contrasted so pungently with her aristocratic *hauteur* when besieged by unknown gossips and culture-vultures, is well in evidence in her description of a crucial event in her grandmother's life: 'One evening, at the beginning of November, my grandmother (who was then at Londesborough Lodge in Scarborough) went up to bed with her hair of the usual brown colour. Next morning when she came down, at eleven o'clock to an enormous breakfast (eggs and bacon, cold grouse, ham, cold partridge, home-made buns and buttercup-coloured cream and butter, hothouse peaches and grapes), the autumnal hue of her hair had changed to the most snowbound of winters. My aunts, not daring to appear conscious of this phenomenon, stared at their plates. My grandfather concentrated on the breast of a cold partridge. The footmen seemed to be bound, more than ever, in a spell of silence.'

Of the deep influence of Scarborough, in the lives of all three children, I shall write later.

Undoubtedly the dominant influence in the early lives of the three was their father, Sir George Sitwell. A learned eccentric, so obsessed with the Middle Ages that they became more real to him than the age in which he lived, he concentrated more and more as the years went by on his schemes for landscape gardening, on which, at Renishaw and later at the Tuscan castle of Montegufoni which he bought, he was prepared to spend huge sums. Both Edith and Osbert give the impression that he gradually withdrew from actuality, perhaps owing to a sense of failure to communicate with other human beings; he was both insistently present and almost completely absent. Edith writes of him with a mocking bitterness: 'I was unpopular with my parents from the moment of my birth, and throughout my childhood and youth. I was in disgrace for being a female, and worse, as I grew older it was obvious that I was not going to conform to my father's standard of feminine beauty. I in no way resembled a Pekinese, or one of those bloated pink imitation roses that my father (who had never forgiven himself for marrying a lady) admired. Instead, I had inherited the Plantagenet features and deep-set eyes of my grandmother Londesborough. . . . My friends were my dear old nurse Davis. (When I think of her now, I see her like a phrase in my friend Gertrude Stein's *Geography and Plays*, "a shadow, a white shadow, is a mountain". She was at once a white shadow and a mountain. And her real name was comfort.) And my other friend — my father's valet Henry Moat — whose friendship with my brothers and me lasted until his death.'

It is interesting to notice that the celebrated description of Sir Henry Rotherham in Edith's novel *I Live Under a Black Sun* is, in fact, a portrait of Sir George Sitwell, because in the novel the passage about Sir Henry's eccentric habits is almost word for word the same as in *Taken Care of*: 'He was exceeding active physically, and he had adopted this custom of pacing the passages because, he said, by cultivating such a habit one ceased to trouble or even notice if the days were wet and cold, or torrid and weighted by the heat, if the days were drawing out or drawing in. . . .

'When pacing the passages, he walked very slowly, occupying as much time as possible in order that the house should seem even larger than it was — for he liked to feel that it was very large. Occasionally, about once or twice a day, he would pause outside a door, if he could hear voices in the room beyond — not because he wanted to eavesdrop or to spy, since there was nothing he could hear, now, that would interest him, but because he was enabled in this way to touch, for a moment, the world in which others moved, thought, acted, without being obliged to become a part of it, and this made him feel real to himself, real in his isolation, in the separation of his identity from the world that he could yet touch at will. He would, too, spread various objects belonging to himself all over the house, in the many rooms — his hat in one room, his stick in another, his spectacle case in a third, because when he came face to face, once more, in the course of his wanderings, with these records of his own personality, he was reminded of himself,

Sacheverell Sitwell: drawing by Wyndham Lewis, 1922

Edith Sitwell: drawing by Wyndham Lewis, 1921

Renishaw family group: Sacheverell, Sir George, Georgia, Reresby,
Lady Ida, Edith, Osbert

which was pleasant, and because it enabled him to stake his claim on every room in the house as sole inhabitant.'

Osbert's descriptions of his father are much kinder, though equally extraordinary. While savouring to the full Sir George's eccentricities, he gives the impression that, in spite of constant misunderstandings and failures of *rapport* in their relationship, a deep bond of affection united them. He writes of him with a slightly malicious humour, but the malice is tempered with warmer vibrations. As *Left Hand, Right Hand!* progresses, Osbert lets himself go on the subject of his father more and more; until one can say that by the end of the fourth volume, *Laughter in the Next Room*, he has become one of the great comic characters of our time.

At the very beginning of the first volume, Osbert has a bravura passage on Sir George, which one can place beside the passage from *Taken Care of* which I have just quoted: 'My father is very fond of walking, extremely rapidly, in these gardens he has made. All day long he can be found in them: and this year, into which I lead you, he is there for a longer time than ever, because to him the Middle Ages are the model for all life to follow — hence the isolation you noticed, for he lives behind invisible barriers of pedigrees and tourneys and charters and coats-of-arms, and all round him hang its shields and banners, all round him sound its discordant trumpets and the battle-cries of armoured men — and since every medieval romance opens in a garden at the hour of sunrise, he has, this summer, chosen to be called every morning at five. . . .

'He walks up and down, surveying his work, which will never be finished, his head full of new projects of sun and shade, but never of flowers, measuring the various views with a stick to his eye or a pair of binoculars. Sometimes he is planning a boat of stone upon the lake, or a dragon in lead, writhing for a quarter of a mile through its level waters, or a colonnaded pavilion upon another island, or a Roman aqueduct in counterfeit to frame the prospect with its elongated arches, or a cascade to fall down a stone channel for a hundred and fifty feet, from the water to the garden below: and, for such projects as these, though most of them never materialised, he would cause wooden towers, built up of planks and joists and beams — like an early machine for siege warfare or a drawing by Piranesi — to be erected here and there at the right points of vantage. In the summer he would spend many hours aloft on these platforms, with a large grey hat or grey umbrella to shield his light-coloured skin and eyes from the sun, and with a telescope to his eye, enjoying the air and also, perhaps, the feeling of command which such an altitude above the ground affords. . . . All my life, these have been his ways, in one place or another. He made the great garden lay-out at Renishaw just before I was born, and I grew up, year by year, with its yew hedges.'

However much he might treat his father as a figure of fun, both during his life and in his autobiography, Osbert's devotion to him and confidence in his wisdom went deep, and his father had a sympathetic understanding of his problems as a boy. In a later passage he describes how, at a time when his father had been suffering from a long illness, and was therefore playing a rather remote part in his children's lives, he had become more and more oppressed by the tormenting puzzles of a young intelligence faced with conventional Christian tenets. Was Hell real? If it was, and if he was as wicked as he was constantly told he was, how could he avoid burning for eternity? It was his father who rescued him from this purgatory of religious fear. One day, when he happened to feel better, he sent for Osbert and took him out for a drive. Osbert writes: 'We had not met for some weeks, and though he was so ill himself, he noticed, directly he saw me, that something had gone wrong, and contrived to persuade me to tell him my secret agony. And I have always been grateful to him for the triumphantly clever and subtly imaginative manner in which he dealt with it. He realised at once that it would be no good to enter upon long theological discussions with a small boy, and that the whole matter must be tackled from a different angle and with a different point of view. On the other hand, it would not do to dismiss the matter too lightly. So he said, in serious tones, "My dear boy, if you go to hell, you'll certainly find all the people you most admire there already — Wellington, Nelson and the Black Prince — and they'll discover a way of getting you out of it soon enough!"'

This answer completely banished Osbert's anxieties, and thereafter he indulged happily in fantasies of his favourite heroes organising and disciplining the demoralised legions of hell; though he still remained slightly confused as to whether this discipline would bring about their eventual pardon on the part of heaven.

3

I N her decidedly farcical description of her birth at her grandmother's house in Scarborough, Edith wrote: 'A short way from the house, the sea crawled like a lion awaiting its prey, so softly you could not guess of what tremendous roars that seemingly gentle creature was capable across the lion-yellow sands.'

The image of the lion was always one of Edith's favourites, reaching its most beautiful invocation in one of the masterpieces of her later period, *Heart and Mind*; and here — for this is surely a recollection of childhood vision — one sees it presented to her imagination in her earliest years. She has also told us that the wild seas of the Yorkshire coast had a profound effect not only upon her imagery but also upon her sense of rhythm. 'My earliest recollection,' she wrote, 'is of the tides, the wild rush of waves, the sweep onward, heard night and day, so that it seemed the sound of one's own blood.' Under all her poetry, as it matured, it is surely not fanciful to hear the long, slow beat, now lazy in halcyon calm, now wild in equinoctial storm, of the waves upon those northern cliffs.

But Scarborough made a profound and lasting impression upon all three Sitwell children. In their childhood they spent much of autumn and winter there; first, at their grandmother's, Londesborough Lodge, and then later at Wood End. This latter home, 'a singular, oblong house, built in 1820 of orange-yellow stone', with an enormous palm in the middle of the conservatory, was bought by Sir George Sitwell's mother in 1870, and he himself could remember playing with his tutor in the garden there in the summer of that year. Later, Lady Sitwell moved to Hay Brow, a few miles outside Scarborough, and Wood End remained empty until she gave it to Sir George and he moved in with his family in 1902. They spent much of every year there until the bombardment of Scarborough in 1914 by the German fleet; so that the background of this house and its surroundings was as important as Renishaw during the formative years of Edith, Osbert and Sacheverell. Londesborough Lodge, where they stayed before 1902, was not far away, was in fact visible from the windows of Wood End on the eastern side.

In his childhood, the atmosphere of the house seemed to Osbert, in some indefinable way, evil and he was often frightened there at night. 'My bedroom was cut off from the main body of the house by the conservatory, through which you had to pass to reach the library — which had been built by my father on the model of the library at Renishaw, some twenty years before — and then climb up a small staircase to the room over it.' He was a highly strung boy, and like many other boys of similar temperament was sometimes unable to get to sleep and would creep out of bed, as late as ten or eleven o'clock. He would stand in his night-clothes at the top of the stairs, hoping to gain comfort from the sound of voices issuing from the room down below where his governess and tutor were accustomed to sit after dinner. Often he could not make out what they were saying; it did not matter, because the sound alone gave the re-assurance of a human world he needed. On one occasion, however, he heard them discussing his father and his illness 'without much apparent sympathy, and remarking how extraordinary it was to have a nervous breakdown just because you could not get your own way in everything ...'.

Osbert has also described the impression made upon his childish imagination by the beggars and eccentric local characters of the town: 'At Scarborough the night nursery was at the top and back of the high old stone-pillared house we then occupied, and looked out above a narrow alley. When the rushing and bellowing winds of the winter ceased for a moment to roar down this passage made for them, tearing the words from the throats of the speakers right away into the void, and only the background of tumultuous seas remained, you could hear very distinctly what was said below. In the winter dawn, before it was fully light, these houses resounded with the loud cry, "Rags and Bones! Rags and Bones!" And so it came about that these words were the first I learned, and who knows that such counter-signs to mortality, pronounced at an impressionable age, may not have influenced my mind, making me seek behind the flattering disguise for the mortal and immortal core.' This cry came from an old man who, with flustered, jerky movements pushed his barrow along the alley, the battered, derelict top hat that crowned his bearded face completing the effect of a scarecrow driven forward by a violent wind. ' "Rags and Bones" the old man used sometimes to shout, sometimes to insinuate slyly, in a voice that was between a song and a whine, into the frozen air, beneath where the fleeces of the sky were now showing their flayed and bloody edges.'

There were other eccentric or derelict figures of the Scarborough of his childhood who remained in Osbert's memory. They seemed innumerable: foremost among them was a Negro, known in the town as 'Snowball', who limped through the streets, trying to sell small bunches of flowers or buttonholes at times when they were most scarce. To Osbert he appeared strangely exotic, as if he had been exiled from some warmer, gladder climate, condemned to haunt the 'prim, northern streets, with their frozen gutters and their roofs saw-edged with icicles'. Then there was a bearded tramp, apparently half-witted, known as Lousy Peter, who was persecuted by cruel gangs of urchins: they would belabour him whenever he fell asleep, curled up in his rags, in the early evenings, empty buckets of water over him or snare him into other booby traps it was their special pleasure to devise for him. There was also a forlorn character known as the 'Cat Man', who could be heard mewing to himself on the sands, a truly frightening portent to an imaginative child; not to mention the Italian organ-grinders with their dressed-up monkeys, and — as weird and alarming as the beggars — the occasional cretinous child of a rich family.

Osbert was equally impressed by the working life of the town, above all by the fishing fleets and the fishermen who formed its main population. He would walk down to the quays around which the ships were crowded with their brown sails furled, and sometimes see the fleets coming in, from far out, under full sail. 'Nets bursting with fish, and empty barrels stood upon the stone platform, and the air was strong with the smell of salt and rope and fish, and tar and wood-smoke. The fishwives roared to each other across their tables, slimy and running in the morning sunlight, and the pavement itself was slippery from the catch, soon to be smoked and dried. . . .

'When the great storms of December began to break, and

the rolling, gigantic waves bellowed and roared far out to sea and shook the whole town as they battered and pounded, and the houses seemed caught, themselves, in a net of finely spun spray from the breakers, snowy and mountainous or creamy with sand, I have seen the impassive faces and stoic endurance of these women, waiting for their husbands and fathers, and themselves so well able to value the dangers run, since not one woman in the fishers' quarter but had lost during the passage of the year some relative . . .

'The frequent storms gave, indeed, an awful and vivid excitement to life in winter. For days and nights at a time you could hear the pounding shudder of the vast forces throwing themselves upon stone walls and cliffs, and above it, the distress signals that sounded dull and vague, but infinitely sad, in this upheaval of air and water, these wastes into which the avenging spirit had descended, and in the morning I would listen to Martha telling Davis that the lifeboat had been ordered out seven times in the night, but that once it had been too rough for it to put to sea. . . .' The ocean seemed to him terrifying in its overwhelming power, but nevertheless he responded to it with an almost physical passion, feeling himself to be reinvigorated 'in every cell of the body' as he stood watching it on the cliffs or listening to it at night. He loved all its sudden, violent, changing moods, but especially the exhausted mornings that followed the nocturnal storms when mysterious and unforeseeable treasures had been tumbled on to the sands as the waters receded, 'sea fruit and weed and strange shapes in wood and bone and in a substance black as jet and weighing as light'.

The proof of the deep impression that Scarborough made on the young imaginations of the Sitwells is not only in what they have written, reminiscently, about it, but in their creative works. One of Osbert's earliest short stories, *Low Tide*, published in *Triple Fugue* in 1924, is his first attempt at satirical portraiture in fiction, in this case of the conventional middle-class life of the town. The sea is a continual presence in the story. He describes how his pathetic-ridiculous heroines, the Misses Cantrell-Cooksey, loved to walk together along the sands in winter: 'Especially after a storm would they enjoy walking along the lonely winter sands. Their scarlet hair, their faces so badly made-up that the expression of each side would vary as if one half of the mask was tragic, the other comic, their absurd and complicated dresses, looked all the more fantastic for this submarine setting; and such it seemed after a storm, some strange undersea view. The sloping, pebbly border of sand and sea would be littered with a wild disarray of broken glass, worn down to round gleaming jewels by the constant fret and foaming of the breakers, of starfish, sea-urchins and queer-shaped monstrosities, heaped up with seaweed like small brown palm-trees or the long black matted hair of mermaids. There were so few people about, and the few there were would haunt the sands each day. . . . Most interesting of all, after a storm there would gather together those men who make a living by combing the golden sands. What profession they followed in between the gales, or where they came from, it was impossible to find out. . . . They would rake over the slope of pebbles and the sands beneath, just at that point where the high tide deposited its hostages. It was a gentle but fascinating exercise, and one requiring very competent eyesight and a certain agility of mind. The sisters would stand there for many minutes watching the alternately romantic and prosaic treasury which the storm precipitated on these bleak sands. As the men combed, they

would find silver pennies of the Plantagenets, old biscuit
tins full of sea-biscuits, gold coins from Spain, a piece of
rusty armour that had been gnawed by the waves for centuries, coppers that had been thrown down to the pierrots
in the summer, a glass bottle with a faded message in it —
the family to which this agonised scrawl was addressed had
been dead these ten years! — a bit of a weighing-machine
that had stood on the sands in the summer, a Dutch cheese
still round and fresh and cherry-coloured, a long clasp-knife
with a curious tortoise-shell handle — all the trifles that
time and the cruel tides had left over.'

If one were to comb through Osbert's works for extracts,
one could build up a fascinatingly detailed picture of Scarborough, its natural phenomena and its inhabitants of all
classes, from the fishermen and the beach-combers to the
regular denizens of the lodging-houses and the Grand
Hotel. By far the most complete picture he ever attempted
is in his novel *Before the Bombardment*, in essence a more
extended satirical picture of upper and middle-class life in
the town in the years just before the First World War.

It is possible to think that his novel is rather heavy-going
in its opening chapters, the innuendo of the satirical portraits a little too monotonous and continuous. This is
largely, I feel, due to Osbert's fictional method, almost
entirely composed of description as opposed to the present-
day dominance of dialogue. As one reads on, however, the
characters begin to develop a three-dimensional reality, and
the descriptions of 'Newborough' to acquire depth and a
haunting solidity. Above all, the sea begins to invade the
book, so that by the end the sound of the raging waves is
loud in one's ears and the most impressive memory one is
left with.

Early on in the book, he writes: 'Our story must be told to the monotonous accompaniment of waves beating like the drums of gathering armies: an accompaniment so tremendously out of scale that its very force adds, as it were, a certain mad interest to the varying trivial and human events which the tale describes.' These notes are repeated, gathering in strength, until in one of the penultimate scenes, where the 'paid companion', Miss Bramley, is struggling with feelings of jealousy about her employer's favouritism towards her new 'relation' and protégé Cecilia, they reach a crescendo:

'The drawing-room was too large and dark to be in by oneself for long: and dismal, looking over so rough and threatening an ocean. The sound of sea and wind rushing and jostling rose up too sharply at the large windows. It quite got on one's nerves. For, far down below, the waves were hollowing out every kind of crevice, vault, cave, coffin and cavern, every place imaginable in which to secrete bleaching bones, every form of tube and hollow instrument, upon which the wind could play an accompanying and awful music. The prospect was full of the aerial commotion caused by all this labour, full of white foam, the steam given off by this titanic and terrible machinery. The vast, grey, undulating backs rolled sideways against cement walls, rocks, cliffs and precipices, acting as inspired and living hammers. These monsters pushed and heaved against each other, and then with an added force rammed at the obstacles interposed between themselves and humanity, meeting them with an unimaginable dull and forceful thudding, while, in the very act of clashing with them, they uplifted feline white claws by which to grab hold of the hated, hard objects obstructing them. Still dully roaring, they clambered up with unexpectedly lithe and sinuous movements. For a moment they clung tenaciously, held their own; then, unable at present to lift up the whole, enormous weight of their bodies, fell back gurgling and snarling to recruit themselves for another leaping attack.'

In the *Municipal Review* for October 1958, Sacheverell contributed an article of his reminiscences of the years at Wood End, which some years before had been bought by the Scarborough Corporation and turned into a Museum of Natural History.* His most vivid and haunting memories were of the sands, which with their pools among the sea-weed-hung rocks formed a marvellous playground for his childhood. He never forgot to wait for the sea to roll right out on the tide, when he would scramble over the uncovered rocks. Sometimes the spring tide would carry the water back right beyond the harbour 'unveiling as it were new continents to explore', and filling his mind with dreams of Captain Cook's voyages — for Cook came from nearby Whitby. He remembered the wonderful impression he had looking down on the whole wide sweep of them from the Esplanade. And on that Esplanade he also remembered the great church parades of Sunday mornings, 'so many people one could hardly move', a scene resembling a Manet painting. On week-days there was another attraction: the pierrot troupes upon the sands, which Charles Laughton, also born in Scarborough, told him had made him determined to go on the stage. Even now, Sacheverell can remember the look of individual pierrots and the songs they sang. Years later, these childhood memories were brought

* Wood End, which had been empty for twenty years, had actually been bought in 1934, but the war interrupted the Corporation's plans, and it was not until 1951 that it was reopened in its new capacity.

back to him by the drawings of John Leech which seemed exactly to capture the spirit of those days, even though the strollers on the sands were ladies in crinolines and men in tweed suits of a forgotten fashion and long whiskers; a spirit that Rowlandson's earlier drawings could never so poignantly evoke for him. 'I had always believed that it was my mother who invented the little jockey carriages that were a feature of the town; but I now remember to have seen them in earlier drawings and paintings. How can one ever express the fascination of a Spa to a small child? That wonderful stone terrace built right into the sea with those theatrical buildings behind it. . . . Then, of course, the fore-shore was an unending attraction — and the lifeboat! My mother's family used to give a dinner for the lifeboat men and my brother as a small boy was taught to dance the horn-pipe by the coxswain of the lifeboat.'

Apart from this brief impression, Sacheverell has been shy of revealing himself in public. His one autobiographical book, *All Summer in a Day* (from which I have already quoted), is a mixture of direct reminiscence, characteristic flights of imaginative appreciation of art and artists, and semi-fictionalised evocations of youthful scenes. The de-scriptions of Renishaw I have already recorded; but the whole of the second part is devoted to a fantasia on the theme of the Scarborough scene, the sea, the ragged children and the pierrot shows he mentions in the article for the *Municipal Review*.

It is when he comes to these pierrot shows on the front, that he writes most vividly of the sea: 'They blew into a shrill and exaggerated life for one moment more, and it was as if one had blown upon red embers till some resemblance of flame came out of that dying struggle. I heard the loudly rattling piano again and felt that glass wall of air between my world and theirs. Everything was hurried in the last few minutes of their performance: and why? Because the sea, glittering all over its huge mass, was slowly creeping towards them over the crackling sands, which, themselves, shone with such a transparent fire under the sun's eyes that you could readily believe how important an ingredient sand might be towards the making of glass.

'The turn of tide one did not notice, but over a great stretch of what had not long ago been sand, the blue sea now shook and played in its tidal strength. It would besiege one rock after another, running back again so as to have the pleasure of once more surrounding and taking it. The actual shelves of sand it ran down as quick as wind bends the corn, but even this easy conquest it repeated again for its pleasure. It was shaking a thousand cymbals, rattling a thousand silver coins in each wave that broke; and this slighter music came out above those tumbling, sleepy moves of its great mass.'

It might be thought, because Sacheverell has almost completely avoided, in his writings, any political partisanship or zealous reforming advocacy, that he is indifferent to suffering and injustice in the world around him, except, as it were, as part of a dramatic backcloth. This would be to do a highly sensitive human being, all too easily moved to tears, a gross injustice. All through his work there are passages which show the alertness of his sympathetic eye and the quickness of his compassion.

As, for instance, in these descriptions of the poor children of Scarborough: 'The gutters were choked with the rubbish from cheap sweets or fruit and were the chosen playground for dozens of small flaxen-haired children. They were all

shouting out the same clatter of dispute as I passed them by
and walked past the opening of street upon street of coffin-
like houses, the front of each house having a door, as it
might be a mouth, and windows arranged like the nose and
eyes to this staring, senseless face. There must be some half-
dozen of these children to each brick tomb, and I could in
my mind see them pouring out at pale, twittering sunrise
and playing first of all upon the doorstep and then on the
drab threshold of the room as night turned cold and stern.
These children had, for the most part, the long Danish skulls
and the groundsel or bird-seed hair that I noticed in an
early part of this book when describing the miners' families
in Derbyshire who were looking for blackberries in the
September hedges. The cheapness of their toys made them
more pathetic than it is possible to imagine.'

A little later he describes the profound effect made upon
him by the sight of two small children, of the same 'long-
headed flaxen type', who, being from a very slightly higher
stratum of the working population, played alone: 'I could
see the hazards, their little strange chances, lying out before
them like the few poor effects of a soldier at a barrack-room
parade of his kit. . . . How could anyone climb out of this
black quicksand of ugliness and poverty; how could they
find foothold, even for a moment, in this sliding horror of
hopelessness! . . . Even the idea that they would think the
slum children from the town dirty and not fit for them to
play with was an anguish, because this argued that they must
see themselves as something apart and of a higher life than
those urchins of the street-corners. To be brought up in any
belief about yourself that is based on such tenuous defences
as a weekly wage is so near to the precipice edge as to give
one vertigo and an insensate longing to fall over; this

seemed to me to be as close to the abyss as it is possible to stand balanced.'

He concludes this long reflective and descriptive passage with the moment he arrives at his hotel door: 'As if in last reminder of my thoughts I found myself in that short space between hotel and station besieged by a rabble of small children. These were so vociferous, and so pale and starved, that it was impossible to believe one was in England; they were of all ages up to fifteen, the oldest and tallest among them showing incipient moustaches and long hairs on the face that wanted a razor. They were all shoeless, hatless, and in rags, and they made a gaunt and horrifying file, like one limb of a guard of honour, while I went through the swing-door of the hotel on my way to the groves and pavilions of comedy.'

4

EDITH was born in September 1887; Osbert in December 1892; and Sacheverell in 1897. If Edith, the strange child who did not fit, had been born second or third, when there was already a male heir, one cannot help feeling that her childhood might have been much happier. Their mother may have been frivolous, irresponsible, extravagant (as well as beautiful), and given to unpredictable fits of rage, but that she was capable of great fondness for her children is shown by Osbert's relationship with her in his earliest years. 'I was in the happy position as a small child,' he writes, 'of being my mother's favourite. I played on her bed, and upset everything with impunity. I adored her. Yet there were two things about her which I could not understand. The first time she lost her temper with me (I forget about what, but now I deeply sympathise with her), the whole world temporarily assumed a more tragic tone. I had been so sure of our relationship, now growing out of darkness into light, in which neither could do wrong for the other. I would not have believed that such a thing as this could happen, that so radiant and lovely and considerate a creature, always gay and gentle, could contain so dark a shadow within her.' This sudden violence of temper was all the more extraordinary to Osbert, because Lady Ida had a special knack of gaining the confidence of children, and establishing an affectionate intimacy with them, by her habit of treating them as equals and friends and never letting them suspect that she might be finding something they said, or asked, naïvely absurd and a subject for laughter.

In the concluding pages of *Splendours and Miseries* Sacheverell also writes of the deep fondness and love that existed between himself and his mother in his childhood. But it was exactly that affectionate intimacy of which they both speak that appears to have been lacking in Lady Ida's attitude towards Edith. 'I doubt whether any child was ever more mismanaged by her parents,' Osbert writes, and 'where she was concerned, a sense of humour, usually so noticeable a trait in both their natures, entirely deserted them'. Her seriousness, and her habit of refusing to accept the standards of the world in which her parents lived, especially about class, without critical examination, terrified Lady Ida. Edith was, from the first, impossible to mould to any conventional image, was of extreme nervous sensibility, and hated sport. 'You were an exceedingly violent child,' her mother said to her once, many years later. She loved books, and unswervingly followed her own likes in reading, which also alarmed her mother. Indeed one has the impression that fear arising from total incomprehension rather than anger lay behind Lady Ida's constant nagging and her cruel habit of criticising her daughter in public. On one occasion, after Osbert's birth had immediately relegated her to an even chillier second place in the nursery, in spite of the fact that she was five years older, she felt so unhappy that she attempted to run away from home.

The fact that her looks were as unconventional as her nature added to her parents' dismay. They were convinced that she was disfigured by having her nose out of the straight; and then noticed that she stooped slightly and that her ankles were thin and weak. They decided that something drastic must be done to restore her to the normal looks and normal shape that they so desperately desired for her, and sent her to an orthopaedic surgeon. No doubt the fact that Sir George and Lady Ida readily agreed to the treatment recommended by Mr Stout does not, by the standards of that day, imply deliberate cruelty so much as callousness — and perhaps an unconscious desire to compensate for not being able to bend her inner nature by bending her outward physique. To us, however, the treatment must sound utterly barbarous. 'After my first interview with Mr Stout,' Edith writes, 'I was trundled off to an orthopaedic manufacturer and incarcerated in a sort of Bastille of steel. This imprisonment began under my arms, preventing me from resting them on my sides. My legs were also imprisoned down to my ankles, and at night-time these, and the soles of my feet, were locked up in an excruciating contraption. Even my nose did not escape this gentleman's efficiency, and a band of elastic surrounded my forehead, from which two pieces of steel (regulated by a lock and key system) descended on each side of the organ in question, with thick upholstered pads at the nostrils, turning my nose very firmly to the opposite way which Nature had intended, and blocking one nostril, so that breathing was difficult.

'This *latter* adornment, however, was only worn during my long hours in the schoolroom, as it was thought that it might arouse some speculation — even, perhaps, indignation, in passers-by if worn in the outer world.'

In spite of these hideous trials, and the sense that Edith had, during most of her childhood, that her parents were hostile and uncomprehending, she records that after Lady Ida's disgrace and imprisonment, she became 'touchingly reconciled' to her, and forgave her for her existence. A copy of the original edition of *Façade* I have seen, contains the inscription to 'Darling Mother — with Edith's very best love'.

It is recorded that on one occasion in her childhood Edith was asked by a friend of her mother's what she was going to be when she grew up, and promptly replied: 'A genius'. She learned (or taught herself) to read before she was four years old, her earliest literature consisting of the fairy tales of the brothers Grimm and Hans Andersen, many of which frightened her by the coldness and loneliness which seemed to her to pervade them. By the time she was eleven, her organised home education had begun: 'I was subjected,' she writes, 'to a devoted, loving, peering, inquisitive, interfering, stultifying, middle-class suffocation, on the chance that I would become "just like everybody else".' Before she was thirteen, she had been 'kept in' Saturday afternoon after Saturday afternoon, because she refused to learn *The Boy Stood on the Burning Deck*, as the fact that he remained on the deck when everybody else had left it struck her as idiotic. About the same time, however, according to her own account in *Taken Care of*, she had found a poem which she fell in love with and learned by heart — Pope's *The Rape of the Lock* — 'secretly at night when my governess was at dinner — sitting up in bed, bending over, poring over it'. It is possible that when she wrote her memoirs at the end of her life, Edith ante-dated her enthusiasm for Pope's masterpiece by several years, for it is her brother Sacheverell's recollection that nothing in the eighteenth century pleased her until he pointed out the special beauties of Pope some years later. In any case, *The Rape of the Lock* taught her a lesson about poetry that she never forgot, and was to come back to again and again in after years, whenever she wrote about her own poetry or that of the poets she most admired. 'From the thin, glittering, occasionally shadowed, airy, ever-varying texture of that miracle of poetry, the instinct was instilled into me that not only structure, but also texture, are parents of rhythm in poetry, and that variations in speed are the result not only of structure, but also of texture.'

About the same time she was given the works of Shakespeare and of Shelley, and learned great chunks of them by heart. A year or two later, she discovered Swinburne's *Poems and Ballads*, an event that seems finally to have decided her that she must be a poet. In a letter to me she once wrote: 'I had an absolute mania for Swinburne as a girl, and learned a lot about vowel-techniques from him.' One must assume that at this time she began her immense reading in the English poets. Her artistic emancipation, however, had to wait until the arrival of her governess Helen Rootham in 1903. 'She was the first grown-up person,' writes Osbert, 'to seize the quality — though even then, perhaps, not at first the gifts — of this young girl, with her face of brooding and luminous melancholy, with her lank, golden-green hair, and her features, of so distinctive a kind, but which her character, though developing so fast, had not yet fully carved out of the soft matrix of childhood.' She was young, she had a passion for the arts, especially music, and considered them of more importance than anything else in the world — a revolutionary view in the society in which Edith and her two brothers were growing up. 'At that moment,' writes Osbert, 'my sister, whose character was fast developing, found it harder than ever to please my parents: but in Helen Rootham she found a champion, and we all gained a friend.'

In his 'Tribute', which introduced the programme for
the concert given in celebration of Edith's 75th birthday in
1962, Sacheverell wrote of his sister in these early years:
'My earliest memories evoke the figure of a young girl,
thirteen or fourteen years old, tall and thin, and already
copying out reams of poetry into her notebooks. Ten years
later she was forever reading aloud to my brother and myself from these notebooks. She started writing herself a
little later than this, having been delayed by circumstances
neither propitious nor happy. But, also, she was absorbed
for a time by her musical enthusiasm, and her love for playing the music of Chopin, Schumann, and Debussy.'

Helen Rootham remained the closest of friends of the
three Sitwells until her death in 1938, though from 1929
she had been ill in Paris, where Edith devoted herself to
looking after her, and records, sadly, the change in her
character that her illness caused.

Meanwhile, however, Helen Rootham encouraged by
every means Edith's dawning love of music and poetry.
When Edith was about twenty they started travelling together; first to Berlin, and then to Paris, where Edith was
able to indulge and develop her taste for French poetry,
above all of the Symbolists. She had, I believe, already discovered Rimbaud, and shared a particular love of *Les
Illuminations* with Helen Rootham, who was later to make
an excellent translation of this difficult and highly charged
work. All her life Edith was to find inspiring treasures in
Rimbaud's poetry and prose poems.

In 1914 they returned to London, and took a small flat
in Pembridge Mansions, Moscow Road. It was at the top
of the building, with a fine view of the trees in Kensington
Gardens. Osbert, when on leave from the Front, collected

furnishings for their two sitting-rooms. 'Helen's sitting-room,' Edith records, 'was hung with green and silver, mine with red and gold.' They lived there at first very quietly, because they were poor. Edith worked at the Pensions Office in Chelsea, for twenty-five shillings a week: it was extremely little, but at least it made her independent. Every summer, however, during and after the war, until 1932, she returned home to Renishaw.

At last, poetry began to stir in her. Her first verses were published in the *Daily Mirror*, and her first small collection, *The Mother*, as I have already mentioned, appeared in 1915. She was already twenty-eight.

Osbert's schooldays appear, in his autobiography, as a desert in which he found scarcely any oases at all. Of Eton he says: 'I liked Eton, except in the following respects: for work and games, for boys and masters.' He cared neither for athletic pursuits, nor for intellectual distinction in the approved categories. If he liked Eton, it was because it gave him, as few other public schools at the time did, the opportunity to read and educate himself in his own way. Also, he made some friends who were to last him a lifetime.

After he had left Eton, instead of moving to Oxford he had been sent to a military crammer, as he was considered too backward and unteachable for any other career. He had failed his examination for Sandhurst, but managed to get a commission in the Yeomanry (the Sherwood Rangers, in 1911, attached to the 11th Hussars). He had escaped this to travel in Italy, and then eventually to find himself with a commission in the Grenadier Guards. By the end of 1912, then, though he had not yet written anything he considered more than schoolboy trash, he was already enjoying

himself as a young man about town, a Guards officer with a
keen interest in the arts. Edith, five years older, was still
in the hands of her governess and spending much time
abroad; Sacheverell was still at Eton; yet both of them,
whenever possible, joined Osbert in exploring art galleries,
theatres, concert halls and opera houses where new movements were stirring. Sacheverell, the most precocious of the
three, was already devouring every book he could lay his
hands on, and writing reams of juvenile poetry — mainly,
as he has said, 'to please Edith'. It was an intoxicating time
in London, the five years or so before the outbreak of the
first World War, and the three Sitwells drank to the full.
When Sacheverell was on holiday from Eton, he would join
Osbert in exploring the art exhibitions: so eager was his
curiosity about all new movements that, even when only in
his mid-teens, he was writing to the leaders of the Vorticist
and Futurist movements, and exchanging views with them.
He was well over six feet in height, with a straight nose and
pinched-in nostrils typical of his mother's family, and the
air of 'a farouche young shepherd, but a shepherd of lions
rather than of lambs. He was already immersed in his lifelong search for knowledge, infused by a passionate love for,
and divination of, beauty.' Osbert declares that his range
and depth of learning, when at that early age, put him to
shame. Almost inseparable from his elder brother, he went
with him not only to see whatever was new in the art world
but also to the opera and ballet. Together they heard Chaliapin, 'at the very height of his powers, in *Khovanshchina*'.

Two years before, the famous Post-Impressionist Exhibition, held at the Grafton Galleries and organised by
Roger Fry, had startled and infuriated the conventional art
world of England. 'The public in 1910,' writes Virginia

Woolf in her biography of Fry, 'was thrown into paroxysms of rage and laughter. They went from Cézanne to Gauguin and from Gauguin to Van Gogh, they went from Picasso to Signac, and from Derain to Friesz, and they were infuriated. The pictures were a joke, and a joke at their expense.' Wilfrid Blunt thought that, apart from the frames, the whole collection wasn't worth more than £5. Roger Fry himself observed, with amused detachment, that his exhibition had caused the biggest outbreak of militant philistinism in England since Whistler. The modern movement had broken through, and the noise of splintering glass was horrific.

This event deeply impressed the young Osbert. 'The galleries in Bond Street and elsewhere,' he writes, 'though they could not, in so far as modern pictures were concerned, vie with those of Paris, showed for the most part eighteenth-century English pictures, Italian old masters, and modern English as well as French paintings: for the dealers had struck the Pre-Raphaelite camp, in which they had dwelt for so long, and moved on. England possessed its own painters again, and a ferment such as I have since never felt in this country prevailed in the world of art. It seemed as if at last we were on the verge of a great movement.' He goes on to describe the hope inspired by the work of Sickert, Nicholson, Steer, Orpen, McEvoy and Spencer Gore, and many other English artists 'then with a future, who today have no past'. One day in the winter of 1912, he visited the Chenil Galleries which consisted at that time of a small room of the simplest sort near the Post Office in the King's Road, and saw for the first time a collection of paintings by Augustus John. He was deeply impressed, and tried to persuade his father to purchase the whole exhibition: but in vain.

Of all the exciting artistic and literary manifestations of

the time, for the young Osbert, and his brother and sister, undoubtedly the most impressive was the Russian Ballet, which perhaps more than any other force revolutionised taste and artistic creation in Western Europe in the years before 1914. 'It becomes inevitable,' Osbert observes, 'when writing of it at this time, that the word *genius* should recur with frequency, almost with monotony, in these few pages, for no other word can describe the quality of the chief dancers or the influence at work: Stravinsky, Diaghilew, Karsavina, Fokine and Nijinsky.' In the three years, 1912, 1913 and 1914, so many new operas and ballets were being produced that it seemed to the Sitwell brothers that almost every evening they attended there were new experiments in dancing and music, a new artistic vision was being presented to them. Osbert describes his first experience of the revolutionary event, on a night up from Aldershot, a performance to which he went alone, having little or no idea of what the programme would be, or indeed of what ballet could be apart from the ballet interludes conventionally interpolated into operas: 'I did not reach the theatre until the moment when the curtain was going up, for the first time in London, on *L'Oiseau de Feu*. I had been so tired by the day's riding that I had nearly decided not to go — but directly the overture began to be played, I came to life. Never until that evening had I heard Stravinsky's name; but as the ballet developed, it was impossible to mistake the genius of the composer, or of the artist who had designed the setting; a genius plainly shared, too, by the chief dancers and the choreographer. Genius ran through the whole of this ballet. Nevertheless, Stravinsky towered above the others, a master. It may be that today the music of this particular piece sounds almost traditional when compared with his later work, such as *Le Sacre du Printemps* or *Les Noces*, but as I heard it and watched the accompanying dances, I was aware that for the first time I had been given the opportunity of seeing presented upon the stage a work of art, imbued with originality and with the spirit of its own day . . . a work of art that could not have existed before, and would cease to be given in its perfection, within the brief season of the dancers' finest span. Because, for the first time, I was able to watch, in addition, the dancing of great artists, Karsavina, and Adolf Bolm, who was superb in the part. Karsavina, so beautiful today, was then at the height of beauty and of her career, the greatest female dancer that Europe had seen for a century.'

In addition to his intellectual and aesthetic pursuits, Osbert was enjoying a full and extremely varied social life. His duties as a soldier kept him to Wellington Barracks or the Tower of London; from there he might go to Downing Street or Lambeth Palace or his Aunt Londesborough's establishment. After a dance or a late evening reception, he might eat a quick supper in a cab-shelter, or visit the Cabaret Club, where famous stars and lesser stars of the theatre mixed with painters and writers and the more adventurous officers of the Brigade of Guards. The Cabaret Club was a 'low-ceilinged night-club, appropriately sunk below the pavement of Beak Street', near the police station and the now famous Carnaby Street. It was 'hideously but relevantly frescoed' by Wyndham Lewis, and 'appeared in the small hours to be a super-heated Vorticist garden of gesticulating figures, dancing and talking, while the rhythm of the primitive forms of ragtime throbbed through the wide room. Over it presided Madame Strindberg, the third and not least exceptional of the great writer's wives.'

At the other end of the social scale, he was a constant guest of Margot Asquith in Downing Street, and frequented the splendid houses of Lady Brougham, his aunt Lady Londesborough, Lady Sackville and Mrs George Keppel, where the intellectual fare was certainly more conventional than in the Cabaret Club. Another hostess to whom he was especially faithful was his cousin, Mrs George Swinton, whose house was always full of painters and musicians, and whose reputation as a singer was then at its height. But in the musical world there was above all Lady Cunard's house at 20 Cavendish Square (almost entirely destroyed during the second World War), where Osbert met, among many other celebrities, Delius, Sir Thomas Beecham and George Moore, Lady Cunard's eccentric daughter Nancy, and Lady Diana Manners, whose beauty and personality, Osbert has written, 'placed her alone in the English scene'. 'The social world,' he comments, 'was more miscellaneously composed than ever it had been: it offered the most singular contrasts, while the ready friendliness found in so many places provided for me a lively intoxication. Indeed, the London of which I talk possessed such warmth and life, and existed, comparatively, so short a time ago, that I am continually surprised at its complete disappearance and extinction.'

In discussing the brave new worlds of ballet and music which were exciting the London audiences in those years, Osbert makes the interesting observation that he was able to enjoy them, to be among the first on the scene, so to speak, because he 'came from the stalls, from the wrong side of the house'. Opera and ballet were for the rich, and it was the rich that Diaghilew, for instance, cultivated in order to support his visionary enterprises. The 'stalls' were suspect in the eyes of the advanced writers, painters and musicians, 'convinced that nothing aesthetically good could come from such a quarter'. So it was that those who stood most to benefit from these new worlds, on whom they would have the most stimulating and fertile influence, failed to become properly aware of them until after the war.

Some years before this, another influence, of the utmost significance, had entered into the lives of the Sitwell children. Before going to Eton, Osbert had been sent to a private school which appears to have been even more crushing to the spirits of gifted and unusual boys than the average run of such schools in England at that time. He dwelt, he tells us, in a deep abyss of spiritual misery, and was only rescued by falling seriously ill, having to leave the school, and being advised to spend the winter in a warmer climate. His parents chose San Remo, where they rented a villa. This was the first, crucial experience of Italy for Osbert: 'San Remo is no more romantic than Margate, but it is, in landscape and people, Italian. And the very first morning that I woke on Italian soil, I realised that Italy was my second country, the complement and perfect contrast to my own. As I looked out of the window of my room, I knew that this was how I had always hoped the world would appear. . . . Light! Light was everywhere again, spattering ceilings, walls and floors, even through the narrow slats of the green Venetian shutters, which were kept closed throughout the middle of the day, light from the sky and light from the sea again — but how different a sea from that of Scarborough —, trembling, moving, affording an infinite richness of texture to every plain, dull surface. . . . Light vivified everything, there was no need for defiant colours. Since every stone glittered as though it were of gold, and every patch of lichen, even, swam in almond-husk green or rose, the vegetation here was darker, more grey than green, so as to afford contrast to the flowering skies and to the Mediterranean, with its tessellations of wine-colour and azure and copper, holding its hints of gold, and of a green more intense than that which clothed the land. And, as if the life-giving, creative light, besides calling out this entire range of colour, this wide vision of form, penetrated, too, to the heart of every human being, purifying it, I discovered the simple and unspoiled nature of the people of Italy, who laugh and cry and sing — or sang in those days — so easily.'

Osbert expatiates at some length on these first impressions of Italy in his convalescence and on subsequent visits in boyhood, a honeymoon that became a marriage when in 1909 his father purchased (in Osbert's name) the Tuscan castle of Montegufoni. He sums up: 'I mention at some length the effect, and lingering influence, of Italy on my brother, my sister and myself, because it provides a clue to the work which later we set ourselves — or which set itself for us — and have since striven, however imperfectly, to accomplish. By this path we came to the classical tradition, through the visual arts, rather than through Greek or Latin. In a sense, as artists, we thus belong to Italy, to the past of Italy, hardly less than to England, to that old and famous combination of Italian influence and English blood. We breathed in, without being wholly conscious of it, the space and proportion of Italy which for centuries gave grace to Western Europe and even to the Marches.'

It was an earlier vision of light that first awoke in Osbert the desire to become a writer. When he was about five years old, on a Saturday afternoon in June, after fearful scenes at

home (in Scarborough) with his father and his Swiss govern-
ness, due to his passionate desire to get out into the golden
afternoon rather than do his lessons, he was at last allowed
to go for his usual afternoon promenade with his nurse
Davis, about six o'clock. 'I ran to the edge of the pre-
cipitous cliff and stood there looking straight in the face of
the evening sun. The light bathed the whole world in its
amber and golden rays, seeming to link up every object and
every living thing, catching them in its warm diaphanous
net, so that I felt myself at one with my surroundings, part
of this same boundless immensity of sea and sky and, even,
of the detailed precision of the landscape, divided from it by
no barriers made by man or devil. Below me and above me
stretched the enormous merging of blue air and blue water
with golden air and golden water, fathomless, and yet more
and more fervently glowing every moment, the light
revealing new avenues and vistas up into space or out towards the horizon, as though the illimitable future itself
opened for me, and, as I watched, I lost myself. . . . All this
must have endured only an instant, for presently — but
time had ceased to exist — I heard Davis calling. The eye
of the sun was lower now. The clouds began to take on a
deeper and more rosy hue, and it was time for me to return
home: but this strange peace, of which poetry is born, had
for the first time descended on me and henceforth a new
light quivered above the world and over the people in it.'

Osbert calls this revelation 'seeing the salamander',
referring to an episode in the *Memoirs* of Benvenuto Cellini,
and adding that the salamander is the symbol of all art. The
next glimpse he gives us of his development as an artist is
the moment when he wrote his first real poem, in the middle
of the first World War.

As an officer in the Brigade of Guards, he was called up on the outbreak of the War. He is reticent about his experiences, which were chiefly of boredom and misery, enlivened by fantastically irrelevant letters from his father.

Sir George had always rather hero-worshipped the Kaiser and had a profound respect for Germany's military might, a feeling that was only increased by the naval bombardment of Scarborough in December 1914 — the very day before Osbert left England for the Front. The experience of this bombardment led him to send some advice at once to his son in France in case shells were being aimed at him too: to keep warm, have plenty of plain, nourishing food at regular intervals, and a nap in the afternoon. Apparently it never occurred to him that a soldier on active duty might have difficulty in following this advice.

Nevertheless, in the intervals of action, sleep came to mean much to Osbert: sleep and reading. He read *The Brothers Karamazov*, *Crime and Punishment* and *The Idiot*, and then turned again to his beloved Dickens. While re-reading *Our Mutual Friend* it occurred to him how well Dickens would have understood the squalor and misery of trench life, how brilliantly he might have rendered the atmosphere of the 'coffin-like ditches', the rats and the mud and the ruins and the atmosphere of mortal decay and death in which everything was plunged — as in the obscene alleyways of 'Tom-All-Alone' in *Bleak House*. He kept up a regular correspondence with Edith and Sacheverell: the war drew the three of them, who had always been very close, even closer together. And this closeness was reinforced by the long drawn-out anxiety and shame of the financial disaster that was gradually engulfing their mother at this very time.

Osbert and Sacheverell: sketch for the cartoon by Max Beerbohm, 1921

Mr Osbert Sitwell watches the Victorians step by: cartoon by Max Beerbohm

Osbert did not see himself as a particularly efficient officer, but all the same army life, even at the front, seemed to have advantages that he had not found in school life, especially in the civilised *camaraderie* of the Guards. His memory, as he gazed out on to the desolate landscape of no-man's-land from the trenches, kept on echoing the beggar's cry of 'Rags and Bones' which had filled him with such a sense of desolation in his boyhood in Scarborough. An involuntary censor, he finds, has wiped out much of the suffering and horror, though leaving the deepening sorrow of the loss of friends. Nevertheless, one entirely personal experience remains in vivid detail. He was going through his second period in the trenches. During one of the brief spaces of rest, in a billet not far from Ypres, what he describes as 'a combination of feelings not hitherto experienced' precipitated a poem, in the writing of which, to his astonishment, he found himself completely absorbed and removed from his immediate surroundings and pre-occupations. He admits that he had, like many other imaginative schoolboys, at the age of fifteen or so, started to write poetry which consisted mainly of immense tragedies in blank verse, one of which was a 'rather lurid Oriental fantasy' inspired by Oscar Wilde's *Salome* which he had just come across. But this creative experience was different: he felt that a new power was suddenly, and mysteriously, manifesting itself in him.

He goes on to describe how these verses were shown by a friend, Richard Jennings, leader-writer, literary editor and bibliophile (who was also responsible for Edith's first verses appearing in the *Daily Mirror*), to the editor of *The Times*, and shortly afterwards appeared there under the title *Babel*, in May 1916. To Osbert, this appeared as an overwhelming stroke of luck, surely 'the sole instance of a first effort by a young author being printed in an organ of such national and international celebrity, so that, in so far as writing was concerned, it can be said that my muse was born with a silver pen in her mouth'.

The experience was crucial. 'From the moment of my beginning to write, my life, even in the middle of war, found a purpose. Within the bounds of a few years, the new power revealed to me had sharpened my character, late, like that of all the members of my family in the past, in developing. To me hitherto work had always been a bugbear, something wan and listless, like a ghost, to be avoided, haunting the end of every spell of freedom and pleasure. I had acquired through my education no ability to concentrate. My mind rambled dully if I sat behind a desk. In short, I loathed work with all my heart, whether at school or later, and wherever possible evaded it. . . . But now I discovered my greatest pleasure — yet pleasure is not the correct term —, my greatest concern, an immersion and a transport, in this labour that had been revealed to me for my own.'

This is perhaps the place, before I move forward again to consider the place of the three Sitwells in the English intellectual and artistic world of the twenties, to call attention to two basic attitudes, characteristic of all three from the very beginning of their public careers, and most notably expressed in the works of Edith and Osbert.

Describing the excitement of discovering that he was a poet, an artist, with a brother and sister who shared his sense of dedication, Osbert writes: 'Yet fortunate as I was in this respect, fortunate above all others in my generation,

there was always hereafter a lurking duality: the excitement and interest to be derived from the lives we led, intellectual and devoted to art, and, underneath, the knowledge
of the powerful enmity of many . . . the bitter loathing of
the Philistine, and its continual symptoms in the press. For
I was never under any illusions as to the hostility of the
great book-hating public: a large and powerful body. All
this I believe I understood instinctively, as well as from the
results of experience, and better than most of my calling.
I realised that everything I said or wrote would be misunderstood by a great many — and my heredity, coming as
I do on all sides of stock that for centuries have had their
own way, and have not been enured to suffer insolence
passively, made it hard for me, and for my brother and
sister, not to fight back: (so it was, I am inclined sometimes
to think, as I survey the past three decades, that we gave as
good as we got!). We knew, in addition, all three of us, that
henceforth the sillier, more spiteful acquaintances of my
father's and friends of my mother's, who never tired of
mischief-making, would misrepresent every line we wrote
and every opinion attributed to us, and that this would be
reflected in our parents' conduct to us.'

Not only did they sense from the first the hostility of the
Philistines; but they saw through and despised the characteristic pursuits of their kind: 'They were scarcely at ease out
of the saddle,' writes Osbert describing the male guests at
the family gatherings of his youth, and likening them to the
leaders of Tamerlane's Golden Horde, 'and tended to fall
asleep if they entered a house and sat down for a moment,
except at meals. . . . Though in their fashion they were most
kind, yet if during the daytime a spare moment not already
occupied with slaughter occurred, it, too, must necessarily

be devoted at once to killing: otherwise they would consider they had wasted their time. No small creature on four feet, no feathered thing with wings, as it ran over the snow, was safe; neither the fox — but that was a lengthy business and very ritualistic — nor hare, shrieking its soul out like a human being, nor pheasants, designed so splendidly for a brief autumn, nor partridges, more discreetly clothed than those who shoot them, nor the dank, long-beaked birds of the marshes, snipe and woodcock, nor the ducks, with their hints of water in white and blues and greens, their bright features that might, when wet, so well be scales — none of these could hope for much mercy: while as for rabbits, they were collected by the attendants, put in sacks, and emptied out of them at a moment when there was no other killing to be had, so that tweed-clad hordes of men, and the women, many of whom accompanied them, could set their dogs on these confused, bolting creatures, and knock them on the head with sticks. . . .'

The Sitwells seemed to be born with the knowledge that attack, and repeated counter-attack, is more effective than the most dogged defence; these two basic attitudes, so closely connected with one another, were like a trumpet-call that was to be heard again and again in the ensuing years as the Sitwells charged into their latest fray.

5

IN his autobiography Osbert Sitwell makes great play with the family portrait group that his father commissioned from Sargent. It was intended to be a worthy modern pendant to the famous ancestral group of 'The Sitwell Children' painted by J. S. Copley a century before.

For a long time, after the birth of his three children, their father, Sir George, had been increasingly obsessed with the idea of having a family group painted, and, rather comically, wrote to his agent Peveril Turnbull in the spring of 1899 to say that he found himself slightly better off than he anticipated, and proposed therefore to realise at last his deep-seated ambition to immortalise his family. Turnbull was to ask his friend, the artist D. S. MacColl, to recommend a suitable painter. MacColl suggested Jacques-Emile Blanche; but meanwhile Sir George's cousin, George Swinton, had introduced him to Sargent, who seemed to Sir George exactly the right person to execute the desired masterpiece with sufficient panache and elegance. Sargent was invited up to Renishaw, and inspired to emulation by the sight of the Copley group, agreed to undertake the commission for £1,500.

Sargent insisted on doing the work only in his studio, and so all the accessories which were to appear in the background, the grand Brussels tapestry, the exquisite Adam commode, and a silver racing cup won by an ancestor at the Chesterfield Races in 1747, had all to be packed up and transported to London, accompanied by Sir George, Lady Ida, Edith, Osbert, Sacheverell and Yum the black pug, together with the Copley portrait for Sargent to keep the proportions right and his sense of emulation at the right pitch.

Osbert gives a very funny description of the painting of the group, and his father's constant attempts to interfere and teach the artist his business. 'My father held strong views concerning the relationship of the patron to the painter, who ought, he inwardly maintained, to occupy the same position as a bone to a dog — or, as for that, of a mouse to a cat —, being created and placed before him to be worried, gnawed and teased.' These interferences eventually provoked Sargent to outbursts of rage, which delighted Sir George, because in his opinion every artist worthy of the name should be capable of showing temperament. Differences of opinion appear to have become more acute as the work went on, but nevertheless Sir George's pleasure in it was great. Reporting to Turnbull in the middle of March, he wrote: 'Sargent's picture is going on famously and will I think be finished in a fortnight. We are all very much pleased with it. Lady Ida is standing in a white and silver evening-dress arranging flowers in that old silver bowl on a little first Empire table. Osbert and the baby are on the floor to her left, giving the black pug a biscuit. I am standing to her right in dark grey and with brown riding-boots with one hand on Edith's shoulder — she is in scarlet. The tapestry and old French chiffonier make a most satisfactory background. We have put Lady Ida in a black "shadow" hat, something like that in Copley's picture, with white feathers and red ribbons. . . .'

Edith's comments on the group are terse and caustic.

Of her father's riding dress: 'He never rode.' Of her mother's attitude, arranging flowers in the bowl: 'She never arranged flowers, and in any case it would have been a curious occupation for one wearing a ball-dress, even if, at the same time, she wore a hat.' And finally of herself during the sittings: 'I was white with fury and contempt, and indignant that my father held me in what he thought was a tender paternal embrace. (I was freed from my Bastille during the period of the sittings.)'

If one were to try to imagine a portrait group of the three Sitwells in the early twenties, at the time of their first impact on the English literary and social scene, one would, I think, see them, not exactly holding hands in a ring-a-ring-a-roses or lying side by side in a supernal swoon, as in the ingenious period photographs of Cecil Beaton;* nor entirely as in the well-known drawing by Max Beerbohm, where Osbert in white tie and tails and Sacheverell in dinner jacket address one another through the parrots perched on their respective wrists in mutual laudation. Perhaps a little of both aspects would be present, to emphasise their close-knit unity in the siege they had opened on the fortresses of

---

* It may seem a little unfair to call them 'period', as this particular style of photography was in fact created by Mr Beaton; but I do not believe it could have flourished at any other time in our century than the mid-twenties. In *Photobiography* he records enthusiastically the debt he owed to Osbert and Edith, whose readiness to pose in all the fanciful positions he invented for them set him off on his successful career. Of Edith he writes: 'With her etiolated Gothic bones, her hands of ivory, the pointed, delicate nose, the amused, deep-set eyes, and silken wisps of hair, I considered she must be more remarkable than any model that I would ever have the fortune to find. . . . Suddenly I found myself busy taking all sorts of exciting photographs. All at once my life seemed fulfilled. New and wonderful friends seemed to appear from nowhere.'

culture, the slight touch of aristocratic difference that always characterised them, that sense of belonging to the stalls, 'the wrong side of the house' in spite of their iconoclastic intentions, and, last but by no means least, the impression that they were playing a hugely enjoyable game, of poking fun and being rather rude to the Establishment of the time in the interests of their own publicity.

As this is a family group, they would of course dominate the foreground. Immediately behind them, to the left, would appear the leading lights of Bloomsbury, now in the heyday of their influence, E. M. Forster (a little detached), Virginia and Leonard Woolf, Maynard Keynes, Lytton Strachey, Roger Fry, Desmond MacCarthy (with his back turned to them), Clive and Vanessa Bell, Aldous Huxley, T. S. Eliot with the diffident smile of the guest, and, gambolling at their feet such ardent youthful figures as Raymond Mortimer, Duncan Grant and David Garnett. The background on this side would be of those eighteenth-century residential districts in the neighbourhood of the British Museum from which the group derived its name: Tavistock, Brunswick, Mecklenburgh, Bedford and Gordon Squares.

The picture would suggest a certain rather more than formal diplomatic inter-relationship between the foreground Sitwell group and the Bloomsbury group in the nearer middle distance, such as the relationship between two states who respect and yet at the same time suspect one another; an amicable conversation on a high level by the leaders, with a distinct undertone of snide criticism at a lower level.

On the right side of the picture, at a slightly further distance, would be depicted that group of poets, novelists and critics who came to be known as the Georgians, with the

elegant, slightly affected but genial figure of Sir Edward
Marsh as the focal point. The background here, changing
rather abruptly from the Bloomsbury square beside them,
would be of traditional English cricketing fields, with
ancestral elms and oaks on their boundaries and week-end
cottages peeping from the low, rolling hills behind them.
Arranged round Eddie Marsh would be such figures as
Harold Monro, W. H. Davies, Lascelles Abercrombie,
Gordon Bottomley, Edward Shanks, Edmund Blunden,
Robert Nichols, John Drinkwater and Sir John (then plain
Jack) Squire; Hugh Walpole casting ardent glances in the
direction of Bloomsbury; and a chubby Yorkshire boy,
Jack Priestley, at their feet. Separate, but nearer to the
Bloomsbury group, would be a small cluster of Irish bards
and dreamers, W. B. Yeats, James Joyce, 'A. E.' and James
Stephens. Away in the background would be the seated
Olympian figures of Joseph Conrad, Rudyard Kipling,
H. G. Wells, Bernard Shaw and Arnold Bennett; and
somewhere between them all, thumbing his nose in most
directions, a bearded young Nottinghamshire faun in
gamekeeper's costume, D. H. Lawrence.

Like those zephyrs that puff from the corners of Botticelli's pictures, arranged in the sky at various points would
be the symbolic figures of the Ladies Emerald Cunard,
Ottoline Morrell and Sybil Colefax; while from behind a
tree, with forked tail and mephistophelian grin, intent on
spoiling the fun of all these groups, Percy Wyndham Lewis
would be sharpening his satiric arrows.

This sounds rather a crowded canvas; and to be strictly
fair, of course, a number of equally notable figures in
their time, not mentioned by me, should also find their
places. Where, for instance, to place Mr William Somerset

Maugham? Mr Walter de la Mare? Mr John Masefield? Mr Ronald Firbank? Or Miss Katherine Mansfield and Mr John Middleton Murry? But for our purpose, if we are taking the Sitwells as our foreground, I believe the arrangement would be illustrative enough.

These early years after the first World War were a period of exciting literary experiment and discovery. As the Sitwells had already started their counterblast to the Georgian poets with *Wheels* in 1916, while the war was still raging, so Wyndham Lewis's *Blast*,* Eliot's *Prufrock*, James Joyce's *Portrait of the Artist*, D. H. Lawrence's *The Rainbow*, Lytton Strachey's *Eminent Victorians* and Virginia Woolf's *The Voyage Out* had all appeared before the peace was signed at Versailles. All these authors, however, were to reach the high tide of their creative activity in the twenties. By 1923, when the first performance of *Façade* took place, Huxley had published *Limbo* and *Crome Yellow*, Joyce *Ulysses*, Strachey *Queen Victoria*, Eliot *The Waste Land* and Virginia Woolf the first of her novels in the new manner, *Jacob's Room*. If one takes into consideration what was being published by French and American authors at the same time, Proust, Gide, Hemingway and Dreiser for example, I do not think we can find in our century a short space of years so crowded with innovating achievement.

The Sitwells' relations with Bloomsbury were, as I have already suggested, ambivalent. Part of the reason, one cannot help suspecting, was that Bloomsbury was founded on Cambridge, and neither Edith nor Osbert ever went to an University. Osbert has written: 'The great figures were Roger Fry, Virginia Woolf, Clive Bell, Vanessa Bell,

* The first number of *Blast* appeared in 1914 before the war broke out. *Tarr* appeared in 1918.

Lytton Strachey and Duncan Grant. After them followed a sub-rout of high-mathematicians and low-psychologists, a tangle of lesser painters and writers. The outlook, natural in the grand exemplars, and acquired by their followers, was one of great tolerance: surprise was never shown at any human idiosyncrasy, though an amused wonder might be expressed at the ordinary activities of mankind. . . . No less than by the sentiments themselves, the true citizens of Bloomsbury could be recognised by the voice in which they were expressed. The tones would convey with supreme efficacy the requisite degree of paradoxical interest, surprise, incredulity: in actual sound, analysed, they were un-emphatic, save when emphasis was not to be expected; then there would be a sudden sticky stress, high when you would have presumed low, and the whole spoken sentence would run, as it were, at different speeds and on different gears, and contain a deal of expert but apparently meaningless syncopation.'

Osbert, with his insatiable interest in exploring the intel-lectual and artistic world of his time, even if this as often led him to satirical comment as to enthusiasm, was more often to be found in the company of the Bloomsbury 'Junta' (as he called it) than Edith. 'I do not think I should have "fitted into" the closely serried company of Bloomsbury,' she observed. 'I was not an unfriendly young woman, but I was shy, and yet, at unexpected moments, was not silent — and silence was much prized, sometimes to the embarrass-ment of persons outside the inner circle of Bloomsbury.' Nevertheless, she added, 'the company of Bloomsbury were kind-hearted, and from time to time I entered it on sufferance'.

For Virginia Woolf, high priestess of Bloomsbury as

many saw her, both Osbert and Edith have confessed to great admiration and respect. Osbert has written of her as being 'notably beautiful with a beauty of bone and form and line that belonged to the stars rather than the sun', and that she 'manifested in her appearance, in spite of the modernity that was also clearly hers, a Victorian distinction. She made little effort to bring out the quality of her looks, but she could not destroy it. It has often occurred to me, when I have seen Roman patrician busts of the fourth century, how greatly she resembled them, with her high forehead, fine, aquiline nose and deep-set, sculptural eye-sockets. Her beauty was certainly impersonal, but it was in no way cold, and her talk was full of ineffable fun and lightness of play and warmth. I have never known anyone with a more sensitive perception of the smallest shadows cast in the air around her: nor could I ever understand why people were — but certainly they *were* — frightened of her; because, though there was, and I am sure she would have admitted it, a human amount of malice in her composition (and how greatly the dull-minded would have complained if there had not been!), there was very much more, and most unusual, gentleness.'

Edith was also immediately struck by Virginia Woolf's appearance. She noted that she 'had a moonlit transparent beauty. She was exquisitely carved, with large thoughtful eyes that held no foreshadowing of that tragic end which was a grief to everyone who had ever known her. To be in her company was delightful. She enjoyed each butterfly aspect of the world and of the moment, and would chase the lovely creatures, but without damaging the coloured dust on their wings. Whenever anyone present said anything pregnant, she would clasp her long delicate hands together and laugh with pleasure. In her own talk she always went straight to the point. For instance, on the first occasion when I met her, at a dinner party given by Osbert and Sacheverell, she asked me "Why do you live where you do?" "Because I have not much money." "How much money a year have you?" I told her. "Oh well, I think we can do better for you than that," she said thoughtfully.'

The earliest picture Osbert gives us of meeting Lytton Strachey is at a party to celebrate the end of the first World War in Monty Shearman's rooms in the Adelphi, at which Bloomsbury had turned out in full force. 'I remember the tall, flagging figure of my friend Lytton Strachey, with his rather narrow, angular beard, long, inquisitive nose, and air of someone pleasantly awaking from a trance, jigging about with an amiable debility. He was, I think, unused to dancing. Certainly he was both one of the most typical and one of the rarest persons in this assembly. His individual combination of kindness, selfishness, cleverness, shyness and sociability made him peculiarly unlike anyone else. As I watched him, I remember comparing him in my mind to a benevolent but rather irritable pelican.' After this, it is clear that they met frequently, at least in the early years after the war, and Osbert became an admirer of his work, especially in its aspect of debunking the formerly unassailable heroes of the Victorian era.

Edith, on the other hand, did not find his work sympathetic, nor, I suspect, the man himself. With Roger Fry, however, her relations were much closer and her feelings warm. She sat to him for several portraits. 'For one of these I wore a green evening dress, the colour of the leaves of lilies, and my appearance in this, in the full glare of the midsummer light of midday, in Fitzroy Square, together with the appearance of Mr Fry, his bushy, long grey hair floating from under an enormous black sombrero, caused great joy to the children of the district as we crossed from Mr Fry's studio to his house for luncheon. . . . Mr Fry was a most delightful companion, learned and courteous; he had a great gift for attracting and retaining friendship. Warm-hearted, generous-minded and kindly, he was always espousing some lost cause, championing some unfortunate person, rushing at some windmill with a lance. In other respects he was dreamy and vague, incapable of noticing any but a spiritual discomfort.' For Osbert and Sacheverell Roger Fry was not only a friend but spiritual mentor, hierophant and powerful ally in their enthusiasm for modern art.

Undoubtedly the closest friend among the Bloomsbury group for all three Sitwells was Aldous Huxley, who having been born in 1894 was rather younger than the leading figures, in fact of their own generation. They had met him and his first wife Maria for the first time after they had invited him to contribute to *Wheels*. He had replied by inviting Edith to luncheon at the Isola Bella restaurant in Soho, 'in a dreamlike golden day in June'. Edith was struck by his willowy tallness, his full lips 'and a rather ripe, full but not at all loud voice. His hair was of the brown, living colour of the earth on garden beds. As a young man, though he was always friendly, his silences seemed to stretch for miles, extinguishing life, when they occurred, as a snuffer extinguishes a candle.' In contrast to these silences, when he did speak she found him one of the most accomplished talkers she had ever known. His long monologues, which might be sparked off by almost any conceivable subject under discussion, were brilliantly erudite, elaborate and entertaining, and also frequently of an absurdity that seemed to her deliberate.

'The animal and vegetable world became endowed, under the spell of his talk, with human characteristics, usually of a rather scandalous nature. I remember one monologue of this description on the subject of the morals of the octopus tribe — the tribe in question being, according to Aldous, conversant with Ovid's theory of love. He expatiated on the advantages possessed by the octopus in every amorous adventure . . . so many arms with which to enfold the beloved! His enthusiasm grew as he proceeded. We were, at the moment, on a platform in Sloane Square underground station. It was Sunday morning, the platforms were crowded, and the passengers waiting for trains listened, spellbound, to the monologue.'

These were his lighter moods. At other times, she records that he would discuss with her and her brothers, with endless zest and erudition, many artists, musicians, painters and sculptors who had been out of favour with an older generation but were now — to a large extent owing to his own enthusiasm — coming into fashion again. She describes Maria as having 'beautiful blue eyes like those of a Siamese cat', and a gentle and endearing manner. They were near neighbours, and if Osbert and Sacheverell were not in town, they nearly always joined forces for social occasions.

Osbert also records the fascination of Aldous Huxley's conversation and the depth of his silences. He describes how he and Lytton Strachey used to come to visit him in hospital, after he had been demobilised in the winter of 1918–19: 'The silent elongated forms of Aldous Huxley and Lytton Strachey could occasionally be seen drooping round the end of my bed like the allegorical statues of Melancholy

and of a rather satyr-like Father Time that mourn sometimes over a departed nobleman on an eighteenth-century
tombstone. Lytton's debility prevented him from saying
much, but what he did say he uttered in high, personal
accents that floated to considerable distances, and the queer
reasonableness, the unusual logic of what he said carried
conviction. . . . As for Aldous, Nonchalance, perhaps, more
than Melancholy, should have been the image we took him
to represent. He was then very young, I think twenty-three.
Though often silent for long periods, he would talk for an
equal length of time with the utmost fascination. Versed in
every modern theory of science, politics, painting, literature
and psychology, he was qualified by his disposition to deal
in ideas and play with them. Nor would gossip or any
matter of the day be beneath his notice: though even these
lesser things would be treated as by a philosopher, with
detachment and an utter want of prejudice. But he preferred
to discourse of more erudite and impersonal scandals, such
as the incestuous mating of melons, the elaborate love-
making of lepidoptera, or the curious amorous habits of
cuttlefish. He would speak with obvious enjoyment, in
a voice of great charm, unhurried, clear without being loud,
and utterly indifferent to any sensation he was making.
Thus the most surprising statements would hover languidly
in air heavy with hospital disinfectants.'

Very early on the Sitwells made up their minds not only
to be in the van of what was new in English literature in the
early post-war years, and to be closely associated with the
other leaders, but also to lead in the appreciation of the other
arts, particularly where the English seemed to be lagging
behind other countries. Sacheverell, young though he was,
had already developed a great enthusiasm for Italian opera

The Copley group: Frank, Mary, Hurt and Sitwell Sitwell

The Sargent group: Edith, Sir George, Lady Ida, Sacheverell, Osbert

Edith Sitwell by Pavel Tchelitchew

Design for mural at Montegufoni by G. Severini

and singing, and Osbert relates an amusing occasion when they decided to honour Madame Tetrazzini, who had returned to sing at Covent Garden, by presenting the great prima donna with a wreath of bay and myrtle in the name of the 'young writers of England'. Tetrazzini agreed to receive the deputation, which consisted of seven or eight persons including Osbert, Sacheverell, Edith and Aldous Huxley — who prepared the speech with them at dinner the night before.

The next day, after luncheon, they assembled at the Savoy, and were shown up to Tetrazzini's private suite. She was evidently determined to make the most of the occasion, for the sitting-room had been filled with white lilac, and the press alerted. Several journalists were present, and a camera-man with a high-mounted camera in the fashion of the day and an assistant for the flashlights. They had not long to wait before 'the bedroom door was flung open, and the famous prima donna entered. Short, fat, age-ing, wearing an over-elaborate brown *crêpe* dress, with much lace attached to it, she nevertheless had a captivating air of kindness and good-nature, and walked as one used to receiving acclamation. She advanced slowly, making a conventional theatrical gesture of greeting and pleasure, with her right hand to the poets, drawn up in line, and with her left hand to the camera-man, up his ladder ready to pull the trigger, and to the journalists, their pencils poised. The tall figure of Sacheverell, very young — just over twenty — stood heading our number, with Aldous, over-topping him, just behind. Slowly, very slowly, she continued to move toward us. The camera-man was just giving the signal, when suddenly the great singer caught her foot in a rug and fell flat! . . . There are those, I know, who hold that no fall, whatever the circumstances of it, can ever be funny. All I can say is that I disagree with them. . . . Fortunately, she had come to no hurt, and still more oddly, seemed singularly undiscomfited by her misadventure. She was helped up, and straightened her dress: the poets straightened their faces: the camera-man again got ready: Sacheverell was just going to read our message, when, this time impelled I suppose by curiosity, Tetrazzini snatched the paper from him. Sacheverell, who dislikes speaking in public, was nevertheless determined to go through with it, so he snatched it back, saying at the same time in his deep voice, "Prego, Divinissima," and began to read. The camera clicked — and so thus a delightful occasion remains, enshrined in the dusty office files of newspapers.'

Nothing daunted, the 'young writers of England' made another, equally melodramatic–hilarious (and equally uncharacteristically English) appearance on a parallel occasion described by David Garnett in *The Familiar Faces*. Francis Birrell arrived in their bookshop one day to announce that he had promised Osbert that morning to present a laurel wreath to Chaliapin. 'At half-past eleven our little party punctually assembled and was shown into a vast ballroom at the back of the Savoy overlooking the Thames. It consisted of Osbert and Sacheverell Sitwell, William Walton, Frankie, Raymond Mortimer who had just come down from Oxford, and me. But if the poets and writers and musicians of England were select and few, the photographers and newspapermen made up the numbers. Osbert was carrying an enormous laurel wreath such as visiting sovereigns lay on the Grave of the Unknown Soldier or the Cenotaph. He formed us up in line at one end of the vast room and sent word to the great Russian singer that we were waiting.

Twenty minutes later we were informed that Chaliapin was very nearly awake. His breakfast would be sent up to his room shortly. We broke formation and entered into conversation with the reporters. Three-quarters of an hour went by. Some of the reporters looked anxiously at their watches, several of the photographers disappeared. Osbert sent up another message and after a long period of waiting a messenger came down to say that the maestro was having his bath. At half-past one I began to feel faint and even Frankie had exhausted his topics of conversation. Just before two o'clock word came that Chaliapin was on his way. Osbert hurriedly arrayed us in line dressed by the right. Then, as Chaliapin came into the ballroom and crossed the vast floor, he stepped smartly two paces forward, said a few words and presented the wreath in the best Brigade of Guards manner. It was most appropriate, for at close quarters one saw that Chaliapin was built on the lines of the Cenotaph. He over-topped even Sacheverell. The great Russian seized the wreath and with extraordinary *savoir-faire* did not even glance at it but sent it spinning away behind him across the polished floor. Then, taking Osbert into his bear's hug, he embraced him warmly, kissing him on each cheek and then holding him at arms' length, gazed with delight at seeing a poet so close.'

Alas, by the time Chaliapin appeared the patience of the photographers had been exhausted: they had all gone, and the great occasion failed to be recorded for posterity. There is no record that the 'young writers of England' ever made a third attempt to honour a foreign *artiste* in so solemn a manner.

The earliest major offensive mounted by the Sitwells on behalf of the modern spirit in art was the Exhibition of

Modern French Art at Heal's in the Tottenham Court Road in 1919, organised by Osbert and Sacheverell with the aid of Zborowski, the Parisian dealer, and the sympathetic encouragement of Roger Fry. This was certainly the most important such exhibition since Fry's own Post-Impressionist exhibitions in 1910 and 1912, already referred to. The name was, perhaps, a little misleading: it was a selection of the work of the contemporary School of Paris, which of course included Belgians, Russians, Spaniards and Italians as well as native Frenchmen. Osbert has described the excitement of the preparations, so soon after the war:

'The days before the opening of the Exhibition are memorable to me because of the interest of seeing the pictures unpacked, and of hanging them. During the war it had been for so long out of the question to see modern French pictures at all, except for a single specimen at some gallery, that considerable excitement now evinced itself. The July evenings were very hot, and after dinner, at about nine o'clock every evening, while my brother, Zborowski and I supervised the hanging, friends would come in from the Eiffel Tower Restaurant and from Fitzroy Street nearby, to watch. Among those present at these unveilings would be our hierophant, Roger Fry, who walked round from his studio. The Exhibition, though by no means enormous, included pictures by — among others — Othon Friesz, Vlaminck, Derain, Matisse, Picasso, Modigliani, Survage, Soutine, Suzanne Valadon, Kisling, Halicka, Marcoussis, Léger, Gabriel-Fournier, Ortiz, André Lhote, Utrillo, and Dufy, and sculptures by Archipenko and Zadkine. Derain and Picasso had both made their personal appearance in London that summer, when Diaghilew had produced the two finest ballets of his second period, *La Boutique Fan-*

tasque, and *The Three-Cornered Hat*. I had been present at
the first night of both performances, and shall never forget
the excitement of first seeing truly modern works of scenic
art upon the stage.'

In spite of the fact that Roger Fry's revolutionary exhibitions were almost a decade away in the past, the practic-
ally *de rigueur* explosions of philistine outrage followed in
the press, though, as Clive Bell has told us in *Old Friends*,
Zborowski did very well with the Exhibition, and 'supply
hardly met the demand'. Osbert and Sacheverell, in the
hope of preventing the anticipated explosion, had persuaded their friend Arnold Bennett, with his well-known
practical sense and high contemporary reputation as a
pundit, to write the preface to the catalogue. Their plan
failed. Osbert records: 'Every day the public tantrums,
whether inside the Mansard Gallery or outside it, in the
columns of the newspapers, increased. For the most part
the critics showed themselves impressed, at the lowest were
civil: it was in the news and correspondence columns that
riots and mutinies broke out. A notably irate series of letters,
arising out of a favourable account of the pictures by Clive
Bell, appeared in the *Nation*, and continued for six weeks, a
fortnight after the Exhibition had closed! Throughout, the
attackers maintained a strong moral note, and one of them
declared that at one moment he had felt the whole collection
of pictures to be "a glorying in prostitution"!'

Osbert goes on to describe a comic encounter with one
of the most furious of the Philistines, W. H. Mallock, once
well known as the author of *The New Republic*, and at that
time an elderly fellow-guest of Osbert and his brother,
during the hot August days which followed the opening of
the Exhibition, at Mrs Ronald Greville's house at Polesden

Lacey. The two Sitwells used to go up to town every morning to attend to the business of the Exhibition, and return to Polesden Lacey every evening in time for dinner. On one of these occasions, on arriving at Bookham, the station for Polesden Lacey, they found an elderly gentleman looking in rather a distraught manner for the car which should have been there to transport all three of them to the house. This was Mallock, described by Osbert as an 'Old Chinoiserie tottering about in the heat in a state of despair'. The Rolls failed to turn up, so the Sitwell brothers offered to carry his luggage on the one and a half mile walk. To their dismay they very soon discovered that their polite and self-sacrificing efforts on his behalf had in no way soothed the rage about their Exhibition that seethed in his breast.

'He proved to be an ingenious and assiduous organiser,' writes Osbert. 'Each evening, when Sacheverell and I returned to Polesden, no less tired out by the heat of the days than rendered uneasy by profitless argument in the Gallery, and by the ferocious attacks delivered on us in the evening papers, which we had just read, unsuspecting, in the train, we would find the bulk of the guests assembled to meet us, grouped either just outside the front door or on the stone steps of the loggia. They were fresh as if they had just issued from a rest-cure, yet fiery in spirit as only bridge and golf can make people. . . . This chorus of ambassadors, political peers, retired Speakers, ministers and their wives, were ready for us: the figureheads had been supplied, if not with arguments, at least with sentiments of an unimpeachable respectability, by one more wily, though generally speaking less well preserved, who had contrived by a little judicious meddling to make them associate in their minds a political regime they disliked with certain works of art. . . .

I think it was the photographs of the Modigliani portraits, appearing now nearly every day in the press, which furnished Mallock with his chief weapons: just as the pictures themselves exacerbated the public.'

One of the great services which the Sitwells rendered through this Exhibition was, as Osbert justly claims, the introduction of Modigliani's pictures to the English public. Osbert suggests that though it had been possible, before the Exhibition, to appreciate this highly original artist's drawings, the oil paintings showed, to those who had eyes to see, what a master he was of the medium of oil, and the extraordinary sculpturesque quality inherent in his nudes and portraits. He records that beside the table in the middle of the Gallery at which he and Sacheverell and Herbert Read took their turns to sit and act as information bureau, was 'an enormous wicker basket full of sheaves of Modigliani drawings, from which the visitor could choose a specimen for a shilling'. He also records that the Parisian dealers allowed him to choose one painting for himself as reward for his services in organising the Exhibition. He chose a superb *Peasant Girl*, for which he paid four pounds. He and his brother were so excited by the Modiglianis on show, so deeply moved and convinced of the artist's essential worth, that they tried to persuade their father to buy the whole lot for something under a thousand pounds — a ridiculously low price, in view of the value Modigliani paintings were very soon to be fetching on the international market. The move failed; but a few years later, a friend persuaded Osbert, who was badly in need of money, to part with *Peasant Girl* for eighty pounds, pointing out that this represented a profit of nearly two thousand per cent. A week after the transaction, Osbert discovered that this

friend had re-sold it for two thousand pounds. And, to point
the giddy rise in Modigliani values even more clearly,
Peasant Girl was on sale a few months later at a famous
Parisian dealer's shop for four thousand pounds.

Modigliani was dying at the time; but in the sphere of
music, at almost the very same moment, the Sitwells were
about to lend their support and enthusiastic appreciation to
a boy of sixteen who had just entered Christ Church and
already (to their minds) showed unmistakable signs of the
musical genius which is now universally acknowledged.
Sacheverell, fretting at Oxford, one day told his brother
that the sole redeeming feature of life at the University was
the discovery of this boy, William Walton, who had so impressed the organist, Dr Henry Ley, and the Dean, Dr
Strong, of Christ Church, that the latter had managed to
have the rules relaxed in order that he should pass directly
from the Cathedral Choir School to the college at this, for
modern times, extremely early age. I have already described
how, in 1923, Walton appeared as the collaborator of the
Sitwells in *Façade*, still thought of as one of his most
brilliant musical achievements; but the friendship and
association had been close, and ripening fast, during the
intervening years.

The first occasion on which Osbert met him was when,
after leaving hospital early in 1919, he went to Oxford to
see Sacheverell and Siegfried Sassoon, who had been the
first of their friends to meet the young musician, through the
Canadian poet, Frank Prewitt. They were all four invited
to tea by Walton, and Osbert records that 'sensitiveness
rather than toughness was the quality at first most apparent
in him. He appeared to be excessively shy, and on this
occasion spoke but little, for I think he was rather in awe of

us, as being his elders.' To relieve the constraint, his guests asked him to play some of his own compositions, of which, though he was only in his seventeenth year, a number already existed. Comically enough, their impression was that he revealed 'a lack of mastery of the instrument that was quite unusual', and so they were unable to judge the quality of what he was playing. 'It was, indeed,' Osbert concludes, 'as impossible that afternoon to estimate his character or talents as it was to foresee that for the next seventeen years he would constitute an inseparable companion and friend, and an adopted, or elected, brother to Edith, Sacheverell and myself.'

The Sitwell brothers moved into what was to be Osbert's home until long after the end of the second World War, No. 2 Carlyle Square, in November of 1919; but between their meeting with Walton at the beginning of 1919 and that move, he was given a room at the top of the house in Swan Walk, for which a piano was hired for him and where he could work at his compositions, and, according to Osbert, 'sat by the window for long periods, eating black-heart cherries from a paper bag, and throwing the stones out of the window, down on the smooth brown-tiled pavement outside the door'. Osbert's housekeeper, Mrs Powell, became very attached to him, and looked after him 'with much imaginative tact and consideration' for the next twelve years until her death.

From that time, Walton accompanied the Sitwell brothers when they travelled to Renishaw and Scarborough, and further afield on their expeditions to Italy and elsewhere in Europe. They brought him together with Bernard Van Dieren, the brilliantly gifted young composer of mixed Dutch and French blood who died in 1936, with Gerald

Berners, and the young Constant Lambert, 'at the age of seventeen a prodigy of intelligence and learning'. Osbert observes that, keen though he and Sacheverell were to do all they could to advance Walton's chances and genius, the concrete results seemed to them very small. 'In the end, perhaps, all that we were able to accomplish directly for him was to have prevented his being sent to one of the English musical academies and to have lent him, as a musician, what prestige we ourselves possessed in the world of art and writing at a time when he lacked supporters, and when, in consequence of our attitude, we incurred a certain amount of odium, both from those who did not believe in him and from those who did. . . . We were able to keep him in touch with the vital works of the age, with the music, for example, of Stravinsky, and to obtain for him, through the kindness of our old family friend E. J. Dent, an introduction to Busoni, a modern master of counterpoint. . . . He also at times had the benefit of consulting Ernest Ansermet on various problems of composition. Moreover, by travelling in our company in Italy, Spain and Germany, he soon acquired a knowledge of the arts, both past and present, belonging to those countries. It was noticeable from the first that he manifested an innate feeling for the master-pieces of painting and architecture, no less than of music.'

One should, I feel, add — what Osbert does not in fact mention at this point — that association with the Sitwells was the direct cause of the creation of that early masterpiece *Façade*.

During these years, all three Sitwells would migrate for long summer periods to the family home at Renishaw. 'There were relays of very young writers, musicians, poets, painters, whom my sister, my brother or I had asked,'

Osbert relates. Frequent among these visitors were William Walton, Constant Lambert and Peter Quennell. Evelyn Waugh, who was first invited there in 1928, was fascinated by Sir George, and described him as 'slightly estranged' from the large party his children had invited. He noted with fascination during his stay 'how his beard would assume new shapes with his change of mood, like the supple felt hat on an impersonator. Sometimes he would appear as King Lear on Dover cliffs, sometimes as Edward Lear on Athos, sometimes as Mr Pooter at Margate. Tonight he was Robinson Crusoe. I think it was in his mind, then, that rather than being, as he was, a rare visitor to Renishaw, he lived there uninterruptedly all the year round and had in consequence lost touch with the life of fashion which was his birthright.'

Osbert has painted a picture of the family at Renishaw at the time, a *conversazione* piece in his mother's boudoir, during one of the occasions when Lady Ida persuaded her Swiss maid, Frieda, to give a performance of yodelling — which she would only consent to do from behind a Japanese screen. 'My sister would be sitting on the bed. Now a person of the utmost distinction and beauty, with her long slender limbs and long-fingered hands, and the musing but singularly sweet expression which always distinguished her, she belonged to an earlier, less hackneyed age, in which the standards of Woolworth mass production did not exist. . . . My mother, who had so cruelly ill-used her, had come to love her society, her wit and perception, and it was symptomatic of Edith's fineness of character that she responded and, now that my mother was growing old and her spirits flagging, set herself, at a great waste of her own energy and time, to amuse her — and there was little else one could do for her. Edith, then, would be sitting on the bed: while on a very straight Chippendale chair, but thrown backward and supported in front by his own two long legs, Sacheverell would balance his tall frame. His appearance at that age — twenty-five or six —, his very handsome head, with hair curling at the sides, and with its cut and contours so Italian in essence, but so northern in colour, translated perfectly the strange power and intensity that have always been his, the generous warmth of his temperament, so genial and impulsive, the passion of many kinds that burns in him — passion for people, for books, for learning, for works of art, for old lamps that can be lit again at his fire —, the wit, distinguished and apt, which he despises in himself and does nothing to cultivate, instead preferring the jokes of others which he so immensely enjoys: the flash, deep as bright, of his anger, large as the scale of his mind and frame, but never enduring, breaking down eventually into a smile, though by no means an easy smile. Meanwhile, I with my rather heavy mask and build, would be seated in an armchair opposite. Frieda's shelter was in front of the door, and sometimes, just as her voice had reached the top of a high mountain, and was preparing to receive answer from another, my father, attracted by the sound and always liking to know what was going on, would bolt in and find himself enclosed with her behind the Japanese screen.'

Meanwhile, in the middle twenties, Osbert had persuaded his father to emigrate to Italy. He alleges that he took this step mainly in order to get rid of him, for the sake of the future careers of himself, his sister and brother: Sir George's constant presence, his fussing interference, domineering alternating with touching dependence, and his inescapable eccentric schemes, made, they decided, a really free life for themselves as authors impossible as long as he was at hand in England. One cannot help feeling, however, that Osbert was almost as much inspired as his father by the idea of developing an estate in Italy. The Castle of Montegufoni had been purchased by Sir George in 1909, in Osbert's name, at a knock-down price. It constituted an enormous complex of ancient buildings, at one time the house of the Acciaiuoli family (who had been a reigning family in Greece at the time of the Frankish occupation in the thirteenth century), and now in a state of considerable disrepair. A terraced garden and an intensively cultivated estate consisting mainly of vineyards surrounded the castle. Sir George described his purchase in an enthusiastic letter to Osbert, explaining that: 'We shall be able to grow our own fruit, wine, oil — even champagne! ... The purchase, apart from the romantic interest, is a good one, as it returns five per cent. The roof is in splendid order, and the drains can't be wrong, as there aren't any.' After the announcement of this extravagant purchase, the letter, to Osbert's bewilderment, ended with an admonition to his young son to avoid 'that miserable career of extravagance and selfishness which has already once ruined the family'.

In a letter to his agent at the time, Sir George said that he proposed 'to put some rooms to rights, and perhaps go there for a few weeks in the vintage time, to see the champagne made'. He was, one feels, trying to present an entirely romantic purchase as the action of a practical man of affairs. Nevertheless, for the next twenty or more years, the visits of the Sitwells to their new castle were only fitful, and immense rebuilding and improvement operations were set in motion. Osbert describes his first impression of the estate that had been bought in his name at the age of seventeen, which resembles love at first sight: 'as, at the end of the twenty-mile drive, we motored down the steep hill between the stone lion and the stone greyhound — supporters of the Acciaiuoli coat of arms —, I was astonished to find that I not only knew, as I did from photographs, the garden façade, but that I also recognised the other, north side, so different in aspect and architecture, from having seen it in a dream.'

In *Great Morning*, Osbert reveals how early and how deeply his love of Montegufoni took root. He rhapsodises over the gardens, which, in mid-October, resembled those of an English June; filled with roses, carnations, verbena, ranunculus, plumbago and lemon-trees in flower, with the blue-green and emerald-green lizards darting out over the walls covered with tufts of rose-coloured snapdragon and wild caper blossoms, and the air filled with wild bees and butterflies, while everywhere the cicadas were 'playing selections, day and night, from their voluptuous repertory of music'. He tells us that, in spite of its antiquity and charm, it possessed no features of outstanding architectural interest, though it atoned for this deficiency by the beauty of its vistas of painted rooms, the romantically designed terraces, and a general atmosphere 'overwhelmingly touched with poetry'. When he first saw it, 'Over a hundred people — men, women and children — were still living in the house, yet every day new features came to light in rooms that had recently been quitted and were beginning to be restored. For the next twenty-eight years, except at the very climax of the two wars, the noise of hammering, scratching and scraping was to rise up from dawn to dusk at my father's command. Already many of the rooms echoed with it, and a cloud of dust hung over the Court of the Dukes of Athens;

the existence of which, for it had been filled up with a warren of rooms, had only lately been revealed. . . . As plainly as the grapes of the valley belonged to the vats in the vast old cellars, the Castle — a construction, rather than a house — belonged to the landscape, dulcet but poignant, in which it stood, crowning a little hill in a wide valley that rose on all sides again toward the horizon.'

In 1925, when Sir George finally decided to make his main residence in Italy, Montegufoni had, after the incessant alterations and improvements, an entirely different look from its dilapidation in the early years of the century. The higgledy-piggledy accretions of buildings that had continually spread to house all the peasant families who had moved in through the generations, had been cleared away, and vistas of courtyards and façades could be seen from every room in the house as originally planned. The terraces, which had become vegetable gardens for the peasants, were finally cleared of their maize, tomatoes, beans and lettuces, and Tuscan roses bloomed in their place. One outstanding feature of the grounds, an ancient pink oleander the size of a sturdy tree, had been replanted in the middle of the Cardinal's Garden at the western end of the terrace (where it still stands). All this, however, was only the first stage of Sir George's teeming plans for the 'vast labyrinth of a building'. For thirteen years, since he had bought it, there had been the ceaseless work of opening up and making discoveries each one of which fired his imagination to new schemes. Now, for the next fifteen years, it was 'never to know an hour's rest from structural repairs and decoration: it was continually being carried back, pinned down to a past that — like the present — only existed in my father's mind. During this period, both my mother and father were to find a comparative contentment, even happiness, they had never yet known, for my mother liked the climate, and the life in Florence, and my father enjoyed the absence of life in the house.'

Here, when his father and mother were established in residence, Osbert would from time to time bring some of his friends to stay, and in particular William Walton and Constant Lambert when *Façade*, with a new curtain design by Severini, was performed at the International Music Festival at Siena in 1928. Osbert records that at that moment Edith had just written *Gold Coast Customs*, and was 'at the zenith of her first period of poetic achievement — and famous everywhere except in her own home'. Her father was afraid that her satire and experiments would 'offend people'; but Sir Edmund Gosse, who, according to Osbert, once bade the three of them farewell with the words 'Goodbye, you delightful but deleterious trio!', had written to Siegfried Sassoon: 'I feel that she is a sort of chrysalis, in a silken web of imperfection, with great talents to display, if only she can break out into a clear music of her own. There is no one I watch with more interest, and her personal beauty and dignity, which are even pathetic, attract me very much.'

6

IT is time to take a closer look at Edith's development as a poet.

'Ever since my earliest childhood,' she has stated, 'seeing the immense design of the world, one image of wonder mirrored by another image of wonder — the pattern of fur and feather by the frost on the windowpane, the six rays of the snowflake mirrored in the rock-crystal's six-rayed eternity — seeing the pattern on the scaly legs of birds mirrored in the pattern of knot-grass, I asked myself, were those shapes moulded by blindness? These were the patterns used by me, consciously or unconsciously, in certain of my early poems, *Bucolic Comedies*. . . . In most of these early poems, *Bucolic Comedies*, the experiments are less dealing with rhythm than with sense-transfusion. It was said that the images in these poems were strange. This was partly the result of condensing — partly because, where the language of one sense was insufficient to cover the meaning, the sensation, I used the language of another, and by this means attempted to pierce down to the essence of the thing seen, by discovering it in attributes which at first sight appear alien, but which are acutely related — by producing its quintessential colour (sharper, brighter than that seen by an eye grown stale, and by stripping it of all unessential details).'

It might seem at first sight that in this passage, written at the end of her life, Edith Sitwell was attempting to correct the view she took at an earlier date, that her earliest poems were inspired by a desire to challenge and change 'the rhythmical flaccidity, the verbal deadness, the dead and expected patterns, of some of the poetry immediately preceding us'. And yet this is not strictly so. The early poems were remarkable for 'sense-transfusion', as well as for the use of strong rhythms which suggested dance measures, waltzes, polkas, foxtrots; and these strong rhythms were not confined to the poems originally included in *Façade*, because, as I have already demonstrated, in the light of the rearrangement that the poems presented under that heading were constantly receiving, it is more or less impossible to consider *Façade*, *Bucolic Comedies* and the other early poems in separate compartments. In fact, two of the most memorable and delightful poems from the rhythmic point of view that appear in the final canon of *Façade*, *Popular Song* and *Polka*, were originally part of *Bucolic Comedies*. What is more, the interpretation I have just quoted from *Taken Care of*, appears in various passages of the 'Notes' that introduce her pre-war *Selected Poems*.

In his study of *The Three Sitwells* (1927) R. L. Mégroz wrote: 'As a realisation of artifice in poetry, from their metrical virtuosity, to evocative music, *Bucolic Comedies* is one of the most astounding and revolutionary volumes of modern verse.' These early poems were, however, remarkable for another quality which was, I cannot help thinking, as much responsible for the success of *Façade* in its performance as the strong rhythms, so brilliantly interpreted in the music by William Walton, and the sense-transfusions of such images as 'the light is braying like an ass'. All through these magical poems there is an extraordinary free association of images, drawn from classical and biblical mythology, fairy-tales, nursery rhymes, historical reading, and the poet's own childhood surroundings, in Renishaw, Scarborough and the Londesborough houses. Purists may object to the images brought together in these lines:

> Where reynard-haired Malinn
> Walks by rock and cave,
> The Sun, a Chinese mandarin,
> Came dripping from the wave.
>
> 'Your hair seems like the sunrise
> O'er Persia and Cathay —
> A rose-red music strange and dim
> As th' embalmèd smile of seraphim.'

Nevertheless as Shelley observed in his famous *Defence of Poetry*, it is the business of poetry to startle established ways of thought and enlarge the imagination by bringing images, ideas and persons of legend or history together that have never yet met. And as Shakespeare once thought nothing of giving a sea-coast to Bohemia or presenting a company of Elizabethan English yokels and artisans in a 'wood near Athens', so Edith Sitwell, following the creative instinct of her imagination, could write that

> The harsh bray and hollow
> Of the pot and the pan
> Seems Midas defying
> The great god Apollo!

The richness and originality of these poems derives from the fact that Edith Sitwell tumbled all the heaped stores of her mind into them, a mind where Midas and Apollo and Chinese mandarins and goose-girls and 'Grisi the ondine' and the 'dog-furred' leaves of strawberry beds and 'Mahomet resting on a cloud of gold' all lived together in a republic of poetic fantasy:

> The trees were hissing like green geese . . .
> The words they tried to say were these:
>
> 'When the great Queen Claude was dead
> They buried her deep in the potting-shed.'
>
> The moon smelt sweet as nutmeg-root
> On the ripe peach-trees' leaves and fruit,
>
> And her sandal-wood body leans upright,
> To the gardener's fright, through the summer night.

In an essay published in his book *Transition* (1926), Edwin Muir wrote: 'No other poet of our time has written so many lines which delight the imagination and give us a sense of magical freedom.' Speaking of her transposition of imagery, he remarks that the danger of deliberate adoption of such transposition is that her poetry may often appear as the 'poetry of method rather than of imagination. But at its best that poetry has the flash of divination, the sudden view of fresh worlds, which art exists to give us.'

In the majority of the poems of *Façade* the association of images is deliberately slanted towards producing effects of satiric gaiety or absurdity:

> Where the waves seem chiming haycocks
> I dance the polka; there
> Stand Venus' children in their gay frocks, —
> Maroon and marine, — and stare

To see me fire my pistol
Through the distance blue as my coat;
Like Wellington, Byron, the Marquis of Bristol,
Buzbied great trees float. . . .

And bright as a seedsman's packet
With zinnias, candytufts chill,
Is Mrs. Marigold's jacket
As she gapes at the inn door still,

Where at dawn in the box of the sailor,
Blue as the decks of the sea,
Nelson awoke, crowed like the cocks,
Then back to the dust sank he.

This is nonsense poetry of the most inventive and delightful kind, all the more effective because, as in Edward Lear's nonsense poems, a romantic note of sadness and mystery comes hauntingly through every now and then, as in *Jumbo Asleep*. Indeed, the parallels with Lear, in mood and method, are often strikingly close. It is not easy to produce specific examples, because the resemblances are scattered through the work of the two poets, but here is an example, I think sufficiently telling:

The Amazons wear balzarine of jonquille
Beside the blond lace of a deep-falling rill;
Through glades like a nun
They run from and shun
The enormous and gold-rayed rustling sun;
And the nymphs of the fountains
Descend from the mountains
Like elegant willows

On their deep barouche pillows,
In cashmere Alvandar, barège Isabelle,
Like bells of bright water from clearest wood-well.
Our élégantes favouring bonnets of blond,
The stars in their apiaries,
Sylphs in their aviaries,
Seeing them, spangle these, and the sylphs fond
From their aviaries fanned
With each long fluid hand
The manteaux espagnols,
Mimic the waterfalls
Over the long and the light summer land.

That quotation from *Valse* is surely from the same kitchen of the imagination as Lear's *The Cummerbund*:

She sate upon her Dobie,
    To watch the Evening Star,
And all the Punkahs as they passed
    Cried, 'My! how fair you are!'
Around her bower, with quivering leaves,
    The tall Kamsamahs grew,
And Kitmutgars in wild festoons
    Hung down from Tchokis blue.

Below her home the river rolled
    With soft meloobious sound,
Where golden-finned Chuprassies swam,
    In myriads circling round.
Above, on tallest trees remote,
    Green Ayahs perched alone,
And all night long the Mussak moan'd
    Its melancholy tone.

And where the purple Nullahs threw
   Their branches far and wide, —
And silvery Goreewallahs flew
   In silence, side by side, —
The little Bheesties' twittering cry
   Rose on the fragrant air,
And oft the angry Jampan howled
   Deep in his hateful lair.

Bucolic Comedies was published in 1923. *The Sleeping Beauty* followed in 1924, *Troy Park* in 1925 and *Rustic Elegies* in 1927. In the last three of these volumes, she turned away from the satirical gaiety of *Façade*, and exploited the elegiac, romantic vein that had already made its appearance in *Bucolic Comedies*. I think myself that the work of this period, such poems for instance as the *Elegy on Dead Fashion*, full though they are of wonderful passages and flashes of beauty, and certainly remarkable all through for Edith's highly developed sense of poetic texture are, in the end, cloying to the mind and imagination. The note is too unvaried, and the riches are poured out in too indiscriminate a profusion. By this time she could spin beautiful verses out of herself with what seemed an inexhaustible ease (though one is in fact well aware that she took immense trouble with every line). One's objection is that this power has been too little checked by a sense of intellectual structure; a doubt imposed by the fact that the poems do not, in general, have their crystallisation point in actual, concrete events or emotions. One must, however, make certain important exceptions: the arcadian, nostalgic poem of romanticised autobiography, *Colonel Fantock*, the crystal fairy-tale purity, as another example, of the song called *The Strawberry*, and, best known

of all, the rustic elegy *The Little Ghost Who Died for Love.*
This poem, founded on the story of Deborah Churchill,
who, at the age of thirty in 1708, was hanged for shielding
her lover in a duel, has reappeared in anthology after anthology, but still haunts one with its piercing note of sadness:

'Fear not, O maidens, shivering
As bunches of the dew-drenched leaves
In the calm moonlight . . . it is the cold sends quivering
My voice, a little nightingale that grieves.

Now Time beats not, and dead Love is forgotten . . .
The spirit too is dead and dank and rotten,

And I forget the moment when I ran
Between my lover and the sworded man. . . .

The poem rises to its climax where the village girl, who
'could never understand the justice of her sentence',
prophesies a doom hanging over the world for its cruelty
and corruption:

'. . . . so I sank me down,
Poor Deborah in my long cloak of brown.
Though cockcrow marches, crying of false dawns,
Shall bury my dark voice, yet still it mourns
Among the ruins, — for it is not I
But this old world, is sick and soon must die!'

Some of the critics, in this phase of Edith Sitwell's poetic
development, complained that her imagery varied very
little from poem to poem, coming, as it were, from the
same garden of flowers, strange though many of them were
and peculiar to herself. This is in part true; but I doubt

whether it is an altogether valid criticism. One can point
out that a number of famous poets, among them Shelley
and Edith's beloved Swinburne, have had a special vocabulary
of images which they are fond of repeating in poem after
poem. What is important, surely, is the intensity with
which the imagery is felt and the conviction it carries. In
considering this point, it is interesting to observe that there
are many passages in the poems of this period which foretell
the new phase which was to begin in 1940. If I had not, for
instance, been reading Edith Sitwell's poems for some time,
and was asked where the following two stanzas (from
Romance) came in her work, I should find it difficult not to
assume that they were from one of the long poems in *Green
Song* or *A Song of the Cold*:

> And still their love amid this green world grieves:
> 'The gold light drips like myrrh upon the leaves
> And fills with gold those chambers of the South
> That were your eyes, that honeycomb your mouth.
>
> And now the undying Worm makes no great stir,
> His tight embrace chills not our luxuries,
> Though the last light perfume our bones like myrrh
> And Time's beat dies.'

Colonel Fantock is, it seems to me, one of the most durable
of the poems of this phase, because of its inspiration in
the personal childhoods of herself and her two brothers,
who appear as Dagobert and Peregrine. 'Colonel Fantock'
was a real person, and Sacheverell devoted one of the best
chapters in *All Summer in a Day* to him. He was, in his old
age, a tutor who earned his living by teaching small boys,
and was appointed to look after Sacheverell's education,

mainly during the Sitwell family's yearly sojourn in Scarborough, where he lived, but also occasionally at Renishaw.
Sacheverell seems to have been fond of him, and found him
'a true teacher, not overloading my own mind, but allowing me to travel about in his experience, where I could find
an answer to every question I wanted to ask. He could tell
me anything between 1840 and the summer before last. . . .'
Sacheverell describes long walks with him in Scarborough,
and boating expeditions on the lake at Renishaw, during
which he would discourse on the Duke of Wellington's
funeral, having seen him lying in state, or the uniforms of
the Cent Garde of Napoleon III, politics, the history of the
Gentlemen's Club, amateur theatricals, the organisation of
public balls and other charity occasions, and the lives and
background of almost every single inhabitant of the town.
He had been married twice, and had twelve children, all of
whom had left for other parts of England or the Colonies;
as they had numerous children of their own, Colonel Fantock never asked them to help him in what was, in fact, a
situation of extreme genteel poverty. 'The furniture of the
room in which he taught became, every year, scarcer and
more simple, as though philosophy had taken a stern and
austere hold upon his conscience. . . . It was in very fact the
cell of a philosopher, for but few thinkers can stand their
rooms full of objects that distract the attention; but this
ideal setting had imposed itself, and philosophy was no more
the agent than it was the object of his simplicity.' Sacheverell also tells us that he was an enthusiastic amateur gardener, often helped in the pruning of their own garden, and
delighted in spring to walk by and inhale the perfume of the
beds full of wall-flowers in the Corporation gardens: 'I have
only to bend down, at any time or place, to pick a stem of

wall-flower, and its smell, as I draw in breath, carries me straight away till, in the space of a flash of light, I am with him again, just above, and in the full yellow furnace heat of, the massy bed of these same flowers that is like the pylon, the electric tower, that receives my message and gives me my answer.'

In *Colonel Fantock* Edith Sitwell abandons her more elaborate tropes and conceits, and writes with a moving simplicity:

> ... I saw this
> Old military ghost with Mayfly whiskers, —
> Poor harmless creature, blown by the cold wind,
> Boasting of unseen unreal victories
> To a harsh unbelieving world unkind:
> For all the battles that this warrior fought
> Were with cold poverty and helpless age —
> His spoils were shelters from the winter's rage.

The poem is especially interesting for its portraits of the three Sitwells as Edith saw them in their youth:

> But Dagobert and Peregrine and I
> Were children then; we walked like shy gazelles
> Among the music of the thin flower-bells.
> And life still held some promise, – never ask
> Of what, — but life seemed less a stranger, then,
> Than ever after in this cold existence.
> I always was a little outside life —
> And so the things we touch could comfort me;
> I loved the shy dreams we could hear and see —
> For I was like one dead, like a small ghost,
> A little cold air wandering and lost.

She then describes how Colonel Fantock had all three of them for audience when he told his stories of 'old apocryphal misfortunes', and glories of past military victories in which he had played his signal part, while all his present victories were over 'little boys who would not learn to spell':

> All day within the sweet and ancient gardens
> He had my childish self for audience —
> Whose body flat and strange, whose pale straight hair
> Made me appear as though I had been drowned —
> (We all have the remote air of a legend) —
> And Dagobert my brother whose large strength,
> Great body and grave beauty still reflect
> The Angevin dead kings from whom we spring;
> And sweet as the young tender winds that stir
> In thickets when the earliest flower-bells sing
> Upon the boughs, was his just character;
> And Peregrine the youngest with a naïve
> Shy grace like a faun's, whose slant eyes seemed
> The warm green light beneath eternal boughs.
> His hair was like the fronds of feathers, life
> In him was changing ever, springing fresh
> As the dark songs of birds . . . the furry warmth
> And purring sound of fires was in his voice
> Which never failed to warm and comfort me.

Edith's travels with Helen Rootham on the Continent came to an end in 1914, when she was twenty-seven. At that date the two of them established themselves at 22 Pembridge Mansions, Moscow Road, in Bayswater, and Edith lived there for the next eighteen years, though during most of the summers she was at Renishaw. Helen Rootham left for

Paris in 1929, and in 1932, largely owing to the increasing seriousness of her illness, Edith went over to France to join her at 129 rue Saint-Dominique.

During the most creative first period in her life, therefore, from 1915 to 1929, during which she wrote *Façade, Bucolic Comedies, The Sleeping Beauty, Troy Park, Rustic Elegies,* culminating with *Gold Coast Customs* which was published in 1929, she was working mainly in London. She had a circle of friends who came to visit her in Pembridge Mansions, she dined out with people she especially admired and liked, such as Aldous and Maria Huxley, Sir Edmund and Lady Gosse, she came to know intimately many of the Bloomsbury figures, such as Roger Fry, she had her enthusiastic fans among the younger writers such as Peter Quennell and Harold Acton; and yet one has the impression that the period was one of loneliness and struggle in its main outlines. She needed the warmth of sympathetic admiration for her talents to flower, she was acutely sensitive to criticism, which was constantly directed at her by a certain section of the press, and by fellow-writers who ought to have known better. The image of the Sitwells as '*enfants terribles*' (in Frank Swinnerton's words) may have been useful in their early assaults upon the literary establishment, but one cannot help feeling that all three, and Edith in particular, became the prisoners of the image of 'Sitwellism', and tried too often, misguidedly, to live up to it by reckless and wounding, though often witty, attacks on those on the other side of their own, constantly shifting firing-line. In the gossip-columns of the daily papers and illustrated fortnight-lies and monthlies of the time, her own war-cry is repeated, parrot-like again and again, that 'in early youth she took a dislike to simplicity, morris-dancing, a sense of humour, and every kind of sport except reviewer-baiting'. The particular Sitwell brand of '*épater les bourgeois*' was especially fascinating to the British public, because it came not from the bohemians but from the dissident aristocrats.

Often they provoked, for the sheer pleasure of having a row with the Philistines; sometimes they were provoked in their turn — and never forgot it. Noël Coward had been invited to the performance of *Façade* at the Aeolian Hall. Though already established as a daring young playwright and wit (he was twenty-three years old), he failed to see the point, and wrote a parody sketch in a revue, in which 'Hernia Whittlebot', a poetess with grapes in her hair, was quite obviously meant to be Edith. It took nearly forty years to heal the breach, Osbert refusing to forgive until Noël Coward had obtained Edith's forgiveness. Typically, when she forgave, she forgave wholeheartedly, sent him her *Shakespeare Notebook*, and a warm letter of friendship. By then she had become a Roman Catholic,* and had confessed to some of her friends that she had taken this step partly because she was afraid of the violence of her instinct for revenge.

Though she courted publicity, in her youth Edith was sensitive about her unusual appearance. The offence of 'Hernia Whittlebot' was aggravated by the suspicion of mockery on this count. Robert Herring remembers that, one autumn afternoon during the thirties, he accompanied her to a party at Marjorie Bowen's. It was a few days before the fifth of November, and as they got out of the car a small urchin ran up to them and said: 'Penny for the guy, miss!' Edith drew herself up and replied: '*I* have been a guy all my life — it's about time someone gave *me* a penny!' Immedi-

* She was received into the Catholic Church in August 1955.

ately after, she turned to Robert Herring and said: 'Robert, I shouldn't have said that. Here's my purse.' She instructed him to give the urchin half a crown.

There is also a story that one day in Paris, at about the same time, two *gamins* began to make disrespectful remarks about the strange tall figure who was passing them. With great dignity, Edith turned round, and said in accents to strike terror: '*Souvenez-vous de Waterloo!*'

Edith was courted to write articles in the newspapers on a variety of subjects, any subject — the important thing was to have her as a contributor. Editors, however, did not always realise what a Tartar they had caught. In January 1927 she wrote to Tom Driberg, apropos a series of 'causeries on the three arts' she had arranged to write for the *Weekly Dispatch*: 'The Editor-in-chief has just returned from the South of France in a vile temper. He *won't* have anybody under 80 mentioned, unless I say what they look like. Also, it is a case of England for the English. I mustn't mention Matisse, or Picasso, or Stravinsky, because the readers of the *W.D.* have never heard of them.'

She was ready at any moment to write a newspaper article on such subjects as 'Would I change places with the man in the Iron Mask?', 'Freak Parties' or 'Amusements that amuse and Amusements that do not'; the point of which, for the editors who commissioned the articles, was simply to encourage her to throw a few more coconuts at the well-known Sitwell Aunt Sallies. At one moment she and Osbert would publish a notice in the personal column of a well-known London newspaper, announcing that 'Miss Edith Sitwell and Mr Osbert Sitwell have much pleasure in announcing a general amnesty. This does not apply to habitual offenders.' At another a stuffed owl in a glass case would be sent to the editor of a weekly newspaper they considered insufferably boring or lacking in respect for their talents. This was quite a good gambit when first thought of, but having started the game they had to keep it up. A certain sense of strain was evident when, in the autumn of 1938, in an atmosphere very different from the carefree, iconoclastic fun of the twenties, they instituted the 'Annual Minerva Prizes' for what they held to be the worst, or dullest literary productions of the year; the prizes including a case of mothballs, a stuffed and glazed barn owl, and a stuffed fish.

These campaigns may have been mounted as a 'turn' by what sarcastic press commentators sometimes referred to as 'the Sitwell troupe of performing literary lions', but the aim was not always innocent. Edith was always the most loyal and devoted of friends to those who she felt sincerely admired and cared for her; but often the most venial of lapses, or indeed a purely imaginary slight, a piece of gossip misunderstood or exaggerated, would lead her to substitute, in the twinkling of an eye, and to the baffled confusion of the victim, condemnation for praise. In this she betrayed her lasting sense of insecurity, and a conviction, which had hardened in the sufferings of her childhood, that only her own uncompromising readiness to do battle would get her through. Most authors learn to ignore, or stoically to endure mean and even partially libellous attacks by reporters and reviewers in the press; but Edith and Osbert never. Their readiness to reply in kind, and even to take legal action, caused them to be accused of instituting a reign of terror among reviewers. When one considers the number of times such critics as Geoffrey Grigson insulted them with legal impunity, one must hold this to be an exaggeration. Nevertheless, they did from time to time instruct their lawyers, and in February 1941 they won a libel case against *Reynolds News*, before Mr Justice Cassels.

The offending sentences occurred in a review of *Edith Sitwell's Anthology*, which had recently appeared: 'Among the literary curiosities of the nineteen-twenties will be the vogue of the Sitwells, sister and two brothers, whose energy and self-assurance pushed them into a position which their merits could not have won.

'One brother wrote amusing political verse. The sister produced a Life of Alexander Pope. Now oblivion has claimed them, and they are remembered with a kindly, if slightly cynical, smile.

'Miss Edith Sitwell has been occupied in collecting her favourite pieces of poetical writing, and has published 812 pages of them in *Edith Sitwell's Anthology* (Gollancz 7/6d). It would be a delightful bed book if it were not so heavy to hold. The 160 pages of "critical introduction" might well be omitted from future editions.'

There was plenty here designed to prick the Sitwells into counter-attack, but they based their case essentially on the imputation that since 1930 (when *Alexander Pope* appeared) they had fallen into oblivion, which they considered a slur on their reputations and injurious for their professional livelihood. Edith pointed out that she had written or edited nine books during those ten years, all of which had received long reviews; Osbert pointed in particular to his novels and travel books, all of which had been remarkably successful, and Sacheverell to his biographies and also to his travel books. The Judge agreed, and the Sitwells were awarded £1,050 damages (one-third to each) and costs. Even so, one cannot help wondering whether it was worth it: the kind of dignified and crushing reply that Osbert was later to make to James Agate's attacks might have been better for their public image in the long run.

Apropos this event, Edith wrote afterwards to Lady Aberconway: 'I gave what I consider a really beautiful performance of a sweet, sunny-natured old lady, stinking of lavender and looped with old lace, in whose mouth butter, even in the palmy days when it could be procured, would not have melted.'

When Edith's great triumphs came to her during the forties, this acerbity, so at variance with the rich vein of human sensitivity and compassion which runs through all her serious poetry, and which was always evident in her conversation, gradually began to dissolve; but her hypertrophied alertness to injury, real or fancied, never entirely left her. It was the inspiration of some of her wittiest and most comic observations; but also of her occasional lapses of fair judgment.

I have already described the flat in Pembridge Mansions, with its view over Kensington Gardens, where Edith and her governess friend lived for eighteen years. In *Memoirs of an Aesthete*, Harold Acton records an early visit to them in their fastness, a few months before the first public performance of *Façade*: 'One climbed for ever, pitying anyone forced to live in such an eyrie. Remembering the magnificence of her father's mansion at Montegufoni, rising above an ocean of olive groves and vineyards, I wondered at the contrast. The view of chimney-pots and slate roofs from the window of her small sitting-room had been standardized by the London Group of painters.' Harold Acton's heart sank at what seemed the utter joylessness of these surroundings, particularly on a raw December morning. The atmosphere changed, however, the moment Edith glided into the room in a dress of emerald brocade. 'A rare jewel, a hieratic figure in Limoges enamel, I thought, clamped in some tin biscuit box, but rarer, more hieratic against this background. The pale oval face with its almond eyes and long thin nose, had often been carved in ivory by true believers. Her entire figure possessed a distinction seldom to be seen outside the glass cases of certain museums. Physically, she was an extraordinary survival from the Age of Chivalry. And when she spoke, how musical her enunciation, with a complete absence of pedantry, of that feministic challenge so many women writers hurl at men!'

It was at this time that another observer, Sewell Stokes, wrote that Edith 'appeared to be chipped from marble, a walking piece of smooth, magnificent marble'. To Harold Acton, Edith Sitwell's appearance and manner, her whole ambience seemed inseparable from her poems. 'She did not suffer fools gladly, and her descriptions of lectures to provincial poetry societies and of the people who "nearly bored her into her tomb" with letters of advice, abuse and unintelligent gushing, were prose variations of her "Bucolic Comedies". She complained of the insolent stares to which she was subjected. Even the boor sensed that he was in the presence of a poet, and as true poetry is anathema to the mob, or was then, Edith was continually persecuted in one way or another. But the tale of this persecution as she told it, rippled with ludicrous highlights: she could appreciate the grotesque element in her fortuitous encounters.'

Edith's relations with Harold Acton when he was a young man at Oxford are a remarkable proof of her sincere and generous concern for other, struggling poets even when she was in the midst of the struggle herself. For instance, she writes to him in Oxford from Pembridge Mansions: 'I am so glad my review gave you pleasure; "Contrasts" is very well done indeed, and I am glad Mr Stephens agrees with me that it is the best poem in the book. You know, it is a very good thing if a young poet *can* do that kind of work, and it should certainly be encouraged. You are infinitely better at that kind of work than you are at the kind of work I do, for instance. You see, my work is (apart from its technique, which is the result of many things, including terribly hard work) very much the result of my particular personality; and it is, therefore, not a suitable medium for other people. Every poet must find out what is his own *personality*, and then act upon it. I do not mean that he must parody himself, or imitate himself, but he must cultivate that particular style. Your personality finds its best outlet in poems like "Contrasts". Persevere in that style, and you will find in it your best development.'

Another memory of Pembridge Mansions days comes from Peter Quennell, who to the best of his recollection was introduced to Edith by Edward Marsh, to whom he had in turn been introduced by Richard Hughes. The first visit took place late one summer afternoon. He remembers how, after climbing 'several flights of dusky stairs', they halted 'slightly bemused and breathless' in front of the topmost flat. 'Behind that dark uncommunicative door lay the enchanted realm I longed to enter.'

He was not disappointed by his first glimpse of this poetic paradise. Edith Sitwell herself, about whom he had heard so much, who had occupied his imagination for so long, answered the bell, 'tall, attenuated and elegant as one of those sculptured saints and martyrs who keep guard around the portals of Chartres. Sheathed in a garment of gold brocade, wearing a toque of gilded feathers and a large jewelled cross which, I afterwards learned, had originally belonged to Cagliostro, Miss Sitwell raised a finger to her lips — on her long pale distinguished hand were several impressive rings set with big fragments of semi-precious stone — and murmured warningly, before we advanced, that there was a madman in the room beyond. Again, I was not to be disappointed. On the end of a small sofa crouched a haggard foreign poet — the demented Northern bard, nicknamed "The Icelander" . . . describing the horrible and fantastic visions that pursued him when he walked abroad, notably a band of little dark men, carrying large un-rolled umbrellas, who perpetually dogged his footsteps, and harried and threatened him wherever he fled. On the oppo-site end of the sofa perched an elderly lady, entirely clothed in black velvet, and visibly quivering with alarm beneath a wide black picture-hat. Her profile was aquiline and boldly whitened; her lips were summarily painted a brilliant red; and from under the brim of her hat appeared an array of yellow Gorgonian curls.' Later, Peter Quennell discovered that this terrified lady was none other than the once fashion-able novelist Ada Leverson, whose fame today rests so much more on the heroic kindness she showed to Oscar Wilde — who had christened her 'The Sphinx' — at the dark mo-ment in his career when he was waiting for his second trial at the Old Bailey, than on her own writings. Though deaf, she enjoyed talking; but on this occasion she had been re-duced to silence by the madman who, with eyes glittering as he recounted his hallucinations, edged ever closer to her across the sofa, while 'she shrank away from him against its arm, doing her best to seem attentive and making tremulous propitiatory gestures'. This, for the young poet, was the supreme touch: he felt he had at last entered the true literary world, 'in which beauty, lunacy and genius were woven together into the pattern of everyday life'.

Already, in the early twenties, it is clear that Edith Sitwell was manifesting her lifelong talent for attracting lunatics. Peter Quennell goes on to record that, subsequently, he was a frequent visitor at Edith Sitwell's receptions, and remembers how she liked to read, not from her poems but from the letters she was exchanging with a retired soldier who lived in the neighbourhood and kept some noisy pets which disturbed her in her work. 'Sometimes these readings were interrupted by the sudden arrival of her two brothers. They did not remain with us for very long, and generally produced the impression of having descended from a different plane. Circling rapidly around the room, and as rapidly shaking hands, "How are *you*?" they would enquire, "And how are *you*?" placing the emphasis upon the last word, in a tone that, although kindly and courteous, did not suggest that they required an answer. Bayswater was not their natural habitat . . .'

Peter Quennell also remembers the buns which were a feature of these tea-parties, 'to which a heavy coating of white-of-egg had given the lustre of antique glazed pottery'. These also figure in Osbert's description of the visits which the poet W. H. Davies made to Pembridge Mansions: 'Davies used frequently to attend my sister's tea-parties, which took place every Saturday, in the two small sitting-rooms of the flat. Here she and Helen fed their friends on strong black tea and glazed, delicious halfpenny buns that seemed for once to have retained the taste and luscious quality of the buns one ate as a child. Owing to the extra-

ordinary mixture of the people she gathered together —
relatives, old friends of my mother's, scared but tittering,
who had never hitherto heard even the name of a poet,
famous poets, school-teachers, the most advanced musicians
and painters, hunting men, doctors, philosophers, zoolo-
gists, economists, and one or two persons who seemed to
exist for no other reason than that my sister was sorry for
them —, these afternoons became renowned for the incidents that they produced.'

Another youthful witness, Tom Driberg, writing in *Encounter* (May 1966), recalls among the literary notabilities
on various occasions, H. G. Wells, Arnold Bennett, Aldous
Huxley and T. S. Eliot, whose 'shyness matched one's own';
Gertrude Stein when she was visiting England, 'massively
commonsensical, like a reliable *Hausfrau*, in brown boots
and black woollen stockings'; Beryl de Zoete and Arthur
Waley; the ever faithful 'Sphinx'; and in the contingent
of his own generation not only Harold Acton but also
Geoffrey Gorer and Brian Howard, who remarked that
Pembridge Mansions looked from the outside like 'an inex-
pensive and dirty hospital'. There were also, he remembers,
visitors from the world of the theatre and music, including
Lord Berners at the time when he and Sacheverell were preparing a ballet for Diaghilew, Constant Lambert, 'an ebul-
lient narrator of the absurd happenings of which he seemed
daily to be the centre and victim', and on one occasion Mrs
Patrick Campbell, who was so disturbed by what she considered the squalor in which Edith lived that she sent her a
dozen silver teaspoons. 'I do not think,' Tom Driberg concludes, 'that any other party of that time — certainly none
so austere in its gastronomic provision, and none of the far
more splendid parties given by the great "lion-hunting"

hostesses of the day, Lady Cunard and Lady Colefax, — attracted so comprehensive an array of genius and talent.'

Tom Driberg, like Harold Acton, was also the recipient of Edith's intense, unselfish partisan interest and sympathy, which she poured out to any young person who seemed to her to have budding talent as a poet. This element in her nature remained constant to the end.

We do not know what led Edith Sitwell to make the drastic change from her elegiac and romantic poems in the manner of *The Sleeping Beauty*, to *Gold Coast Customs*, which, published in 1929, must have been in gestation in 1928, and therefore before the economic crisis of 1929 and long before the appearance of the revolutionary poems of the young poets of the thirties. We do know that from early childhood she had been in revolt against the social world of her home background; we know from *Taken Care of* that during her London years she was contemptuous of the pretensions of rich society hostesses, and enduring comparative poverty herself was particularly aware of the sufferings of the underprivileged; but we can only guess what the point of crystallisation was. The poems of the *Façade* period are gaily satirical nonsense fun that give little hint of a serious social criticism. Suddenly, in *Gold Coast Customs*, the criticism is there, the satire has become focused, and invested with terrifying passionate intensity. Though in *Gold Coast Customs* she again used the strong rhythms, the clashing rhymes and assonances of *Façade*, the effect is far removed from the wit and gaiety of that sequence. The banging, insistent drum-beat that runs through it, the hard explosive consonants, the vivid images of horror, create an almost unbearable atmosphere of brutality, loathsomeness and spiritual death.

'In this poem,' Edith Sitwell wrote, 'the bottom of the world has fallen out. . . . We see everything reduced to the primal mud — the "Rich man Judas, Brother Cain", — and the epitome of his civilisation, Lady Bamburgher, are at one with the slum-ignorance and the blackness and superstition of the African swamp. The beating of their fevered hearts and pulses is no more than the beating of the drums that heralded the Customs, as they were called in Ashantee, a hundred and fifty years ago, when, at the death of any rich or important person, slaves and poor persons were killed so that the bones of the dead might be washed with human blood. So the spiritual dead-in-life cry, in our time, for a sacrifice — that of the starved.'

Gold Coast Customs is characteristic of all Edith Sitwell's longer works, in that it has no precise plot as *Venus and Adonis* or *The Ancient Mariner* has a plot or sequence of happenings. There is, rather, the statement of various themes, their repetition and mingling in a manner that is more reminiscent of music. Structure is there, but it is the structure of images, ideas and emotions that are gradually developed, contrasted and resolved in a deeply moving prophetic cry — as Shelley's themes (though more precisely stated) are resolved. The poet employs considerable skill in the counterpointing of Lady Bamburgher's parties and the heartless nightmare of the primitive African rites, so that each appears as a metaphor of the other; and underlying them both one senses a third, parallel theme, of personal betrayal and love disgraced. The tremendous strength of the imaginative realisation appears from the very beginning:

One fantee wave
Is grave and tall
As brave Ashantee's
Thick mud wall.
Munza rattles his bones in the dust,
Lurking in murk because he must.

Striped black and white
Is the squealing light;
The dust brays white in the market-place,
Dead powder spread on a black skull's face.

Like monkey-skin
Is the sea — one sin
Like a weasel is nailed to bleach on the rocks
Where the eyeless mud screeched fawning, mocks

At a Negro that wipes
His knife . . . dug there,
A bugbear bellowing
Bone dared rear —
A bugbear bone that bellows white
As the ventriloquist sound of light,

It rears at his head-dress of felted black hair —
The one humanity clinging there —
His eyeless face whitened like black and white bones
And his beard of rusty
Brown grass cones.

This atmosphere of macabre horror and cruelty is sustained through nearly sixty stanzas in which the rhythm is varied with the utmost mastery, so that in spite of the terrible compulsion of the underlying drum-beat the mind is never wearied. It is also fascinating to observe with what intuitive power Edith Sitwell uses her favourite device of sense-transfusion, or parallelism to enhance her effects: the light is 'squealing', the dust 'brays white', the bone 'bellows' and so on. Only occasionally does she allow the vision of what is lost, of a fulfilment of longing, to break in:

> O far horizons and bright blue wine
> And majesty of the seas that shine,
> Bull-bellowing waves that ever fall
> Round the god-like feet and the goddess tall!

> A great yellow flower
> With the silence shy
> To the winds from the islands
> Sighs, 'I die.'

It is impossible, in reading this extraordinary poem, not to be reminded at times, in spite of all surface dissimilarities, of the author of *Atalanta in Calydon*; not to remember Edith Sitwell's confession to an early passion for Swinburne. Equally, however, W. B. Yeats was surely right when he said that, reading *Gold Coast Customs*, he felt 'that something absent from all literature was back again, and in a form rare in the literature of all generations, passion ennobled by intensity, by endurance, by wisdom. We had it in one man once. He lies in St Patrick's now under the greatest epitaph in history.'

In her notes to the poem, Edith reveals her debt to Hegel's *Philosophy of History* and Dr George Schweinfurth's *The

Heart of Africa for much of her material detail, and is at pains to insist that the picture she paints of African barbarism only refers to the past, and not to the African races in modern times. Nevertheless, one is led to the reflection that if King Munza belongs to a remote age, Lady Bamburgher does not.

In the great climax Edith Sitwell, having earlier in the poem spoken prophetically of the 'sick thick smoke of London burning', speaks prophetically again, hinting as much at her own coming development, the culminating phase of her art, as at changes in the outside world:

> Yet the time will come
> To the heart's dark slum
> When the rich man's gold and the rich man's wheat
> Will grow in the street, that the starved may eat, —
> And the sea of the rich will give up its dead —
> And the last blood and fire from my side will be shed.
> For the fires of God go marching on.

She herself observed that *Gold Coast Customs* was 'written with anguish, and I would not willingly re-live that birth'.

In one of the most percipient studies of Edith's poetic progress published before the second World War, Dilys Powell pointed out that the themes of treachery, spiritual death and 'Vanity Fair' had appeared in her poetry almost from the beginning though never wrought to such intense effects as in *Gold Coast Customs*. She also pointed out, as Evelyn Waugh was to point out again thirty years later, that though the Sitwells can never really be said to have founded a school, the influence of Edith's poetry in particular may well have been crucial in the development of poetry in the twenties and after: 'I do believe that the emphasis on decoration, on rhetoric in their own work, has restored to English poetry the *possibility* of a richness it seemed to have lost.'

7

AFTER the publication of *Gold Coast Customs* Edith all but abandoned poetry for more than ten years. This must seem strange, in view of the extremely fertile outpouring of the twenties; and the reasons for the long pause remain slightly mysterious. The poetic climate of the thirties may have seemed unsympathetic, even hostile to her; but a more likely explanation can probably be found in the serious illness of Helen Rootham, who had already had a major operation. She decided she would prefer to be with her sister in Paris. Soon after, Edith followed, to help nurse and comfort her. This was without doubt a noble act, because the illness, Edith tells us, was changing Helen Rootham's character — for the worse. Edith has described this period in her life as 'unmitigated hell'.

In a letter to her cousin Veronica (Mrs Frank Gilliatt), in November 1933, she wrote: 'At the moment when I got your first letter, Helen — poor soul — had just been taken off to a nursing home to be operated on again for the same dreadful illness. When she came home — (and they do not keep them long in hospital for an operation to the ——), I did all the nursing (she was entirely helpless), — and all the housework, and it was in the middle of the heatwave, which was worse here than in England. I was up at 6.30 every day, and went to bed at 11, — and was "at it" without stopping.'

It is clear that the atmosphere was far from conducive to the writing of poetry; but in addition to that the expenses of the household were far heavier than in London, and it was imperative that Edith should earn more money. She turned, therefore, to the more lucrative production of prose works and anthologies.

She did not, however, entirely give up poetry, and was obviously longing to get back to it. In December 1932 she wrote to her friend Rée Gorer (Geoffrey Gorer's mother): 'Life here is one long treadmill. I work seven hours a day, and hardly ever go out, as I'm so anxious to get this bore of a book done, and return to poetry. I *have*, by the way, been writing a little poetry, and when it is more advanced I shall send it to you.' This was probably the long poem *Romance*, which she dedicated to Mrs Gorer; though she admits in the 'Notes' to her *Collected Poems* that she also wrote 'one poem in which I was finding my way'.

For the study of Edith's relation to the art of poetry, undoubtedly the most important of the prose works are her biography of *Alexander Pope*, published in 1930, and her one novel — if novel it can be called — *I Live Under a Black Sun*, the central figure in which is the thinly disguised figure of Jonathan Swift.

The book on Pope is informed by great sympathy with her subject, and the most sensitive understanding of his poetry. It was more or less inevitable that Edith should undertake it when she began writing prose books, in view of the special place Pope had held in her affections ever since girlhood. It is highly characteristic of Edith in its reckless partisanship. She is obliged to admit Pope's vanity, his passion for malicious intrigue, and the devious stratagems he employed to call attention to his own works and defame the works of those of whom he was jealous for one reason or another. In spite of all Pope's efforts in the concealment of his tracks, later scholarship has made it impossible not to concede these pettinesses in his nature. Of his most absurd vanity, his habit of altering his letters for publication, Edith writes:

'I do not deny that he was occasionally tortuous in his dealings, nor can it be denied that he was capable of suppressing or altering passages in his letters which might not exhibit him in the light in which he wished to appear. He did alter many of his letters before he allowed them to be printed. But although this behaviour may be called uncandid, yet the reasons for it — and even the excuse — are obvious. Pope knew only too well to what slanders a great man is exposed during his lifetime, from those who are envious of his fame. From what calumnies, then, might he not suffer after his death, when he could no longer defend himself against them. . . .'

Some might call Pope's behaviour over his letters, not uncandid but downright dishonest. And it would seem that there was a very simple remedy if he was anxious not to appear in a damaging light: not to allow them to be published at all. As it is, the damage, as far as posterity is concerned, is double.

Edith, however, must find excuses for the actions of those whose cause she has espoused, even when those actions are thoroughly discreditable. This is the impulse of a loving friend, and not of a scrupulous biographer. And when Edith writes of Pope's longing for friendship and his devotion to his friends, she could be speaking of herself. It is impossible not to read *Alexander Pope* without becoming more vividly aware than ever before of all that was generous and loyal in Pope's nature, and also of the extreme sensitivity that made him react to malicious insinuations or, worse, veiled

hints about his physical deformity with such violence. But
the book is valuable not merely for righting the balance in
our estimate of Pope, and for its revelation of Edith Sitwell's own warmth of heart, but also for what it says about
poetry. Her analysis of Pope's poetic mastery is one of the
most brilliant, and least esoteric, things she ever wrote on
the subject of technique. Her opening paragraphs are a flash
of light:

'It is generally believed, by those whose appreciation of
verse is a platonic one, that poetry springs from the poet's
head, as Minerva sprang from the head of Jove. That is an
easy explanation of the birth of our goddess, but it is not
one which satisfies me. If we were to ask any of the poets of
the past, we should without doubt be told that poetry is just
as much a matter of physical aptitude as of spiritual. The
poet feels, with his poetry, the same certainty yet excitement
as a jockey feels with a race-horse. He has sensitive hands
that feel the horse's mouth, that understand all the variations
of speed, he has a body that is supremely fitted to ride the
horse, a body that is light and that seems like part of this
polished and victorious speed.

'I believe that a poem begins in the poet's head, and
then grows in his blood, as a rose grows among its dark
leaves.'

Sometimes Edith Sitwell's long disquisitions on technique
seem altogether far-fetched, and to obscure rather than to
illuminate the poem. They have, perhaps, a fanciful poetry
of their own, though not audible to every ear; but this chapter on Pope and the heroic couplet is a triumph of imaginative analysis, of an unequalled sensitivity, concerning the
interaction of sound, texture, rhythm and meaning.

It seems likely that her work on Pope, in whose life Swift

figured so importantly, led her to embark on *I Live Under a Black Sun* seven years later.

Edith Sitwell attempted something very difficult, and very daring, in this book. It is characteristic of her attitude to experience that time and place, like the symbols of myth and legend, are interchangeable. It is nothing to her to bring Jonathan Swift into the events of the first World War, or vice versa. She sees human suffering and disillusionment, the struggles of genius against the resisting clay of human torpor, the antithesis of rich and poor, of those who choose and command against those who have no choice but to obey and endure, as constants in human life. Jonathan Swift was a tortured genius, who had a grimly disillusioned vision of greed and stupidity and cruelty at work in human affairs; it is therefore perfectly natural for Edith Sitwell to place him at a moment in history, 1914, when these three elements in human nature were most catastrophically at work.

In her second chapter, she presents this paradox boldly, directly after what is clearly a transposed description of the murder at Sarajevo; 'In the darkness under the trees in the great cities, the young girls held the hands of dead men, pressed lips to lips that were already cold. For the two nations that alone inhabit the earth, the rich and the poor, walking to their death in opposed hordes, had found the only force that could bind them together, a cannibalistic greed, hatred and fear. No longer need they fear each other, for both nations will be swept away.

'Thus began the Plague that was to sweep Europe until it reached the silent house in a forest, where a man sat dreaming of a universe peopled by horses of an infinite wisdom, superior to mankind — imagining, in his ferocious hatred, "twenty thousand of them breaking into our European army, confounding the ranks, overturning the carriages, battering the warriors' faces into mummy by terrible yerks from their hinder hooves". His gigantic laughter falling like thunderbolts or black meteoric stones amid the wastes of the thunderous darkness, he contemplated the grandeur of man. . . . And, in the shadow cast by the giant, pygmy man wrestled with pygmy man under a black sun, their footfalls leaving no trace in the enormous plain of sand, where flows no water, and for shade there is only this aching and hollow waste of rock.'

I do not think it can be said that this extraordinary montage is entirely successful — for a novel. In poetry it would accommodate itself more easily; but where, for instance, one has to deal with Swift's letters, written in the style of the early eighteenth century, while mentioning railways being built and battles on the Western Front, an especially generous 'suspension of disbelief' is required of the reader. *I Live Under a Black Sun* is in fact neither a novel, nor a poem, nor a biography, but rather a fantasia on themes that were to occupy Edith Sitwell as she came to the last phase of her poetry in the second World War:

'Her soul cradled in the night of her body like a small child in its little coffin, Mrs Noon sat among the green branch-like shadows of her kitchen. How ancient was that little child who had never known life. The drops remaining from the far-off Flood had inundated the immense primeval clay in which the coffin was embedded; from the darkness it had heard the Priests of Baal crying to an unhearing God for rain.'

And again, in another mood: 'The country roads look as if they were made of thick gold, it seems as if they must stretch to the end of the world, and as if he and she would drive along them till the end of time, side by side, in a summer that would never fade, under the sun whose great flames seemed stretched across the firmament.'

I have already mentioned the portrait of her father as Sir Henry Rotherham, which she was to repeat, almost word for word, in *Taken Care of* when describing Sir George. Occasionally the imagery of her early poems comes back — even in *Alexander Pope* there are examples of that obsessive fondness for certain images and comparisons which never left her — as in this passage:

'She walked past the potting-shed where Noon, so Jonathan declared, potted out the long-leaved stars for the flower-show — for, he said, they must be stars, they were far too large and too bright to be ordinary flowers and fruit, those huge strawberries shining like fire and freckled with bright gold, under their thick quilted dark leaves . . .'

I Live Under a Black Sun is innocent of plot or probability, but it is written in an elegiac, smoothly flowing prose which rises easily to passages of great beauty of description and reflection. It is deeply steeped in the feelings of compassion for suffering, reconciliation and forgiveness. The portrait of 'Jonathan Hare' achieves a rocky grandeur: it is almost impossible not to believe that Edith herself had at one time felt herself on the edge of madness through disappointed love.

In between these two books, Edith Sitwell wrote a book on Bath, *The English Eccentrics*, and *Victoria of England*; pot-boilers all, in a sense, and yet each volume has some highly characteristic touches. Though it is in reality a kind of annotated anthology from other people's works, *The English Eccentrics* is one of her most delightful — and durable — productions, allowing her to give rein, in her choice of eccentrics and her comments, to her immense, rather

surrealist sense of fun and her delight in the fantastic behaviour of such characters as Lord Rokeby, the 'Ornamen-
tal Hermit' who in later life grew a long beard and became
so fond of bathing that he had a roast loin of veal floating at
his elbow in the Pump Room at Bath; Squire Mytton who
set himself on fire in his nightshirt in order to cure an attack
of hiccups; and Squire Waterton, author of *Wanderings in
South America*, who at the age of seventy-seven was observed scratching the back part of his head with the big toe
of his right foot, and on another occasion was infuriated because a guest remarked that his pet Bahia toad was 'an ugly
brute'. Of the last-named she writes: 'He was a great gentleman, one of a long race of untitled nobles, and showed the
pride and splendour of his race in every action of his long
life. He comes into this book because his very bravery is
born of such an irrepressible sense of fun that it is impossible
to exclude him. He was an eccentric only as all great gentlemen are eccentric, by which I mean that their gestures are not
born to fit the conventions or the cowardice of the crowd.'

Victoria of England is not a work of any particular value
from the historical point of view, because Edith Sitwell relies
entirely on secondary and well-known sources, and skates
rather superficially over politics (with a surprisingly violent
prejudice against Lord Melbourne). Her portrait of Victoria as a woman, however, shows remarkable sympathy
and warmth; and once again, as in certain passages of
Alexander Pope and *I Live Under a Black Sun*, she reveals
her agonised awareness of the underworld of the poor and
the doomed-from-birth, more terrible perhaps during the
early decades of the Industrial Revolution than at any other
time, in a macabre chapter entitled 'March Past'. This chapter opens, curiously, with an echo of *Gold Coast Customs*,

which had been published seven years before: 'Just behind the cannibal mart, where all day long, under the Bedlam daylight's murderous roar, the shambles for souls are set in the street, are the Rookeries of St Giles . . .'

Some interesting light on Edith's attitude to and judgment of the poets of her time is thrown by her *Aspects of Modern Poetry*, which was published in 1934. In this book she also rounded on three writers who had begun to attack her as a poet and as a person with some violence: Dr F. Leavis, the Cambridge don and critic, Wyndham Lewis, and Geoffrey Grigson, poet and editor of the little magazine *New Verse*. In a letter to Veronica Gilliatt, in November 1934 from Paris, she wrote: 'My book on modern poetry is being sent you. All I can say is, I hope the first chapter, which is largely about my enemies Dr Leavis, Mr Grigson and dear Mr Wyndham Lewis, will make you laugh, reading it, as much as I laughed writing it.'

In the case of Wyndham Lewis, it is difficult to know when the quarrel started, because they had begun by being friends. He collaborated with Osbert in the periodical *Art and Letters* directly after the war, and in *Laughter in the Next Room* Osbert has written of him, as he knew him at that time, that in spite of the fact that 'a sense of mystery, a feeling of genuine suspiciousness, emanated from him and pervaded all he did', he was covered with 'bohemian bonhomie, worn like an ill-fitting suit, and he could be, and often was, a diverting companion and a brilliant talker'. He made several portraits of Edith, and one of them, for which she sat in 1923, is now in the Tate Gallery. (It was not finished until twelve years later.) In *Taken Care of* Edith, perhaps not entirely seriously, ascribed the change in his attitude to a disastrous weekend at Renishaw during which he lost his collar, which was eventually tracked down and returned to his neck 'much as a weary and dilapidated blackbird might return to its nest'. However that may be, three years later, in 1930, Lewis published his novel *The Apes of God*.

In this huge and sprawling work, his ostensible object of satire was Bloomsbury. Pierpont's 'Encyclical' of advice to Horace Zagreus on the artistic and social conditions of the London of his time speaks of the 'societification' of art in England, and suggests that the English were actually ahead of the French in this disastrous modern process. 'The notorious *amateurism* of the anglo-saxon mind makes this doubly likely. In *Bloomsbury* it takes the form of a select and snobbish club. Its foundation-members consisted of monied middleclass descendants of Victorian literary splendour. Where they approximate to the citizens of this new cosmopolitan Bohemia is in their substitution of money for talent as a qualification for membership. . . . All are "geniuses", before whose creations the other members of the Club, in an invariable ritual, must swoon with appreciation.' But it was clear that this absurdly distorted condemnation was aimed, beyond Bloomsbury, at many other outstanding literary and artistic contemporaries, including the Sitwells. The huge latter section of the book, 'Lord Osmund's Lenten Party', could not have been mistaken for anything but an attempt to hold the Sitwells up to ridicule, by the simple device of placing them in the centre of a concourse of foolish and frivolous people. 'Blackshirt' tells Dan Boleyn, the innocent epicene young man who is being initiated into the mysteries of London, that 'The Finnian Shaw family group [Lord Osmund, Lord Phoebus and Lady Harriet] I should describe as a sort of middle-aged *youth-movement*. It is confined to a particular family and their dependants. This they have become in their capacity of "rebels" against authority. The danger of the War first must have driven them into that attitude. The idea of "youth" supervened — afterwards. It coloured with a desirable advertisement-value their special brand of rich-man's gilded bolshevism. In the fairy-tales they have spun about this theme ever since, Cockeye [their father] has always been the wicked Giant who tried to kill them during the big bad naughty World War.'

This was a challenge which Edith was not one to fail to take up, and she devotes a dozen pages of the opening chapter of the book, 'Pastors and Masters' to ridiculing Lewis, his pretensions and his poetry. As usual with Edith, it is good knockabout fun, and she gets some shrewd hits in; but it is perhaps open to question whether she was wise to *begin* a book on modern poetry with a personally motivated counter-attack of this sort.* So to a large extent with the making fun of Dr Leavis and Geoffrey Grigson, though in their cases there was the proper excuse that they were both critics who set out to act as guides through the contemporary production of poetry. Dr Leavis had written of her in his *New Bearings in English Poetry*† that she belonged to 'the his-

* Three years later Wyndham Lewis published *Blasting and Bombardiering*, in which he wrote: 'Edith — she is a poetess by the way — is a bad loser. When worsted in argument she throws Queensberry Rules to the winds. She once called me Percy. . . . For all that Edith does liven up the English literary scene considerably.'

† *New Bearings in English Poetry*, the first of Dr Leavis's controversial and influential critical volumes, was published in 1932. In essence, it is a study of T. S. Eliot, Ezra Pound and Gerard Manley Hopkins as leaders of 'a new start' in the English poetry of this century. In an early chapter on 'The Situation at the End of the War' Dr Leavis summarily dismisses the Sitwells in the following words: 'The opposition to the Georgians was already at the time in question (just after the war) Sitwellism. But the Sitwells belong to the history of publicity rather than of poetry.'

tory of publicity rather than of poetry', which, if not the beginning of an antagonism which was to last through the rest of Edith's life, was a major cannonade in the opening phase of the battle. She attacked his prose style, his lack of sensitivity and his critical judgment, pitying Ezra Pound and T. S. Eliot for being hero-worshipped by him, and ridiculing his critique of Milton.

When she comes to her third target, she begins: 'Mr Geoffrey Grigson is not as amusing as Dr Leavis, but there is still considerable pleasure to be derived from contemplating him.' She does not, however, indulge this pleasure for more than two or three pages, mostly devoted to mocking at some of the poetry Grigson was publishing in *New Verse*; a restraint all the more surprising because Grigson had consistently pursued her with blind unfairness and a rudeness that bordered on the libellous — and continued to do so.

All this was vigorous controversial stuff in the best Sitwellian manner; but it is impossible not to feel that it would have been better placed at the end of the volume, for her personal literary quarrels were of small importance compared with the appreciation of the major figures in modern English poetry which follows in subsequent chapters: Hopkins, Yeats, Eliot and Pound. She rightly includes Hopkins, because, though a late Victorian, his work was only published after the first World War. Her technical analysis of his poetry is an example of her own especial genre of criticism at its most effective, and is allied all through to a deeply sympathetic response to what she called his 'raw nakedness and unmitigated violence, in a sort of leonine majesty'.

Her recognition of the power of Yeats and Eliot, and the reasons for it, are equally impressive. There is one passage in particular, where she makes a comparison between

Browning and Eliot, in which she concludes: 'Browning's
verses straddle like a Strong Man [at a Fair]; Mr Eliot's
verses move like the Tyger burning bright; we can see the
splendour of the muscles rippling under the fiery surface of
the skin as the Tyger moves according to the needs of his
nature, seeking the water pools.'

The examination of Ezra Pound is full of admiration —
she speaks of the 'intense vitality' which inhabits his poetry,
'the sharp and clear visual sense, the apparent easiness of
the movement' — but the admiration is by no means un-
qualified. 'I must however confess,' she writes, 'that greatly
as I admire the major part of the Cantos, some of them do
seem to me to resemble the lost luggage office at a railway
station, with the trunks strewn about but carefully labelled.'
And in the rest of his work she finds the frequent contrast
between 'great poetry and an uninspired record' — and
puts her point of view with persuasive force.

There are also less successful chapters on W. H. Davies
and Sacheverell Sitwell. If in the case of the latter her aim
was to put him on the level of the other giants, it is a pity
that her critique was almost entirely and minutely technical.
There is another chapter on 'innovations in prose', discussing the work of James Joyce and Gertrude Stein, which
seems not entirely in place. And finally, an 'Envoi' in which
she examines her younger contemporaries, in particular
Auden, Day Lewis, Bottrall and Cummings (promising a
separate study of Spender for later on). She was largely out
of sympathy with the poetic generation of the thirties, sus-
picious, and even a little bewildered; it is not her most
effective foray.

Aspects of Modern Poetry got Edith into a not unusual
boil of trouble. By defenders of Dr Leavis and Grigson, she

was accused of plagiarism, a charge against which she de-
fended herself with some energy. In a letter to her lifelong
friend Christabel Aberconway,* written from Paris in 1934,
she says: 'I am so very glad you like the book, and that the
first chapter made you laugh. I must say — (there is nothing like laughing at one's own jokes) — I laughed till I
nearly cried as I was writing it.

'I thought it might amuse you to hear some of the reper-
cussions. Lewis is absolutely *howling* with rage. He has taken
refuge with the old ladies of *Time and Tide*, and from the
shelter of their skirts, and amidst the atmosphere of lavender
and old lace, is yelling defiance at me. What has infuriated
him especially is my reference to the fact that he was "formed
to be loved" — and to his sentimentality, and to his age.
(He is revoltingly sentimental. That is the trouble.) A Mr
Stonier — (heaven knows who *he* is) has rushed to the defence of Dr Leavis in the *New Statesman*, and has accused
me of plagiarising Dr Leavis by making the same quotations
from Yeats, and from other sources. . . . (If one writes
about Yeats at all, one *must* quote those particular passages
from *Autobiographies* and *Essays*) and he accuses me, too,
of plagiarising from Grigson by quoting a passage from
Yeats' *Packet for Ezra Pound*. So I have written the Editor
the following little billet-doux. (As they want a fight, they
shall have it.)

'"Sir,

With regard to Mr Stonier's review of my book *Aspects
of Modern Poetry*, may I reply that had I known that Dr
Leavis was the author of Andrew Lang's sonnet *The
Odyssey* (and I think him capable of it) I should have
acknowledged my debt to him. Had I known that he was

* Now the Dowager Lady Aberconway.

the author of Arthur Symons' book *The French Symbolists*, of Villiers de l'Isle-Adam's *Axel*, of Mr Yeats' *Autobiographies* and *Essays*, and of *The Oxford Book of English Verse*, I should have acknowledged my debt. But this is the first I have heard of it. Before we know where we are, we shall find that Dr Leavis is the Dark Lady of the Sonnets. Again, Mr Stonier says that, whilst attacking Mr Grigson, I 'appropriate, without acknowledging' (sic) 'an exceedingly apt quotation from Yeats' *Packet for Ezra Pound*, which Mr Grigson used in a review in *New Verse*.

'"I had not read Mr Grigson's review. Mr Yeats, with great kindness, sent me the *Packet for Ezra Pound*, when it first appeared, with most interesting notations in his own handwriting, and the book is one of my most prized possessions. I was unaware that I had to thank Mr Grigson for this. I thought my debt was to Mr Yeats, who sent me the book.

'"It is right and natural that Mr Stonier should prefer Dr Leavis's criticism to mine. It reminds me of Miss Nellie Wallace's appeal to her slightly denuded feather-boa: 'For God's sake, hold together, boys!' Yours faithfully, etc."

'I send you this, because I don't suppose the *New Statesman* will have the decency to print the letter. . . .'

But they did. G. W. Stonier's review in the issue of the *New Statesman* for 24 November 1934 (which was not without its modicum of praise for certain qualities of Edith Sitwell's book) produced reverberations which went on for some weeks. They began with a long letter from H. S. Sydney Pickering in the issue for 1 December, listing nine alleged plagiarisms of *New Bearings* in *Aspects of Modern Poetry* (though his actual letter specified nineteen), most of which are very difficult to take seriously. They gathered force on 8 December, when Geoffrey Grigson weighed in with a new complaint, that Edith had also been copying from Herbert Read's *Form in Modern Poetry* (1933), and Osbert Sitwell wrote a letter for the defence, the gist of which was that the complaints were no more valid than an accusation of plagiarism of other historians if one said that the Norman Conquest took place in 1066. Edith's letter was published with a long 'reply' from Mr Stonier, which contained yet more complaints which fell into the same category as the others. On 15 December another letter from Mr Grigson appeared, trying, very lamely, to prove that Edith had lied when she said she had not read his review in *New Verse* of Ezra Pound's *Cantos*. There was also a blast from Wyndham Lewis, of more sound and fury than sense, and a spirited defence of Edith from John Sparrow, in which he wrote that 'the fact that Miss Sitwell quotes the same passages from Yeats as does the Doctor [Leavis], and that their expositions of e.g. *The Waste Land* follow very closely the same line, does not prove in her any intellectual dependence on him. Careful study of the "parallel" passages in question will show clearly the truth of this assertion.' He goes on to observe that the real point of *Aspects of Modern Poetry* is to contrast Edith Sitwell's attitude to modern poetry with Dr Leavis's, and that 'no two views could be more radically opposed; the Doctor thinks of poetry as a sort of moral hygiene, Miss Sitwell sees it rather as a means of creating beauty in language.' The controversy closed with a letter from Edith on 22 December, not as funny or as characteristic as her first letter, but scoring a valid point against her opponents.

The next year, in a letter to Ronald Bottrall apropos the reaction of Grigson and Lewis to her book, she wrote: 'I'm shortly going for them again in a pamphlet, which is to be

called *The May Queen*, and my theme songs are two. The
first is that Mr Lewis resembles that other starry-eyed
adolescent, the heroine of Lord Tennyson's poem *The May
Queen*, inasmuch as both of them are always just *going* to be
crowned Queen of the May, or *were* crowned Queen of the
May a year or two ago, but neither of them are ever Queen
of the May at the moment. . . . The second theme-song is
that for years Mr Lewis has been howling that if only we'll
pay him sufficient attention he'll produce a rabbit from
under his hat — that, until now, nothing has been produced but an absolute cloud of bats from the belfry — but
that now suddenly he *does* produce a genuine, if very small
rabbit, in the shape of Mr Grigson!'

Further light on Edith's attitude to and judgment of the
poets of her time is thrown by her Northcliffe Lectures, delivered with her brothers Osbert and Sacheverell at the
University of London in 1937. Osbert's two lectures were
on Dickens; Sacheverell's on Palladian England and George
Cruikshank; and Edith's on 'Three Eras of Modern Poetry',
drawing, as she herself acknowledges, to a considerable
extent on what she had already written in *Aspects of Modern
Poetry*, though there is much that is new.

In this *tour d'horizon* she starts with some cracks at the
expense of Austin Dobson, shows an extremely reluctant
and qualified respect for A. E. Housman, and then goes on
to give dignified praise to the three authors she considers
the outstanding poets of the first 'era': Hardy, Yeats and
Eliot, of which the last two are, as she had made clear in
Aspects, her special favourites. She maintains that Yeats's
Words for Music are 'undoubtedly the greatest lyrics of the
last hundred years' and she speaks again of Eliot, in his use
of eight-syllable quatrains, as having 'the muscles of a

jaguar'. She then comes to the poets 'who have been called the Georgian school', long the target of the withering scorn of herself and Osbert, who, she says, 'seem obsessed by the predilection for sheep. . . . There was a good deal of mumbling about Mamble, grumbles because the author had never visited Mamble. There were loud and cheerful if raucous cries for beer, and raptures over cricket. . . .' The curious thing is that as soon as the general condemnation has been made, the number of exceptions begins to multiply. Completely exempted are Walter de la Mare, W. H. Davies and Ralph Hodgson; partially exempted are Sturge Moore, Gordon Bottomley, W. J. Turner, John Masefield, Wilfrid Gibson and Edmund Blunden; Rupert Brooke just manages to be let off with a severe reprimand, James Elroy Flecker is allowed some 'splendid lines' in spite of 'too much Turkish Delight'. Surprisingly, the only other poet she mentions of the 'Georgian school' to be entirely condemned, is Edward Thomas, a judgment which suggests a puzzling blind spot in Edith's sensibility.

It has, of course, to be remembered that the first volume of *Georgian Poetry*, which came out in 1912, did in fact represent an important revolt against the archaic diction and insipid late Victorianism of the poetry of the immediately preceding period. The taste of Edward Marsh, genial editor and impresario, unfortunately narrowed and ossified during the war, and by the time the last of the five volumes came out in 1922 was far removed from the spirit of the age. It was the 'neo-Georgian' group of the last two volumes that gave the whole series, rather unfairly, its bad name, and evoked Edith's satirical strictures. None of this group, except W. J. Turner, figure among her 'exemptions'.

In her second lecture, Edith Sitwell opens with praise

for the three war poets, Isaac Rosenberg, Siegfried Sassoon and Wilfred Owen (though she does not mention Robert Graves). Of Owen, she writes in an interesting aside: 'I can speak with certainty of the care and patience with which he worked, since it was I who prepared his first book of poems for publication. The poems were left in my care by my friend Mr Siegfried Sassoon, who had to go to America and who eventually edited them, and it was I who disentangled, from the highly complicated drafts, the words which I believed Owen wished used.' She then returns to T. S. Eliot, praising him once more with acute critical perception and passionate sympathy; far and away the most memorable passage in the lectures. Immediately after, she switches to an attack on the surrealists, a movement which certainly seems today a dead duck in the history of modern English poetry, in spite of the early advocacy of David Gascoyne — which Edith ridicules. This is followed, characteristically, by an examination of her own poetry, and the poetry of her two brothers. The Sitwells were always the most loyal enthusiasts for one another's work, and one cannot escape a feeling of sheer admiration for reasoned loyalty vanquishing modesty in what she writes here.

Finally, she comes again to the generation of the thirties. It is interesting to observe how difficult, in spite of the fact that she has had three more years to study it, she still finds it to approve *in general* of the poetry written during that uneasy decade, while (rather grudgingly) admitting at this date the limited excellence in the work of W. H. Auden, Cecil Day Lewis and Stephen Spender. She finds nothing to admire in Louis MacNeice's poetry, and gives what seem to me totally inapposite and unperceptive reasons for disliking it. With less qualified praise, at the very end, she recommends the poetry of Ronald Bottrall, William Empson and Dylan Thomas.

Helen Rootham died in 1938, and Edith was released from the servitude she had imposed on herself in her goodness of heart.

In Paris, among her close friends was Gertrude Stein, whom she had got to know in the middle twenties, when she had reviewed one of her books in *Vogue*. Alice Toklas, in her *Autobiography*, says that when Gertrude Stein and Edith eventually met they became friends at once. Edith persuaded Gertrude Stein to accept invitations to speak at Oxford and Cambridge. She arrived in England with Alice Toklas in the spring of 1926. Edith and Osbert both arranged parties for them. 'Osbert was a great comfort to Gertrude Stein. He so thoroughly understood every possible way in which one could be nervous that as he sat beside her in the hotel telling her all the kinds of ways that he and she could suffer from stage fright she was quite soothed. She was always very fond of Osbert. She always said he was like an uncle of a king. He had that pleasant kindly irresponsible agitated calm that an uncle of an english king always must have.'

Among other special friends Edith made in Paris was Allanah Harper (Mrs Robert Statlender), editor of the review *Échanges*, who introduced her to the work of Rainer Maria Rilke, and through whom she met many of the famous contemporary writers and painters. A respectful, rather than a close friendship grew up between her and Jean Cocteau, which lasted to the end of their lives.

It was Gertrude Stein who appears to have introduced her to a person who was destined to become her closest friend, the emigré young Russian painter, Pavel Tchelitchew, and his sister Choura. Gertrude Stein had seen the mark of genius in Tchelitchew's work from the beginning, and brought them together probably in late 1925 or 1927, after the production of Sacheverell's ballet *The Triumph of Neptune*. They remained devoted to one another, in spite of constant rows 'of an unprecedented ferocity' (as Edith herself describes them in *Taken Care of*). In fact, it seems likely that she fell deeply in love with him, though we shall probably not know for certain until the year 2000, when her letters to him, in the possession of Yale University, can be examined. She sat to him for six portraits, of which one, perhaps the most beautiful, showing her in profile with a look of extraordinary calm, gentle intellectual and imaginative power, disappeared for over twenty years and was only rediscovered in the rue Saint-Dominique a year or two before her death. He also made wired effigies of her, in which he used wax with sand over the basic wire structure.

At one period he and Choura took a cottage in which Stella Bowen and Ford Madox Ford had lived in the village of Guermantes outside Paris, and there Edith used to visit him. She also acted as hostess for the *vernissage* of his exhibition at the Galerie Vignon in Paris, an occasion on which he behaved with (characteristic) bad manners, suddenly leaving the party at an early stage, and letting Edith look after the celebrities; a temperamental outburst which Edith, knowing him all too well, quickly forgave.

'He was the most generous man I have ever known,' she confessed, 'a wonderful friend, and tireless in thinking of ways to help others.' They shared a passion for cats. She called him 'the Boyar', and would tell endless stories of his eccentricity, his rages, his violent passing infatuations for people who imposed on him (including English and American poetasters whose works he could scarcely read), and his equally violent impulses of disinterested generosity. In *Taken Care of*, she describes one of the scenes of rage which took place during a period when he had rented a studio in London. 'The floors were particularly slippery. I was sitting to him for one of his portraits of me. Suddenly a storm of particular violence blew up — I do not know — have never known, for what reason, ascribing it, however, to the fact that he had hurt one of his toes the day before, and although I was absent at the time of this misfortune, attributed it to some carelessness of mine.

'In any case, he took to hurling the armchair in which I sat across the slippery floor as if it were a perambulator, at the same time uttering shrieks of rage, and, at moments, hurling bare canvasses past my head. . . .' She was rescued from this scene of unbridled temperament by the arrival of Cecil Beaton for tea.

In the letter to Veronica Gilliatt from which I quoted earlier, she wrote: 'The Boyar and I had some fearful rows in London, and once he locked me in his studio and jumped up and down in front of the door, yelling. But he returned from Spain looking like a melancholy and fairly repentant gorilla, and remembered my birthday for the first time since I have known him. He painted me the most exquisite fan. It is a black fan, and has figures of toreadors on it, and a very strange smoky "torch effect" at the back with long vistas. . . .'

On Tchelitchew himself, Edith had a profound effect from the very beginning. That she should understand, and approve, what he was aiming at in his art, became intensely important to him. He mythologised about her: she became

'La Dame Blanche', one of the archetypal figures in his private aesthetic universe. He felt she had the power of a seer, a sibyl, and awaited her judgments as a suppliant in ancient times might have awaited the answers of the Oracle of Delphi. He called her 'Sitvouka' in his more affectionate moments, which alternated with the rages of which she has written; but beyond the moments of rage and the moments of tenderness, she remained, always, a spiritual presence, reappearing in one transformation or another in many of his most significant paintings. Later on, it seemed to Edith that their relationship, *mutatis mutandis*, could be compared to that platonic yet passionate relationship between Vittoria Colonna and Michelangelo.

Pavel Tchelitchew left for the United States just before the war, and became an American citizen. He wrote to Edith every week. They met again in New York in 1948 (see Chapter 14), but found unhappily that they had grown apart. The breach, however, was healed on his subsequent visit to Europe. He died in Rome in 1957. Edith confessed that 'his power of living was so great that I cannot believe I shall never see him again'. And she adds, as a moving epitaph to one who meant so much to her for so many years: 'Thinking of him now, I see him as I saw him shortly after our first meeting. The snow was thick on the ground, and he was leaping in the air and clapping his large painter's hands together, because the snow reminded him of his childhood and youth, before the misery and grandeur began.'

8

IN discussing *Triple Fugue* and *Before the Bombardment*, I have already indicated my belief that Osbert's outstanding contribution to English literature between the wars was first of all in satire; but also in descriptive writing. The first quality is a dominant characteristic of his verse, the second of his travel-books: but both come together in his short stories, of which *Triple Fugue*, published in 1924, is the first collection, and in his three novels, *Before the Bombardment* (1926), *The Man Who Lost Himself* (1929) and *Miracle on Sinai* (1933).

The essence of Osbert Sitwell's satire is his hatred of the insensitive and the philistine. Anything — a lust for money-making, hunting and shooting elevated to the status of an incessant and exclusive ritual, contempt for subject races, conventional and hypocritically respectable religion, narrow and clan-rigid social snobbery — anything that interferes with the free play and response of the heart and the imagination, is his target. It would be possible to make out a case for Osbert as, supremely, the satirist of the decay of the British Imperial order and the British ruling classes. He *is* that in a certain sense, because his experience as a soldier in the first German war made him passionately contemptuous of the diplomatists, politicians and generals who had blundered into the holocaust and had squandered the lives of a whole generation and the accumulated riches of an industrious century with what seemed to him almost unbelievable ineptitude, callousness and stupidity. The British Empire as a system of world order disappeared between 1914 and 1918, though this was by no means immediately apparent; but Osbert Sitwell would have found his target of insensitivity, repressive respectability, parochialism and philistinism in almost any age, as Shelley and Dickens did in theirs, however different the specific circumstances. Osbert, as we have seen, decided in his early youth to dedicate his life to the pursuit of beauty and the creation of art; and the very fact that he came of a social class where the majority despised such an attitude to life, gave an extra intensity to his satiric vision, an extra impetus to his prophetic wrath. The author of *A Letter to My Son*, published in 1944, is lifting his voice against exactly the same state of mind among his countrymen as the author of *The Winstonburg Line* (1920) and *Triple Fugue*.

Even in his lighter journalistic articles, he maintains an undertone of seriousness, which is not without its apposite interest today. For the New Year of 1929, he was asked to write an article for the *Daily Mail* on 'What I most want in 1929'. Among the wishes he enumerated were:

'That people would realise that another war would destroy everything of beauty, everything that makes life worth living for them, every remaining shred of prosperity in Europe.

'That two plays by Shakespeare should enjoy a long, simultaneous, and successful run in the West End of London.

'That people generally would at last realise that to be intelligent is not only more satisfactory, but also better than to be stupid, and that therefore the word "highbrow" in their mouths is more of a compliment than a reproach; that brains are given us, just as much as the foot, to be used, and that there is nothing intrinsically wrong in using them.'

One might think that, with his passionately held convictions about the social order and public affairs, Osbert would inevitably have taken part in politics; but after his failure to be elected to Parliament in the General Election of 1919 — during which he stood as Liberal candidate for Scarborough — he made no further direct efforts in that direction, having made up his mind that literature was to be his medium and his world. Nevertheless, he has called politics the 'repressed side' of his nature, and attributes to it the profoundly anxious concern he felt when the General Strike broke out in 1926, and the impulse that arose so strongly in him to do something to help resolve the crisis before it was too late. In fact, he managed to play a useful part in setting certain behind-the-scenes negotiations going which contributed more than a little to the final calling off of the strike: an episode which he has described in his autobiography with great fascination.

Osbert Sitwell's satirical method in fiction, its achievements and its weaknesses, can be most effectively studied in his most ambitious novel *Miracle on Sinai*. It is possible to think that *Before the Bombardment* is a better book (as well as one dearer to the author's heart); but *Miracle on Sinai* shows his powers fully extended and at their most varied. *The Man Who Lost Himself*, in its curiously old-fashioned orotundity and conventional approach, cannot, in my opinion, be considered on the same level as the other two novels, remarkable though many of the descriptive passages, in particular of Granada, may be in themselves.

Miracle on Sinai describes the assembling of an hetero-
geneous party in a luxury hotel built by a newspaper tycoon,
Lord Pridian, on the Sinai peninsula, and the adventures
that befall them, in the Peacockian manner that Aldous
Huxley had revivified some years earlier in such novels as
Those Barren Leaves. There is Lord Pridian himself, 'a
placid pot-bellied little mock-Buonaparte' who has deluded
himself into thinking he is a person of importance but is in
fact nothing but 'a money-beetle'. In his party is a young
man, Michael Bettony, a gossip-columnist, a scandal-
scavenger such as had begun to exist in the twenties and is
still flourishing today. Next in importance is Major-General
Sir Rudyard Ramshackle, a retired military buffoon 'who
had quelled the budding mutiny at Melnaimpore by giving
the order to fire into "the dirty, black-faced mob",' and
was now 'on every committee' and 'president of the new,
and very popular, Society for the Prevention of Foreign
Artists from entering Britain or of Native Ones from
Escaping from it'. The General is accompanied by his wife
'Birdie', moving spirit of the Anti-Vegetarian League and
enthusiastic figure in the hunting-field, despite her association with various societies for the prevention of suffering in
animals. Then there is Sir Levy Lollygo, Bart., M.P., a
wealthy Jewish financier, popularly reputed to be a great
philanthropist and national benefactor, but in Osbert's eyes
'the sort of "leading capitalist" who, by his megalomaniac
materialism and blatant irresponsibility, had helped to ruin
capitalism'. His constant cry, is that 'we must learn to think
imperially', and his equally constant chagrin that his son
Stuart Lollygo has become a fanatical pro-Soviet Communist. Among other members of the cast are: Lady Helen
Hornmaker, 'beauty, traveller, and the greatest ornament of

our divorce courts', who 'wearied of men with the same rapidity as she fell in love with them', and was now running a decorating establishment, for which reason she was being employed by Lord Pridian to furnish part of the hotel; Madame Galactic, a celebrated American medium, whose 'control', 'Little Toucan' during her trances 'spoke through her mouth in an eager, pidgin English' and was alleged by Madame Galactic to be a twelve-year-old Negress; and T. L. Enfelon, an author with a 'mild but petulant beard' and 'loose, shaggy clothes clinging to a giraffe-like body' who is obviously based on D. H. Lawrence, but portrayed with surprising charity if one remembers the bitterness with which Edith was to speak of Lawrence in *Taken Care of* and her conviction that *Lady Chatterley's Lover* was an attack on her own family. Finally, there is the Shereef Abdul, famous Arab chieftain, a devotee of *The Forsyte Saga*, and subscribes to the Book Society, travelling with a large harem and attendant household.

Now, the essential object of the gathering together of all these diverse characters in the Aaron Palace Hotel (known to the wits as 'The Golden Calf'), an assemblage that contains representatives of all the main genera of his time into whose breasts Osbert Sitwell delighted to aim his satiric shafts (with the possible exception of a cricketing poet-novelist), is, of course, in Peacockian or Huxleyan fashion, to make them reveal their monstrous, pathetic or ridiculous natures by their inter-action upon one another. The motive power, however — for even a Peacockian novel must have some kind of a plot — is provided by a picnic which is planned at great length, and eventually takes place, on the summit of Mount Sinai. During this picnic a miraculous revelation occurs and new tablets of the law appear out of a mysterious storm cloud. The delightful irony, the sting in the tail of the novel, is that each member of the picnic party reads in these tablets of the law the affirmation and sanction of his own desires or proselytising dreams. T. L. Enfelon, for instance, remembers in particular reading: 'Thou shalt not be repressed, thou shalt not make to thyself inhibition or complex', and 'Thou shalt bow down before Dark Gods and worship Them'; Michael Bettony saw, standing out boldly in clear-cut letters, 'Thou shalt bear false witness against thy neighbour'; while for Lord Pridian the First Commandment ran quite distinctly: 'Buy British'. The final confrontation of these irreconcilable interpretations is prevented by the crumbling into dust of the tablets, and the conviction of the Shereef that what *he* saw upon them enjoined on him the necessity of executing all those male members of the party who refused to embrace the Moslem religion, and of clapping into his harem all the female members. Only Madame Galactic, who manages to fly out before the grand climax when the Shereef's tribesmen surround the Hotel, returns to the Western world.

This serio-comic drama provides Osbert Sitwell with the opportunity of having a great deal of fun at the expense of his victims, and all through the book there are passages which are both extremely entertaining and full of merciless observation of the foibles of his type-characters. What makes the total result less than a first-class success is, I believe, first of all Osbert's habit of *describing* rather than creating his characters — there are, for instance, thirty-six pages near the beginning of the novel devoted to elaborate portraits of the *dramatis personae* one by one, which make one feel that the action will never get going. 'The man *describes* characters instead of showing them,' exclaimed

Arnold Bennett in his journal, on receiving a copy of *Before the Bombardment* inscribed to 'dear good Uncle Arnold from a nephew'. This lack of proportion is also shown in the way Osbert Sitwell lays his satire on with a trowel, exaggerating the absurdities to the edge of burlesque and drawing scenes out long after he has made his point. In the contemporary satiric novels of Aldous Huxley, with which *Miracle on Sinai* inevitably invites a comparison, even the most ridiculous characters are nevertheless three-dimensional human beings; but Osbert Sitwell sees almost all his characters as two-dimensional grotesques. This would matter a good deal less if the descriptions, the musings and the dialogue were cut to the bone, with that dead-on-target satiric terseness of which the young Evelyn Waugh had already shown himself as master in his earliest novels.

Nevertheless, these tentative criticisms must immediately be qualified by the reflection that in the long satiric innuendos with which Osbert Sitwell so richly fills out the portraits of his characters, he is following in the footsteps of the genius of the English novel he so greatly admires, Charles Dickens. By the time he came to write *Left Hand, Right Hand!*, he showed that he could paint portraits with a warm sympathy as well as with mocking critical observation.

Again, *Miracle on Sinai* reveals with exceptional brilliance the author's rare gift for atmospheric description of awe-inspiring natural events and uncommon places. The whole of the journey to the mountain is done with remarkable skill and imaginative power, culminating in the great transformation scene of the miraculous revelation: 'Darker and darker, and yet no cooler, grew the mountain-top; strangely dark, considering its isolation, alone and unshadowed in blue skies. But, tenebrous as was the air, it nevertheless remained transparent, so that, through this deepening though impalpable obscurity, valley and plain, lying in their golden, glossy sunshine, could still be descried; could indeed, perhaps, be focused with more accuracy, as if some object were being examined through smoked glass. The gathering gloom, too, seemed in some perplexing fashion to dull the senses: for few people appeared at first to recognize the metamorphosis which was in action about them, but were content to sit in heavy attitudes, listening in a kind of numbness. There were, of course, exceptions. Lord Pridian, who was in some respects the most, as in others the least, responsive person present, kept on nervously glancing round the circle; and Michael of necessity observed the alteration, although, being a trained journalist, he did not permit its origin or consequences to concern him. T. L. remarked it too: and also that, while this odd diaphanous darkness gained strength, so the cloud, which still lay just within its range, at the back of chapel and mosque, assumed a more ostensible glow, as if the radiant core of it — which even from a distance, he had surmised, was now undergoing some similar and yet reverse process — was beginning to flare up as the light here began to die down, until it glowed like a furnace, its incandescence showing dully but very surely through the enshrouding smoke. . . .'

It is, I think, worth noting that in this book once again Osbert Sitwell reserves his most ruthless satire for an older generation — the generation which, in his eyes, cannot be forgiven for the war. He mocks Michael Bettony's professional activities; but nevertheless he is young, and special excuses can be made for him. In describing Michael's state of mind when Lady Helen Hornmaker agrees to marry him, he writes: 'In love, it was better to exist for the day, and to

leave the examination of motives and principles, and the
personal manner in which they were accommodated, for
the judgment of a cooler, inevitably cooler dawn. They
concerned him no more than — since she had spoken — did
his future: for the generation to which he belonged is precisely the one that most discounts the insensate materialism
of which, by its elders, it is so frequently accused. Brought
up from childhood to support its bankrupt and usually
greedy parents, heedless of the miseries of the morrow as of
the glories of the past, it lurches insecurely from one day to
another: money it desires sometimes for a banner, a token
of success, as once upon a time was a title bestowed, but, if
no longer thus impelled by a sense of inferiority, money becomes valueless to it, except in small quantities and with no
great machinery of living dependent upon it. . . .'

Nevertheless, this must be counted as an unusual moment
of clemency towards the gossip-writer, who does not fare
at all well elsewhere in Osbert Sitwell's works. In 'A Few
Days in an Author's Life', which appeared as a long preface to *All at Sea* — described as 'a social tragedy in three
acts for first-class passengers only' — by Osbert and
Sacheverell (1927), Osbert devotes a section of blistering
invective to the unfortunate subject: 'The "Gossip"
column in the cheaper papers is, generally speaking, one of
Satan's most modern, devilish and devastating devices. . . .
And what is all this "chat" for? To make the suburbs feel
at home in Mayfair and "in the know". To concentrate
their envy and malice respectively on the few peculiarly
fortunate or peculiarly intelligent, and enable them to talk
freely about people they have never met.' Osbert goes on
to suggest, with remarkable prescience, that as time goes on
the gossip-writer, to satisfy an ever-increasing demand for

malicious gossip, will fix his talons more and more ruth-
lessly into the artist and writer. He quotes a delightful
specimen of the abuse to which the Sitwells had just been
subjected in the popular press: 'The latest brainless insult
to actors and actresses the swollen-headed Sitwellian slush
quoted together with players' protests is but one of many
such recent flagrant specimens of "Culchawed" Cant.'*

The same admirable virtues, and the same weaknesses,
can, I think, be found in Osbert Sitwell's short stories — of
which he has written nearly three dozen — as in his long
fiction. I have already discussed *Low Tide* in connection
with Scarborough. The title story of the collection in
which it appears, *Triple Fugue*, is one of his earliest satiric
pieces — and one of the earliest in which he goes for the
gossip-columnist — and is outstanding for the violence of
his caricatures of the English literary 'establishment' of the
time. Unkind is far too mild a word for his portraits of, for
instance, Sir Edward Marsh as 'Mattie Dean', and Lady
Ottoline Morrell as 'Lady Septuagesima Goodley'. The
joke of the story, of the remains of three very different
people who are killed in an air crash being put together to
form a revived composite person, is ingenious but does not
really stand being stretched out to this length; again, it
seems to me, Osbert seriously weakens his effect by reckless exaggeration. Far more effective is the later story *Alive,
Alive Oh!* in which he returns to satirising the same literary
milieu, through the history of Joseph Bundle, the nature

* *All at Sea* was performed at the Arts Theatre Club in November
1927 as *First Class Passengers Only*. It went down well with a smart
audience, and the critics voted it 'an extravagant charade', 'enormously
good fun', but with 'no rhyme or reason as a play'. At one point Edith,
Osbert and Sacheverell themselves appeared on stage as guests at a
cabaret party, and chanted their own poems through a megaphone.

poet who finds that he must pretend to die in order to save his literary reputation. In this story, the rapier is more in evidence than the bludgeon, and there is more affectionate banter than crushing scorn in the portrait of Bundle himself. The whole thing is beautifully handled, and is one of Osbert Sitwell's most characteristic and memorable short stories.

In general, the short stories vary between rather cruel but very sharply observed satiric portraits; occasional pieces that seem to have strayed from his autobiography, such as *Death of a God*, the story of Mr Snowberry, who wound the clocks in all the big country houses round Renishaw; anecdotes and 'after dinner' stories, sometimes about ghosts, which do not always seem quite worthy of the decorative elaboration the author gives them; and others which defy classification. If one reads them all in bulk, one may perhaps be surprised at the number of old ladies, pathetic elderly eccentrics and ruined has-beens who figure as their subjects; and one may feel that all too often they are almost wantonly leisurely, discursive and baroque in the telling. Nevertheless, there are brilliant passages of atmospheric description all through, whether of Italian landscapes and Italian palaces, of exotic animals, or rare collections of *objets d'art*; or of the country house which is the setting for an invalid's murder in *The Greeting* — surely one of Osbert Sitwell's short story masterpieces.

One of his more successful ghost stories, *A Place of One's Own*, about a haunted house in 'Newborough' where an eccentric old lady, subject to fits of madness, had committed suicide — or so it appeared at the inquest — was made into a film in 1945 by Gainsborough. Rarely to be seen nowadays, this film, directed by Bernard Knowles, is interesting for having Margaret Lockwood, James Mason, Dennis Price and Dulcie Gray among the actors.

If his satiric sense is one of the outstanding qualities of Osbert Sitwell's fiction and verse, it is the salt of his polemical writing. No one in our age, I believe, has written with more furious invective against the philistine habits of the British people; but repeatedly the rapier of satiric wit flashes out in the midst of his bludgeoning assault. The shameful under-estimation of the creative artist among his countrymen (in the days before the Arts Council was established) has been a theme he has returned to again and again; the writer, the painter, the musician have found no more constant or courageous defender, and his counter-attack has been all the more deadly because he gives no quarter in his slashing mockery.*

'A Few Days in an Author's Life' is, in fact, a wrathful, wide-ranging pamphlet, his first, against the philistine opponent. 'Never has this unfortunate man,' he says of the creative writer, 'found such a multitude of enemies as in the England of to-day, for he is fighting, usually in the first place his own poverty, owing to the wretched financial state of the country as compared with fifteen or fifty years ago — and poverty is a deadly assassin of the arts, whatever rich people may say to the contrary — and secondly, the stupidity and supreme lack of interest in everything except motor-cars and night-clubs of most of the young super-rich — for if the poor have grown poorer, the rich have certainly grown richer. Then, too, he is battling

---

* Osbert Sitwell did not always write in satirical vein when roused to indignation. His hatred of injustice inspired a moving plea against the condemnation of the Scottsboro Negro boys, in an article in the *Sunday Referee* on 14 October 1931.

against a horde of barbarians of all ages, fear of art the only thing that binds them together: for old Victorian ladies and gentlemen, and the modern cocktail-cosmopolitan, unite on this one point, and this point only. . . . In modern England the artist holds in the community the precise position occupied by the bull in Spain. The argument that the artist, by being baited, has public attention directed toward him applies equally to the bull. But is the attention of the bull-baiting audience the sort of attention, or the sort of audience, that will benefit the bull?'

Sometimes, it must be admitted, Osbert Sitwell's weakness for exaggeration gets the better of him in his polemics, when specific persons are in view: he seems to be setting a pack of hounds to chase a mouse. I would not, however, say that this was true of his attack on Lord Elton (apropos his book *St George and the Dragon*) in his wartime pamphlet (originally published as an essay in *Horizon*) *A Letter to My Son*: he convinces us that every blow was richly deserved.

A Letter to My Son is again a polemic against the Philistine — or rather against all enemies of the artist. Written as it was in the middle of a national death-struggle against the Axis empire, and all the regimentation that struggle involved, it was an act of uncompromising courage. It was also a wittier, more entertaining, and at the same time more profound argument than 'A Few Days in an Author's Life'.

The opening paragraphs in this epistle to an imaginary character are challenging in the manner he had already made his own: 'Our position here is not easy, for not only are we both artists, but we come of the privileged — formerly privileged — classes, and therefore are shot at by both sides; since the kind of people amongst whom I was born

and brought up are still uneducated in aesthetics, only respect pro-consuls and big-game hunters, and, worse still,
have been infected with middle-class conventionality and
worship of money, while the great majority, the voters, are
unlettered, can only read the columns of the daily press,
and are now every day flattered into thinking themselves the
arbiters of all excellence in the arts. As well tell every daisy
that it is a rose!' As a rider to this, a little later on, he adds
the characteristically Sitwellian, paradoxical comment: 'I
would not like to see — though no doubt I shall — here-
ditary wealth abolished. To-day men seem afraid to defend
it. American ideas of ant-labour prevail. But, in all truth, the
only kind of wealth worth having is the kind you do not
earn: it is unassociated with the mean and slavish virtue of
thrift.' This, it is perhaps not inapposite to comment, was
written before the great age of football-pool fortunes.

Inevitably, in his vision of the post-war future, Osbert
Sitwell makes some mis-prophecies. 'It will be harder for
you,' he writes, 'than ever it was for your father. The true
artist has always had to fight, but it is, and will be, a more
ferocious struggle for you, and the artists of your generation, than ever before. The working man, this time, will be
better looked after, he will be flattered by the press and
bribed with Beveridge schemes, because he possesses a
plurality of votes. But who will care for you or your fate,
who will trouble to defend the cause of the young writer,
painter, sculptor, musician?' This has an ironic ring in the
age of the British Council and the Arts Council. Nevertheless, Osbert's vision is not altogether at fault when he goes
on to say: 'At the best, you will be ground down between
the small but powerful authoritarian minority of art direc-
tors, museum racketeers, the chic, giggling modistes who

write on art and literature, publishers, journalists and dons (who will, to do them justice, try to help you, if you will write as they tell you) — and the enormous remainder, who would not mind, who would, indeed, be pleased, if they saw you starve.'

What is best about *A Letter to My Son*, quite apart from its general ultra-partisan tone towards the problems of the artist in the modern world, is the charged epigrams which abound in it: epigrams which were startling enough at the moment when they were coined, but deserve to remain in mind for many decades to come. For instance: 'I would fight — and I know you would — for the right to be idle. We would always oppose the ants in their awful paradise.' And, more trenchant: 'A country is worth dying for, as it is worth living for, because of the flowers its soil produces. Shakespeare out-distances Waterloo as an English triumph. Yet a link may exist between the two: It is possible that had we always been a nation that preferred cross-word puzzles to poetry and the cult of the body to that of the mind, we should not have produced either of these victories.'

As was to be expected, this polemic aroused indignant rage in the breasts of many popular war-time publicists. To say such things at the time of Alamein, when the war-making effort of the British people was stretched to its limit, was, quite definitely, letting down the side, old boy. James Agate waded into the fray, with a hostile review in the *Daily Express*, followed by a pamphlet of his own, *Noblesse Oblige*, in which he attacked Osbert Sitwell's views, as underrating the contribution of the 'common man' to the British cause, and indeed questioning all his arguments. Osbert replied, in an article published in the *Daily Express* on 2 December 1944, in which, after refuting the charge that he underrated the ordinary soldier's sacrifice because the memory of the battlefield of the first German war was always with him, he continues, with considerable dignity: 'I believe — and I repeat it — that it would have been one of the world's most appalling tragedies had Shakespeare died in battle before the age of 30; and I say again that life, as well as death, is important to this country. . . . Atrocities are the result of wrong ways of thinking, as are wars themselves; and it is the great artists and thinkers who train and teach men to see the light. It is well for the ordinary man to bear that in mind. He should also remember that in planning a new world, patriotic emotion, even in time of war, is no good substitute for clear thinking, and that wars will continue as long as hatreds continue. He can best learn to love foreign countries by becoming acquainted with their works of art.'

9

IT is, I think, a matter of fairly general agreement among Osbert Sitwell's admirers that they value him, and believe he has made his distinct contribution to the literature of his time, as a writer of prose; and that his prose *œuvre* reaches its culmination in the unique, five-volume masterpiece of his autobiography, *Left Hand, Right Hand!*

Nevertheless, he cannot be ignored as a poet. It was with poetry that he began his career, in the pages of *Wheels* and in the little book *Twentieth Century Harlequinade* (with some of Edith's earliest poems beside his own), and this was not merely the characteristic start of an imaginative young man who was soon after to opt for fiction or biography or criticism. Osbert Sitwell's poetic production stretches from 1916 over nearly half a century, and the volume of *Selected Poems*, published in 1943 many years before he had finished writing verse, shows how varied his achievement had already been.

The corpus of original poetry (there are no translations or adaptations from the work of others) can, very roughly, be divided into three compartments or categories. There are, first of all, the satires, including the early anti-war poems, which may be viewed as an extension in verse of the pursuit of the 'Golden Horde' and the various other quarry of his indignation and contempt which he hunted with such ruthless zeal (and obvious enjoyment) in his novels and stories. Then there are what one might describe as the general poems, some of them of great beauty, which include such linked series of lyrics as *Winter the Huntsman* and *Out of the Flame*, where the mood is now sombre and prophetic, now festive and full of imaginative colour, now elegiac and reflective. Finally, there are the 'poetic portraits', which first made their appearance in *England Reclaimed* in 1926, and have been described by him as 'written in an effort to form a gallery of rustic characters, and thus preserve their likeness, and commemorate a tradition and a way of life which were even then fast disappearing and have now vanished'. They are for the most part written in a relaxed recitative style, full of shrewd and humorous observations, with a descriptive vigour and a nostalgic music all their own. They are perhaps not quite poetry in the strictest sense, but they are certainly more than light verse. It is difficult not to be captivated by them, and even to feel that they strike an entirely original and memorable note in the literature of our time.

Osbert's earliest poems are very much in the bitter anti-war mood of his contemporary soldier-poets, reviling the stupidity and insensibility of an older generation which he held responsible for the slaughter. He was not yet a master of technique as Siegfried Sassoon and Wilfred Owen were, but the best of them, *Hymn to Moloch*, *Old-fashioned Sportsmen* and *The Next War*, made their mark at the time, and deserve a place in any full-ranging anthology of the poems of 1914–18. *How Shall We Rise to Greet the Dawn* (written in November 1918) has a significant passage that might make an appropriate epigraph for the greater part of Osbert's literary activity between the wars:

Let us prune the tree of language
Of its dead fruit.
Let us melt up the clichés
Into molten metal,
Fashion weapons that will scald and flay;
Let us curb this eternal humour
And become witty.
Let us dig up the dragon's teeth
From this fertile soil
Swiftly,
Before they fructify;
Let us give them as medicine
To the writhing monster itself.

The Next War had a remarkable history, which shows, I think, how truly it echoed the feelings of its author's generation. It was published in England in the late autumn of 1918, after the Armistice, in the *Nation*. In 1919 — it had not yet appeared in the U.S.A. — it was found by the American poet Witter Bynner, as Osbert tells us, 'scrawled in ink upon the marble top of a table in a café in San Francisco'. Bynner was so impressed and intrigued by it that he brought it to the attention of the press. The result was that the mysterious scrawlings on the table-top were photographed, and appeared in a number of newspapers, and the waiters of the café were interviewed in the hope that one of them might remember who had written it, or know who the anonymous author was. 'Eventually, somehow or other, it was tracked down, and Witter Bynner kindly sent me a letter, enclosing the various newspaper cuttings relative to the affair, and telling me the story of the strange adventures of this poem, starred for months as a piece by an unknown hand.'

In his autobiography, Osbert Sitwell makes it clear how closely he was associated with the other soldier poets, and how much they all owed to Robert Ross who drew them together as friends. It was Ross who engineered the first meeting between Osbert and Wilfred Owen, that resulted in an exchange of letters between them over many months, and the offering to *Wheels* of the group of Owen's poems which appeared (as I have already described) in the fourth number. Osbert has described the last meeting between himself, Siegfried Sassoon and Wilfred Owen 'on an afternoon of full summer, a Saturday in July 1918. He had let me know that he was coming to London, and I had been able to arrange to take him and Siegfried Sassoon to hear Violet Gordon Woodhouse play the harpsichord and clavichord, and she made the afternoon stand out as an oasis in the desert of war.' After the performance, Owen, Sassoon and Osbert walked back to the house in Swan Walk, and after tea sat under the mulberry-trees in the Physic Garden opposite. 'It was the ideal of a summer afternoon: various shrubs, late-flowering magnolias and the like, were in blossom, there was a shimmer and flutter in the upper leaves, and a perfection of contentment and peacefulness, unusual in the tense atmosphere of a hot day in London, especially during a war, breathed over the scene. So listlessly happy was Owen that he could not bring himself to leave the Garden to go to the station and catch the train he had arranged to take.' Very soon after, Wilfred Owen rejoined his old battalion in France, and was killed on 4 November, a week before the Armistice was declared.

If the poetry of Osbert Sitwell is compared with the poetry of Edith and Sacheverell, most people will, I think, concede that he only rarely achieves the originality and intensity of the former, or the delicate sense of texture and music of the latter. Nevertheless, *rarely* is a comparative term only in the work of an author whose production has been so copious in all the branches of literature he attempted; and I do not believe anyone can read *Winter the Huntsman* without feeling that in this moving sequence of linked lyrics Osbert the poet has formed his most completely satisfying and individual expression, where content and form are harmoniously balanced. *Winter the Huntsman* was written in 1924, before any of his prose works, and a year after *Out of the Flame* which in its developing poetic power can be said to foreshadow it.

Osbert himself has described the poem's general theme, saying that he had tried to write it on two levels, the upper level telling its own story of the seasons, the more hidden level suggesting the forces which were shaping the ominous future of the times. His idea was to show 'in the simplest terms applied to the most radical and obvious causes, the reasons, as I saw them, of the plight in which we found ourselves; that religion, intuition, even superstition had been banished from the modern world, and a worship of brute knowledge — science — and of material things had replaced them.' Osbert takes as one of the chief symbols of this old intuitive knowledge and numinous sense, the witches and their more modern descendant, expert in country lore, 'Deborah the herbalist', who goes out in the moonlit evening 'to pick a thousand verdigris grasses':

> She can see from her grove
> The far tongues of the furnaces,
> Where the huge red mouths grin
> And bellow bull-menaces, . . .

She does not appeal
To the rational brain,
But to dim, antique instincts
Of fear or faith in man.

She could never distil
From a few cabbage-stalks
Enough force to kill
A million men, . . .

All through the poem the sound of Winter the Huntsman, fanciful and at the same time prophetic image, echoes hauntingly:

Far through the forest
His wild hooves crack and thunder
Till many a mighty branch
Is torn asunder.

And the red reynard creeps
To his hole near the river,
The copper leaves fall
And the bare trees shiver.

As night creeps from the ground,
Hides each tree from its brother,
And each dying sound
Reveals yet another.

Is it Winter the Huntsman
Who gallops through his iron glades,
Cracking his cruel whip
To the gathering shades?

This poem brings to mind the passage in his autobiography where Osbert describes the night terrors from which he suffered as a child, and which began when he first slept alone at Scarborough. And the whole mood of *Winter the Huntsman* makes one realise that in Osbert, under the social satirist and shrewdly observant man of the world, there is a romantic in love with the countryside and the traditional past.

This love came out, so to speak in another key, in *England Reclaimed*, the first volume of poetic portraits, published in 1926, which was later completed by the 'balnearics' of *Wrack at Tidesend* in 1952 and the 'inquilinics' of *On the Continent* in 1958, a large design faithfully adhered to over a third of a century. When the complete work was finally published in one volume in 1965, one could see that he had indeed justified his early claim that the portraits were drawn to commemorate a fast-vanishing way of life. In the course of thirty years and a second World War that way of life had receded even further and faster into the past to the point of being almost totally extinct, but to any reader who had even the most childish memory of it Osbert's 'eclogues' were an evocation as fresh, vivid and true as ever. What is striking about this 'gallery of rustic characters' is the warmth of feeling under the art. The caustically satiric line of the portraits drawn in the novels is replaced by a touch far more tender and sympathetic, that looks forward to the manner of the autobiography. The country folk of Osbert's childhood, who held their sway in village, garden, park and farm, turn to archetypes of myth and fairy-tale. Its verse takes wings as he describes, for instance, the gardener's wife:

Oh, who can describe the grace of Mrs Hague,
A Mrs Noah limned by Botticelli,
'Mid flowering trees, greens winds and pensive flowers ...

Or Luke Kembley, the keeper who jealously preserved the
pheasants all through the spring and summer until October
came:

October was the month,
When the northern air is crystal
And the berries grow all red on the hedges — oh!
When the tall trees grow antlers,
And the three-prong'd leaves of the bracken
Undulate on the pure air
Just as the triple sails of imperial goldfish
Wave through their transparent element;
When even the Sun,
Magnificent Inca,
Wraps himself each evening
For his ceremonial farewell
In gigantic pheasant-feathers.
Then Luke Kembley's breath
Lingered behind him on the air,
As he walked back through the dusk
To find the sharp fingers of the fire
Gilding Mrs Kembley
In the cottage on the hill.

Perhaps the most effective (and the most famous) is the
'Elegy for Mr Goodbeare':

Do you remember Mr Goodbeare, the carpenter,
Godfearing and bearded Mr Goodbeare,
Who worked all day

At his carpenter's tray,
Do you remember Mr Goodbeare?
Mr Goodbeare, that Golconda of gleaming fable,
Lived, thin-ground between orchard and stable,
Pressed thus close against Alfred, his rival —
Mr Goodbeare, who had never been away.

Osbert Sitwell has stated that the poems of *England Reclaimed* were written to be read aloud; and I find it true that if one reads them aloud to oneself one's enjoyment is greatly increased. I particularly regret that, so far, the poet has not made a full recording of them in his own voice. Even if one may have reservations about the over-rhetorical finale, they form, in their own way, as unique an achievement as Edith's *Façade*; and, like *Façade*, they are a reminder that verse can be extremely original, and a landmark of its time, without abandoning gaiety or fanciful extravagance.

Like his brother Osbert, Sacheverell Sitwell has devoted many years of his life to poetry. In spite of the large number of travel books and other miscellaneous prose works he has written — his production has been enormous — he would wish, I think, to be remembered as a poet. He has never written a novel; and even the unique series of essays, appreciations, rhapsodical meditations (it is difficult to find a name that fits them exactly) which he has written in recent years, are more like extended poems in prose than anything on similar themes that Osbert has written. They are, in a sense, travel books of the spirit, explorations in the main of art and artists and reflections that arise from these aesthetic journeys, from *Sacred and Profane Love* to *Splendours and Miseries*. They may throw out interesting and profoundly stimulating critical judgments incidentally, but they are never intended as critical studies, any more than the long series of poems, which they so much resemble and which to my mind form his most successful poetic achievement, *Canons of Giant Art.*

Surveying the whole of Sacheverell Sitwell's poetic *œuvre* (though it is only partially possible today owing to the very large number of poems he has refused to publish),* a hostile critic might say that his extraordinary facility for mellifluous verse-making has led him to a constant dilution of his inspiration, in which the intellectual muscles are too relaxed to produce that concentration of thought, wit and imaginative vision that is the especial province of poetry. Images, I imagine this critic as saying, wander in and out of one another in his poems without any appearance of selective control, and all too little regard for cumulative effect. He delights to elaborate his fancies to such an extent that a great part of his poetry seems to consist of verse-exercises, performed by a technician who has an altogether remarkable delicacy of touch on his instrument.

Now, I think I would find it difficult to refute this criticism in reference to the mass of short lyrical pieces which he has grouped together under the title of *Hortus Conclusus.* Their subjects are the flowers and fruits of garden and the wild countryside immediately surrounding a cultivated garden, with the figures of mythology introduced. Rarely does one feel the poet's heart engaged; but I make one exception at least for 'Derbyshire Bluebells', in which one cannot help being aware of the kernel of a nostalgic feeling for the 'blue flame of love' in springtime round his ancestral home. It has a fresh, almost Elizabethan

* A small selection from his unpublished work has, as this book goes to press, appeared in *The Poetry Review* for summer 1967.

charm, when considered apart from the repetitive pieces that surround it. The same is true of another piece, not included in *Hortus Conclusus*, which was also first published in *The Cyder Feast* (1927), called 'The Renishaw Woods', with its simple, evocative conclusion and precisely defined images of memory:

The miller and his wife have gone.
The cockerel at his fanfare to their last march of sun
Stood on that stone bridge, the highest station for his
    watch,
And was moved in a hen-coop before the sun rose high;
Yet, remembering the collieries,
The noise of a giant forge hid in the trees,
I knew that this pit led to a pit in the deep woods,
A pit with slanted galleries before they sank real shafts,
And the coal-waggons rumbled on that high thin arch
By the mill-stream that worked in great thickets of the
    yellow corn
Crushing out their life into a white bread for men;
Their two paths crossing, their lives led side by side,
Like the nettles and the campion in this summer wood.
By now the 'lords and ladies' in their green hoods
Nod near to sleep,
The coal-pit and the mill are dead, the corn lands are stubble,
But the nettles still hold wine for goats, and the campion
    stands sentinel
Holding the summer wood for ghostly trumpet and black
    shapes of shadow.

Unlike these two poems, the greater part of Sacheverell Sitwell's poetry has been inspired, not by direct personal experience but by the emotions and reflections aroused by

the contemplation of works of art. It is his peculiar idiosyncrasy and gift; where one poet might be impelled to write
by deeply stirring experiences in his own life, or by the
sympathetic hearing of the experiences of others — and I
think most of English poetry lies in these two categories —
Sacheverell's poetic temperament is responsive above all to
great music, dancing, works of painting and sculpture, and
literary masterpieces of the past. It is important to avoid
prejudice here; whatever one's personal preference may be,
it is possible to recognise legitimate inspiration in such
themes. As in the Sonnets and Cantos of other admired
authors, the proof of the pudding is in the eating; and the
proof is most clearly to be found in Sacheverell Sitwell's
Canons of Giant Art, which was first published in complete
form in 1933 (though three of the constituent poems had
appeared in *The Cyder Feast*).

These ambitious *Canons*, long poems the basic rhythmic
structure of which is a loosely organised four-beat line, had
been preceded by *Dr Donne and Gargantua* in 1930. Of
these 'first six cantos', three had appeared from 1921 to
1926: the three new cantos show a striking development of
technical power and thought, and form a direct bridge to the
Canons. The cantos describing the two protagonists taking
refuge on the mountain slopes above Paestum (which was
so familiar a sight to Sacheverell from his window in
Amalfi), and their arrival in classical Sunium, are full of the
most beautiful softly flowing lyrical description, and very
much superior to the rest of the volume. The *Canons of
Giant Art*, whose publication followed *Dr Donne* four
years later, are extremely uneven. The failures are dismay-
ing; one has the impression that the poet is at the mercy of
his inspiration, without a craftsman's coldblooded after-

thought; but when the inspiration really lifts his writing off the ground, the result is exciting indeed.

Among the successes in these twenty pieces, I would put 'The Farnese Hercules', the 'Hermes of Praxiteles', the 'Pastoral' on the Vaphio cups, 'Aeneas Hunting Stags upon the Coast of Libya', the 'Grande Adagio: The Enchanted Palace', and above all, 'Agamemnon's Tomb'. In all these, there is a kind of impetuous movement and proliferation of images that lift the reader to the highest level of imaginative vision. If one takes the last piece, the 'Grande Adagio', one can see how boldly Sacheverell Sitwell brings together the various arts that enchant him: the poem is composed out of the impulse to give words to the most various inspirations: Claude's picture of Psyche's Enchanted Palace, the Grande Adagio in Tschaikowsky's 'Sleeping Beauty', the story of John Keats's last years, and reminiscences of Italian palaces — including the Castello di Montegufoni itself. What is extraordinary in this poem — and proof of Sacheverell Sitwell's innocence towards political happenings—is that it concluded with a brief salutation to the apparently renascent Italy of Mussolini.

The poem on 'Agamemnon's Tomb' stands out because, in it, the poet, more than anywhere else in the *Canons*, and perhaps more than anywhere else in his whole production, appears deeply engaged with his subject. That subject is death, and the horror of death. The tomb is the huge, bee-hive underground chamber that Schliemann discovered below the citadel at Mycenae, and immediately assumed to be the tomb of Agamemnon: obviously the resting place of a great king, there is nevertheless no proof that the body with the golden mask found in the inner room is in fact that of the hero of Homer and Aeschylus. That is of no great importance to the poet, who only refers to the story of the Atridae briefly, being more concerned with the thought that echoes through the poem:

The dead are but dead, there is no use for them,
But who can realize that it ends with breath,
That the heart is not a clock and will not wind once more?
There is something in mortality that will not touch on
    death, . . .

At one point he reflects, with gruesomely realistic detail, on the death-avoiding pretences of the Egyptian Pharaohs:

There's no escape, there is no subterfuge,
Death is decay; nor was it any better,
The mummied dead body, with brain pulled through the
    nose,
With entrails cut out, and all the mutilation
Wrapped in sweet bandages, bound up with herbs:
Death is not aromatic, it is false with flowers,
It has no ferment, it is always bitter;
The Egyptians live for ever, but not like themselves,
They are clenched, tortured, stifled, not the portrait on the
    lid;
They'd be better as old bones, and then might lie at peace.

He describes how wild bees had made their nests in the dome, and how in the spectator this arouses the feeling of peace and comfort in death, as false as the suggestion of immortality in the Egyptian mummies:

How sweet such death, with honey from the flowers,
A little air, a little light, a drone of wings,
To long monotony, to prison of the tomb!
But he did not know it. His bones, picked clean,

Were any other bones. The trick is in our mind:
They love not a bed, nor raiment for their bones,
They are happy on cold stone or in the aching water,
And neither care, nor care not, they are only dead.
It once was Agamemnon, and we think him happy:
O false, false hope! How empty his happiness
All for a fine cavern and the hum of bees.

In the climax of this eloquent and terror-haunted poem,
Websterian in its repeated insistence on the macabre details
of mortality, he comes back to his desperate refrain with
an even more agonised cry, all the more effective for its
apparent artlessness:

You are dead, you are dead, and all the dead are nothing to
us,
There's nothing, nothing, nothing, not a breath beyond:
O give up every hope of it, we'll wake no more,
We are the world and it will end with us:
The heart is not a clock, it will not wind again,
The dead are but dead, there is no use for them,
They neither care, nor care not, they are only dead.

It is interesting to observe how strongly the inter-Sitwell
loyalty has manifested itself in the case of Sacheverell's
poetry, not only on Edith's part, as I have already recorded,
but also on Osbert's. In his Preface to his brothers' volume
of *Selected Poems*, published in 1948, Osbert Sitwell wrote: 'I
have been guided, not by fraternal partiality, but, I acknow-
ledge, by bias; an undoubted prejudice in favour of any remarkable contemporary work that comes my way. . . . As to
the virtues of this poet, I claim for him a prodigious vigour
of thought, of imagery and rhythm, a temperamental fire, and

an ability to produce a sense of prodigality and profusion
in a dingy screwpenny age of pinched and withered talents,
a boldness and largeness that set him apart from most of his
contemporaries. No poet of his time has been similarly
equipped to face his task. The forfeit he pays is that the
very wealth of his invention tends on occasion to dwarf the
immense scale of his work; or at times to lead him to descend into lesser lands, or to stray for a moment into others
just because he has newly created them. His Pegasus is
unduly impatient and wasteful, and quickly abandons
pastures which would have furnished another with material
for a whole career. . . . Yet what an extraordinary power
this poet shows in every line: what a capacity to carry his
readers impetuously along, draw them into his own globes
of fire and air, and point out to them the paths which lead
into the sacred woods: and, in an opposite direction, what a
true and delicious lyricism he manifests.'

Reviewing *Canons of Giant Art* when it came out, Sir
John Squire observed: 'The Metaphysicals were bad
enough, but this lot of young poets are worse. One simply
cannot understand them at all.'

10

In that restless period between the wars, when a large number of brilliant young Anglo-Saxons, including Robert Byron, Peter Fleming, Geoffrey Gorer, and, in various partnerships, Wystan Auden, Christopher Isherwood and Louis MacNeice, were roaming the out-of-the-way places of the world, sometimes inspired by curiosity about people and places, sometimes more by aesthetic or sociological impulses, the Sitwell brothers proved themselves the most assiduous, the most inquisitive and the most idiosyncratic.

Almost every winter they would journey forth, nearly always together before Sacheverell's marriage to Georgia Doble in 1925 (and sometimes afterwards), to new lands, or new corners of countries they already knew, and every spring they would bring back crowded notebooks out of which to fashion their articles and travel books, though sometimes also poems — as in the case of Sacheverell's *Canons of Giant Art* — or novels — as in the case of Osbert's *Miracle on Sinai*.

It is, I think, no exaggerated claim to say that as travellers the two brothers, on the lookout above all for new aesthetic experiences, opened the eyes of their contemporaries and popularised beauties of painting, sculpture and architecture that were unfashionable or neglected at the time. The world, as the saying goes, was their oyster, and they savoured what they found inside with insatiable relish — and made their

public relish it with them. Their taste was catholic, though
with a bias towards the baroque, the rococo and the aristocratic streams of art; I do not remember much in their travel
writings about Gothic cathedrals* or Italian primitives, for
instance, subjects that had already been enthused over in a
myriad books before they reached manhood.

Osbert's first book of travel essays, *Discursions*, was published in 1925. The chapters relating to Italy were, after the
second World War, reissued with a new edition of *Winters
of Content*, first published in 1932 and entirely concerned
with Italy. Just before the war broke out, in 1939, he
published *Escape With Me!*, 'an Oriental sketchbook',
which describes his visits to Angkor and Peking and has
a strong claim to be considered his masterpiece in the
genre.

There is, I believe, no passage which better illustrates the
remarkable qualities which Osbert Sitwell displays as a
traveller, his unflagging curiosity, his capacity to note every
detail of interest, his range of reference, the imagination and
intelligence he brings to bear on his subject and his power
of transforming his experiences into highly evocative and
richly textured prose, than that in which, in *Winters of
Content*, he describes his first sight of Castel del Monte, one
of the two 'incomparable monuments' of the Bari region of
Apulia:

'Castel del Monte I had seen ten years before, unexpectedly. Journeying back from Lecce to Bologna by night,
I had looked out of the window at dawn. The country was

* An exception might appear to be Sacheverell Sitwell's *The
Gothick North*, but the author is in fact mainly concerned with
tapestry, miniatures and the arts of the monastery, particularly in
Spain and Portugal.

utterly deserted, with no houses, but I had then noticed, some few miles away, this majestic work of art on its hill. Even from the clattering train its effect had been sublime. Its elephant-grey bulk rose, strongly defined in the light of early morning, and it resembled no castle one had ever seen before, so organised was its form. Lonely and tragic, so, it seemed, one might perceive for an instant, at this very moment of the day, some mammoth elsewhere in the world extinct. It had the air, too, of a place fabulous and legendary, which might, for all its robustness, fade into earth and sky, and in this it was not deceptive: for a wealth of fable and legend clings to its ruined, but not too ruined, walls. Erected about 1240, this was the very especial creation of that romantic sovereign and very extraordinary man, Emperor Frederick II, King of Germany and King of the Two Sicilies — a man born two centuries ahead of his time, for he belonged to the Renaissance by type.'

Describing his eventual visit to the castle, he goes on:

'As you approach, as you enter the castle, its plan unfolds, continues to unfold, before you with the same inevitable logic (itself, in building, a very rare form of beauty) that characterises the opening of the passion-flower, the petals of which expand, by the most exquisite of all engineering, to reveal what is at once the most symmetrical, complicated, and yet simple of flower forms. Both unassuming and overwhelming, the peculiar eloquence of this architecture at once convinces you. It would, you understand from its loveliness in the distance as much as from its majesty near to, be as beautiful on any scale, as a model in a case, a pavilion, or a skyscraper: albeit if erected in New York, and in fitting proportion to gigantic neighbours, it would shame them: for, in addition to possessing that identical suavely engineered magnificence which sky-scrapers share with expensive cars and battleships, it displays every quality of structural or decorative loveliness possible to a creation of genius. Similarly, as a pavilion, it would outshine the Palazza del Te and the Grand Trianon, making them seem fussy and vulgar.'

It seems to me that the 'peculiar eloquence' of this passage, combining so many of the qualities I mentioned above, would be recognisable at once, in any anonymous anthology, as coming from the pen of Osbert Sitwell — even if it were not for the tell-tale use of the conjunction 'albeit'.

One chapter in *Winters of Content* is devoted to a characteristically fond, persuasive and perceptive eulogy of an unexpectedly chosen trio of great painters: Correggio, Tintoretto and El Greco. Like his brother Sacheverell, Osbert very early on became a profound admirer of the last-named painter, and this study shows his enthusiasm not only at its most subtly reasoned but also at its most imaginative. He is attributing the peculiar quality of the final phase of El Greco's art as much to the landscape round Toledo (which Osbert had frequently observed) as to the 'inky-dark, lank, and defunctive frescoes of Mistra and Mount Athos':

'No: as he lived rather banished by his own temperament from the society of others, he grew more and more to rely on the look of things, which, while he gazed at them at last with complete realisation, it must have seemed to him, with his experience of both worlds, that neither Eastern nor Western artist had fully explored before. So he stared on, from the windows of his house, noticing how the ashen and cinder-coloured hills, so improbably streaked and dappled, altered the shapes of the muleteers, of the townspeople strolling into the country, and even of the beasts that were trying to find pasture on these bare humps; and how, further, the strong light, pouring down, changed utterly in its turn the forms of the hills and of the crenellated walls and sharp, dog-toothed towers of the city, strangled by the silver girdle of its river, until his Eastern spirit rejoiced that in his exile he had been able to discover and interpret in the West something of which no man before him had ever been conscious. Thus he formulated a new system, that could, he knew, be handed on for centuries — but, alas! it was not. With him it died: for, though other artists borrowed his methods and were influenced by his vision, none could combine them. And herein lies the tragic quality that tinges his name for us; in that, like Napoleon or Alexander, he had conquered an empire undreamt of by other ages, but left no heir or successor to consolidate and make permanent their triumphs.'

Osbert Sitwell did not confine his intellectual and aesthetic travels to scenes abroad. In 1935, with the aid of his secretary–collaborator Margaret Barton he published a book on Brighton, as remarkable as any of his other writings in this genre for its wit, its descriptive vigour and shrewd portraiture. Most characteristic, perhaps, most spiced with the aristocratic Sitwellian flavour, is his defence of the Prince Regent against the league of his detractors presided over by Thackeray. 'Perhaps a liking for him,' he writes, after admitting that an element of paranoia began to be increasingly evident in his behaviour as time went on, 'always betrays in those who admit it a preference for talent, even when a little lop-sided, in a prince, and for a love and patronage of the arts, to a regard for the strictest morality. And in the person of George IV England was given, for the first time since the death of Charles II, a king who was entertaining and gay, and who preferred the company of wits to that of half-wits.' He points out that the Prince Regent was the first art-patron to ascend the throne of England since Charles I, himself formed an interesting collection of old masters, and helped to found the National Gallery. As an enthusiast for architecture, he built Carlton House and the Royal Pavilion at Brighton, showed his tact and taste in the rebuilding of Windsor Castle, and 'was responsible for a thousand pillared houses and intricately planned, gracefully curving streets by Nash; the loveliness of which, indeed, we are only beginning, with their destruction, to appreciate. . . . You cannot doubt, in looking at the pictures he bought, and in admiring his architectural feats, that the good he did lived after him, while the evil perished with him; so what concern is it of ours, or yours, to censure him? Further, though not too zealous in paying his tradesmen, who throughout his lifetime took advantage of him in every way, overcharged and swindled him, his generosity to artists, and his punc-tuality in settling their accounts, never failed. And through all his actions, good and bad, gleamed a golden thread of fantastic eccentricity, which set him on one side, a prince apart; for no one was ever to know what whim might seize him next.'

Escape With Me! was, in its own way, an act of defiance, a rowing against the stream highly characteristic of its author. At a time when the taking of sides in politics and the fear of an approaching war were increasingly occupying the minds of almost all writers in England, especially of the younger generation, and colouring so much of what they wrote, Osbert set off to China, as he tells us at once in the preface, 'very largely to escape from Europe, but more especially in order to see China, and the wonderful beauty of the system of life it incorporated, before this should perish. . . . Though I have long carried on a private, one-man campaign against stupidity, and the brutality and greed which are two of its symptoms, I am no soldier of a cause militant.' As if this were not enough, on his return he promptly left for Antigua in Guatemala to write his book there, between January and April of 1939. In a chapter called 'The Element, Earth' in *The Four Continents* (published in 1954), he writes: 'The reason I chose to go there was that after the Munich Crisis I found the mounting war tension in Europe suffocating, and I felt that I must go far away and obtain a draught of fresh air, before war, so claustrophobic in its character, should break out in the autumn. And in Guatemala, nothing then very much interested the inhabitants that took place outside the country. One was bounded in views but free. Never did one hear about politics, except from a few Europeans who ran *fincas* here. One English lady, who was growing coffee on a mountain slope near by, came to stay in the hotel for a few days, and treated me continuously to her views; which were, of course, that the British should make war at once, everywhere and without any weapons'. Osbert concealed his identity, and pretended to 'a complete ignorance and moronic lack of curiosity' about foreign politics and the waging of war. The climax came when she scornfully asked him: 'Have you *never* heard of the *New Statesman and Nation*?' Osbert immediately replied that never, in the whole course of his life, had he heard of this evidently important paper, and was, exactly as he intended and wished, pointedly ignored from that moment.

Escape With Me! is a book of sheer delight for anyone who enjoys armchair travelling and sightseeing; and, though it does not aim to be a learned work, Osbert Sitwell had, as always, taken the trouble to read the essential books by former travellers and scholars, with the result that his marvellously evocative descriptions of things seen and heard, among the crowded noisy streets of pre-Communist Peking as in the bird-haunted wilderness of ruined Angkor, are supported and given depth by historical and archaeological information that is never obtrusive or wearisome. It is highly sophisticated; and at the same time the poetic sense of wonder is revealed everywhere. The volume, he insists in the opening paragraph of his preface, was 'intended for amusement', and it is full of humour as well as poetry. The well-known passage about his visit to the Temple of the Eunuchs is both touching and slyly entertaining; and it is clear that he revelled in the quirks of his Chinese servant, Chang. One cannot, of course, guarantee that his fondness for embellishing a good story to make it even better has not been at work in, for instance, the following passage from his exchange with Chang:

'Often, too, from talking to him, I obtained in part a conception of how the Chinese regard the various actions of men, placing thereon a value entirely different to ours. Thus, one morning, he remarked to me, by way of opening a conversation:

' "Master interested in army?"

' "No."

'Not at all discouraged, he continued proudly, "My uncle a General in Chinese Army."

'I betrayed no surprise, for it was proverbial in the foreign colony here that, since the Civil Wars had started, every

Peking houseboy boasted a father or uncle who was a General on one side or the other; sometimes on both.

' "Uncle very patriotic man," he went on.

' "I am sure he is," I replied commendingly.

' "Yes, the Japanese they offer him one whole hundred thousand dollars to help them."

' "And he refused it," I said, finishing the sentence for him.

'For a moment I saw the shocked expression that always appeared on it when his sense of thrift was in any way thwarted, cross his face, and then he cried out with anguished patriotism,

' "No, no, Master! He take money, and then run home." '

A little later on, in the same chapter, Osbert observes: 'Even so rigid a faith as Communism, if for the sake of convenience it had temporarily to be accepted, would find itself powerless to alter the national character: on the contrary, the national character would very soon modify Communism to suit itself, or even assimilate it, as it has always assimilated foreign conquerors.'

This prophecy, now being put to the test, may well turn out to be true, in spite of all current signs to the contrary. After all, what are two or three decades in the life of a people like the Chinese?

Like his brother Osbert (and sometimes with him), Sacheverell Sitwell has travelled widely and continuously, and written indefatigably on all that he saw and experienced. Apart from his studies of German and Spanish baroque art, and his essays on various parts of Italy, he has made long tours of Mauretania (Morocco, Algeria and Tunisia), Roumania, the Netherlands, Spain, Portugal and Madeira, the Scandinavian countries, Germany, Austria, Greece (as is evident from *Canons of Giant Art*) and various parts of the Orient and the American hemisphere. To each part of the world he has visited, he has brought the same inexhaustible curiosity, sense of wonder and freshness of artistic response, and a human sensibility repelled and dismayed by squalor, cruelty and misery without concealment. Only in irony and humour does he, in these writings, appear lacking by comparison with his brother.

One of his most remarkable travel books, especially for the sense of excitement and discovery it communicates, is *Mauretania*, published in 1940 and written while Osbert was in Guatemala. A keen traveller, particularly one habitually inspired by the exotic, the concealed and the neglected, had reason to be excited: for when Sacheverell first went to Morocco it was only a year or two since many of the regions south of the Atlas mountains had been opened by the French to civilian tourists, and Sacheverell and his companions were quite possibly the first English people to penetrate as far, at least in modern times.

In *Mauretania*, Sacheverell's style as a travel-writer shows at its best. It is lighter, more rapid, less tied to the earth of fact than Osbert's: his writing is more like the zigzag flight of a butterfly, aware from afar of scents and colours to attract it, than the thoroughbred's canter which his brother's resembles. An outstanding, characteristic passage is his description of the Djemaa el Fna in Marrakech:

'At five o'clock, over most of the town if you listen for it, there is a confused murmuring. It is mysterious, like a stirring of the waters, or like something glittering out of a cloud of dust. The noise of it travels on the wind; or, in the lull of that, is deep down in the distance. But it never stops. It is gathering and insistent. It has that kind of excitement towards which it is only natural to hurry your steps. Any moment of delay may be something missed and gone.

'At every corner the noise comes louder. Now it is a beating and a stamping of many feet: the roar of an enormous multitude. It cannot be much further. It is sound that carries and, now, is still a block away. This is it. A huge square with, in the middle, as it were a circus ring. A crowd of thousands moves round it, while its inner side, towards the centre, has circle after circle watching, moving on. Over all, hangs a haze of dust. The noise is such you cannot hear a person speak. In a moment you are lost in it.

'This is the Djemaa el Fna, and there is nothing like it in the world. To begin with, it has no shape. This square, which is to Africa and to the Orient what the Piazza of St Mark's was to the Venetian Republic, the Serenissima, and to all that is implied in that most magnificent of memories, is without any architecture. . . .

'The whole square, for it is now six o'clock, is in the full beat of its life, sending up a noise and clamour which are indescribable. The setting sun makes the dust to be blood red, the red of a blood orange, or of a pomegranate, but gilding the corners of the mean buildings, while it tinges the dirty white of the sempiternal burnouse. But it is not everyone who wears white. There are more soldiers, in varied uniforms, than on the operatic stage. The Spahis, in their Algerian turbans and their magnificent cloaks, red for the Algerian regiments, and blue for the Moroccan, wander in the crowd. . . . In a world from which all, or nearly all, of military glory has gone these uniforms of Northern Africa may remind us of what has been lost, and it is Constantin Guys, in particular, that they recall.'

This passage, I think, illustrates a characteristic that is peculiar to Sacheverell as a travel-writer: it is so often as if, when he is evoking a thing actually seen or heard, he is a person under the influence of opium or lysergic acid, describing brilliant hallucinations as they pass before his inner mind. I have myself travelled in Morocco, as I have travelled in Roumania about which he had written with extraordinary poetic feeling two years before — and can only say Sacheverell Sitwell's two books bring back my memories in heightened intensity. This gift is part of his natural equipment, but the art behind its exploitation is subtler than might appear to a hurried reader; above all, perhaps, in the capacity to leave out what is inessential, or irrelevant, or interesting only to himself.

A glance at Sacheverell Sitwell's *Selected Works*, published in 1955, reminds one that he is an inexhaustibly curious traveller in the worlds of other people's experiences — the experience of artists, the experience of vanished civilisations. I have called them travel books of the spirit. Many of the pieces chosen for this volume appeared in *Splendours and Miseries* (1940), but all, whether of earlier or later volumes, whether celebrations of things seen at first hand, such as the pages on the Dinkas of the Sudan from *Touching the Orient*; or the truly marvellous evocation of peoples and places he had never visited, such as the *Dramas and Dance Cycles of the Islands*, the islands being the archipelagoes of the Pacific; or fantasias which evoke the artistic occasions and social manners of a vanished epoch at the same time, such as *La Vie Parisienne*, the jumping-off point of which is the first night in Paris of Offenbach's comic

*Osbert Sitwell at Renishaw,
1942*

*t the Poets' Reading, May
943: Arthur Waley, Princess
lizabeth, Osbert, The Queen,
rincess Margaret, Walter de
Mare*

Left: *Sachevere[ll]*
Sitwell in his st[udy]
and (below) *Osb[ert]*
Sitwell in his st[udy]

opera of that name in October 1866; all have this power of opening the doors of our imagination to vivid new experiences. They may sometimes be sentimentally romantic; their scholarship may sometimes be faulty (a criticism which has been levelled in more deadly fashion, by major musical experts, against Sacheverell's serious studies of, for instance, Scarlatti, Mozart and Liszt);* one may feel that they are often too discursive and uncontrolled, like protean dreams; one may wonder whether the maximum effect would not rather have been achieved in verse — as in *Canons of Giant Art* — than in this torrential prose form; but there is a vein of liberating poetic vision, unique to the author himself, which runs through all of them.

There is another curious characteristic of Sacheverell Sitwell's writings in this vein, which is bound to strike anyone who reads them attentively. The author constantly acts, as it were, as the impresario of his own evocations, as if he were delighting to manipulate a toy theatre, one of those perhaps that used to be made by Mr Pollock. Take this passage from the opening of 'The Nun's Grille' from *Sacred and Profane Love*:

'It is a morning in the South, early in the year. The almond is in blossom.

'But there is not long to wait. In a moment or two the key has been found and we go into the church. It is long and high, with a Mudéjar ceiling, work which is, at once, the spider and the honeycomb. From its long, thin shape it is more a chapel than a church. The walls are lined with

* The most furious of the disputes arising from such criticism was waged between the veteran Ernest Newman and Sacheverell Sitwell in 1932, and reverberated through the columns of the *Sunday Times* for weeks on end. The occasion was Sacheverell's book on Mozart.

coloured tiles, or azulejos. And there are tombs and canopies and many altars. No one ever comes here. It was with difficulty that the key turned in the door. But listen! listen! What can be that droning? It is like the wings of bees, like the wild bees in the tomb of Agamemnon. There, they come in through a crevice, and their droning is in the dome of the tomb chamber, above where the golden masks lay in the dust of ages. Here, too, it is high up, near the ceiling, close to the artesinado. It keeps to the gilded honeycombs. But no need for more. It is the droning of the nuns.'

Sacheverell Sitwell has a sense of the macabre, pitiable and horrible, as highly developed as his sense of the idyllic and dionysiac: it is the balance and contrast of these two themes that makes the success of *Splendours and Miseries*, perhaps the most impressive of the rhapsodic books he wrote before the end of the second World War.

At first encounter, this book appears to be an extraordinarily diverse assemblage of themes that have little or nothing to do with one another. It opens into a series of seascapes, or rather stormscapes, including a refugee ship heading for Palestine, counterpointed by the Flight of the Earls from Rathmullen in 1607, and a description of the wild and remote cliffs of Slieve League that rise 'two thousand feet sheer out of the dark blue sea'. Then follow accounts of three women who had lunatic visions of horror when their madness attacked them, as it were prefiguring what became actuality in the second World War, and of Pieter Bruegel's phantasmagoric painting of Dulle Griet, with a montage of London blitz scenes. In the next section, there are evocations of picnics 'by the sweet waters of Asia', of Kändler's Dresden china, Redouté's roses, and of the 'golden reign of Saturn' frescoes by Benozzo Gozzoli in the Campo Santo at Pisa. After these idyllic interludes there comes an imaginary picture of a tank battle in the steppe of Russia, a history of the appearance of the 'false Messiah', Sabbathai Zevi, the fantastic Jewish prophet from Smyrna who caused commotion wherever he went in the seventeenth century. The next section consists of fantasias on musical themes, which include the story of the untaught Jewish musical genius, Gusikov, from White Russia, as brilliant in its way as the piece on Farinelli in *Southern Baroque Art*, and a virtuoso celebration of Johann Sebastian Bach's Fugues. The last sections are devoted to an account of Madeleine Smith's non-proven poisoning of her lover, and the drawings of Fuseli, which he calls (I cannot help thinking rather exaggeratedly) the only 'really evil drawings ever done', of the martyred, starving dead of Athens under the Nazi occupation, and, finally, returning to the imaginings of peace and hope, some recollections of childhood and the love between himself and his mother, and the consolations of supreme art.

There is, thus, an extraordinary variety of subject-matter; Sacheverell Sitwell, some might say, has put in what he liked without regard for any sophisticated design of the whole; and yet, to my mind, he undoubtedly creates a powerful over-all effect, communicating an apocalyptic vision of light and darkness of the spirit, appropriate to the times in which it was written. The two dominant themes are interwoven throughout the book, the one mood of darkness:

'This is the reign of madness. The air darkens with steel wings. All men are dressed to match the yellow mud. For the fields are churned and trampled. In the dawn, while the moon is yet shining, the noise of machinery begins. They have started moving. The column of tanks is on the march.

It is a curious and ghostly sound in the cold morning. . . .'
And the other mood, of light:

'Listen to the old enchantment. The antique magic is in
the air. The bird sings on the bough, for rich and poor. The
dear music that we loved, not from the groves and lawns, but
in our immortal minds. We have it in our minds and in our
hands, in our hearts, and in what we surmise to be our
souls, to listen for ever to that music, and obey its rules.'

I I

WHEN Hitler invaded Poland at the end of August 1939 Edith Sitwell was still in Paris and Osbert in Monte Carlo. Osbert cabled to her to leave at once for home, and when he himself got back he found that she had already arrived at Renishaw, having left many notebooks of poetry and other personal possessions behind her in the rue St Dominique.

The war presented the Sitwells with an entirely new situation, though its outline did not become entirely clear until the Nazi air-raids on London began a year later. It should be evident from what I have already written that no one of the trio had felt at home in the climate of the thirties. Neither Edith, nor Osbert, nor Sacheverell was militantly left wing, and they kept away from the political alignments that divided British writers so violently, as the Fascist regimes of Mussolini and Hitler advanced in their seemingly endless push-over game of outwitting the democracies. It was characteristic of Osbert, loathing both war and revolution, and fearing perhaps even more the advantage that a new war might give to his sworn enemies, the Philistines of England, to choose to write an 'escapist' travel book about the vanishing civilisation of China, as the situation grew ominous. Edith had never felt happy about the work of the left-wing 'pylon' poets, Auden, Spender, Day Lewis, MacNeice and their associates; though she found much to admire in the work of at least the first two, her praise — as was

evident in her Northcliffe lectures — was extremely qualified. She disliked the propaganda element, and feared it
might swamp the poetic. She herself had been silent as a
poet during almost the whole decade, for reasons which I
have already suggested, though *Gold Coast Customs* might
have commended itself to her younger contemporaries as
the first major poetic condemnation of an unjust society
they were to attack so fiercely themselves. Nor was she by
any means insensitive to the literature of social protest that
was appearing at the time. Geoffrey Gorer had introduced
her to the work of George Orwell, and in April 1937 she
wrote to Rée Gorer, speaking of Geoffrey: 'It was he who
told me to read George Orwell, and I am really overcome
by his *Keep the Aspidistra Flying*; it seems to me one of the
most moving novels I have read for years and years.'
Again, a month later, she writes to Rée Gorer: 'The horror
of the beginning of *The Road to Wigan Pier* is unsurpassable.
He seems to me to be doing for the modern world what
Engels did for the world of 1840–50. But with this difference, that Orwell is a real born writer, whereas Engels, fiery
and splendid spirit though he was, simply wasn't a writer.
One had to reconstruct the world from his pages for oneself.'

The influence of Sacheverell, whose long poem *Dr Donne
and Gargantua* had seemed to open new vistas for English
poets at the end of the twenties, was almost entirely eclipsed
by the change of direction and taste in poetry heralded by
the arrival of Wystan Auden on the scene. A superficial
observer at the time of the Munich 'settlement' might well
have thought that the Sitwells were finished as a creative
force in the literature of their time. In fact, in a very few
years they were at the centre of interest again.

By the end of 1939 the anti-Fascist movement among the younger writers had broken up, partly because of disillusionment with the behaviour of Soviet Russia, partly because their chief political aim — a stand against the aggression of Hitler's Germany — had at last been achieved. Wystan Auden and Christopher Isherwood had left for America, in total discouragement after Munich. Among those of their colleagues in the movement who remained in England, a sense was growing of the need to emphasise human and civilised values above all in the new situation, at the same time as a sense of national identity overriding former antagonisms. For them, the time had come to 'defend the bad against the worse'. The barriers that had alienated their sympathy for or interest in the work of the Sitwells were falling — and would disappear if they proved that they could give expression to the transformation of the times.

It was easy, as the star of the Sitwells rose again, for detractors to say: 'How clever they are! They were always supreme propagandists for themselves, and they have seized the opportunity of the altered intellectual and emotional climate of the war to push their wares on the public again.' What the detractors failed to realise was that you cannot produce masterpieces by literary–political tactics, however astute.

I have already indicated my view that *Splendours and Miseries*, published in 1943, was Sacheverell's masterpiece in a prose *genre* he had made peculiarly his own. (It had gone, incidentally, into five impressions by 1946.) For Osbert, it was natural to feel that, faced with the possible destruction of everything he cherished, the moment had come to put down on paper, and shape into art, his immense

wealth of memories of the social and artistic scene of nearly
half a century. He began to work on his undoubted masterpiece, his five-volume autobiography, *Left Hand, Right
Hand!* At the same time, as I have already described, he
sensed that the conditions of a new war, however different
in its origins and ideology from the previous war, would
give the eternal English Philistine a grand opportunity to
renew his onslaughts on artists and writers, what Osbert
called 'the members of a despised and maltreated sept'. 'Always at a crisis,' he wrote in *A Letter to My Son*, 'there will
be found a body, hitherto concealed, of critics only too
eager to rush upon the stage and wave a number of trucu-
lent red herrings in order to divert suspicion from the real
authors of the prevailing disaster.' Osbert had trained himself long before as the true mongoose to that particular
snake, and was ready for him when the need came. I know
from my own experience how much this uncompromising
championship of the mind and the creative imagination
meant to thousands of young men in uniform, who were
ready to take their part in the defeat of Hitler — but not on
the Philistines' terms.

In Edith, I am profoundly convinced, the hour and the
poet were matched. Now that the war has receded, and is
not even a memory to many young people in their early
twenties; now that taste has changed again, I can understand
how some of Edith's admirers believe (though I do not
share their belief) that her truly innovating work was done
in the period of *Façade*, or in *Gold Coast Customs*; but there
is no doubt whatsoever in my mind that her war poems,
from *Street Songs* to *The Shadow of Cain*, were of the
utmost significance and value to those who shared the
experience of those years.

Street Songs appeared in January 1942, but several of the most remarkable poems had appeared before, in *Poems Old and New* which was published in 1940, in the *Times Literary Supplement* and *Life and Letters Today* under the editorship of Robert Herring. Two years later *Green Song* appeared, an even smaller collection, with sixteen poems as compared with the twenty-two poems of *Street Songs*. Only about three dozen poems, and yet I think Sir Kenneth Clark was right to call them 'the greatest poems of the war'. Sir Maurice Bowra has written: 'In these two latest volumes Miss Sitwell has brought her techniques to perfection. Her verse moves with unfailing care and flexibility. She has so mastered its intricacies that it seems to respond without effort to any demands that her changing mood may make of it, to be equally effective in long, rolling lines or in the brief tune of a song. Her rhymes come so easily that we hardly notice them, though they make their essential contribution to the final, musical result. Her vocabulary, which looks so unpretentious, has been purified and polished by long, discriminating selection. . . . But the central triumph of this art is that Miss Sitwell has succeeded in her first aim of restoring its texture to her poetry. Her work is first and always poetry and makes its chief appeal to the imagination through the ear and the inner eye. . . . This perfected technique is used to convey experiences of tragic grandeur and intensity.'

Street Songs opens with four poems which were immediately felt to express the profoundest emotions of a time of darkness, agony and endurance against what for most people were incalculable hazards, transmuted by an imagination that ranged far and wide in its search for symbols and used them with consummate mastery. Edith had used the

image of the 'Babioun' before, but in her new Lullaby it is
developed with a nightmarish irony:

> Do, do, do, do, —
> Thy mother's hied to the vaster race:
> The Pterodactyl made its nest
> And laid a steel egg in her breast —
> Under the Judas-coloured sun.

The same tense, bitter irony informs *Serenade*, with its
transposition of Christopher Marlowe's *The Passionate
Shepherd to his Love* into the terms of Europe at war, where
the lover must be unfaithful because he is 'the cannon's
mate' and 'death's cold puts the passion out':

> I'll woo you with a serenade —
> The wolfish howls the starving made;
> And lies shall be your canopy
> To shield you from the freezing sky.

The mood of these two terrible poems is contrasted with
the more oracular, prayer-like *Still Falls the Rain*, written of
the air-raids that began in the late summer of 1940, with its
deep, slow pulse:

> Still falls the Rain —
> Dark as the world of man, black as our loss —
> Blind as the nineteen hundred and forty nails
> Upon the Cross.

In this poem Edith Sitwell openly declares her Christian
faith, and conceives the falling of the bombs during the
blitz as a rain which is at the same time the blood falling
from the crucified Christ's side. In the last line Christ
speaks: 'Still do I live, still shed my innocent light, my
Blood, for thee.'

These poems were published before Dylan Thomas's *A Refusal to Mourn*, Louis MacNeice's *Brother Fire* or Cecil Day Lewis's *Word Over All* had appeared, and their impact was inevitably profound at a time when complaints were being voiced (not without encouragement from the Philistines) that no war poetry worthy of the world-engulfing catastrophe was being written.

The last poem in *Street Songs* was *An Old Woman*: the first of the astonishing series of long odes in the grand manner, which was continued in *Green Song* and *A Song of the Cold* and beyond with increasing artistic assurance and skill. 'Prodigious hymns' Stephen Spender has called them, and noted justly that the first quality which makes them remarkable is that the poet's whole, mature personality is projected into them, that they are *personal* confessions, in spite of their elaboration of imagery and symbol, in a way that is very rarely found in her previous poetry. Underlying their structure is the traditional English iambic line of five beats, but this is occasionally increased to six, seven or eight beats, and at rare intervals curtailed to four or three. There is little end-rhyming, but the lines are full of a subtly disposed internal rhyming and assonance: they are far removed from the free verse of our time. There is rhythmic life and shape in every one of these poems, and they evolve organically, and differently in every instance, out of the heart of the poem's conception. The long, flowing lines, with their apparent ease and simplicity, are the culmination of Edith Sitwell's lifetime of devoted apprenticeship to her art. She had always been intensely aware of the importance of harmonious sound and texture in the making of verse — her studies of other poets' technique are full of observations on this score so subtle and elaborate that it is often extremely difficult to follow them with the patience she expected. In these poems, as Maurice Bowra remarked, she handled sound and texture to create poetic effects of the most astonishing variety and complexity.

The novelist and critic L. P. Hartley has written of these poems: 'They stand up to the most terrible pheno- mena of the present day, the atom bomb and concentration camp; they are indeed the only poems of our time that ac- cept the challenge of the War, that look not unmoved, but undismayed, on "the flag of blood flying across the world", that recognise, without despairing, "the ultimate cold with- in the heart of man".'

Edith Sitwell wrote three poems on the atom bomb. To my mind, *The Shadow of Cain* is the greatest, an ode in which she seems to have presentiment of an unparalleled crisis and cataclysm in the history of man. The poem was written in the spring of 1946, though owing to the slowness of the machinery of printing and publishing at that period, it did not appear (as a booklet by itself) until 1947. Its genesis, however, took place earlier, as Edith Sitwell has described:

'The poem is about the fission of the world into warring particles, destroying and self-destructive. It is about the gradual migration of mankind, after that Second Fall of Man that took the form of the separation of brother and brother, of Cain and Abel, of nation and nation, of the rich and the poor — the spiritual migration of these into the desert of the Cold, towards the final disaster, the first sym- bol of which fell on Hiroshima.

'The poem came into being thus.

'On the 10th of September, 1945, my brother Osbert and I were in the train going to Brighton where we were to give a reading. He pointed out to me a paragraph in *The Times*, a description by an eye-witness of the immediate effect of the Atomic Bomb upon Hiroshima. That witness saw a totem pole of dust arise to the sun as a witness against the murder of mankind. . . . A totem pole, the symbol of creation, the symbol of generation.

'From that moment the poem began. . . . It passed through many stages.'

Remarkable is her confession that two months before she began to write the poem as a whole, certain key-lines of great power came to her in a dream:

> There was great lightning
> In flashes coming to us over the floor:
> The Whiteness of the Bread —
> The Whiteness of the Dead —
> The Whiteness of the Claw —
> All this coming to us in flashes through the open door.

Kenneth Clark has described *The Shadow of Cain* as 'this craggy, mysterious philosophic poem'. These three epithets strike me as admirably chosen: it does indeed seem to move on great, bare heights, the images seem at times to penetrate to regions where reason can scarcely follow. And it is philosophic — but in the way poets are philosophic and not philosophers. In his *Lecture on Proust*, Demetrios Capetanakis wrote that the true philosophers are those, especially artists, who are 'in search of being' and what matters is not conclusions or the making of coherent systems of ideas but the continuous movement of thought inflamed by the 'passion for existence'. Proust, he said, could never be considered a systematic thinker, but his great work is a profound philosophic work. So it is with

Edith Sitwell. The ordering of her symbols, the flashes of her imagination, are often obscure, appear confused, and lack the regular structure of an argument. It is the conjunction of the images, the glow of the vision and the intensity of the rhythmic and musical life which the poet gives to her language that matter. In his obituary notice for Edith in the *Observer*, on 13 December 1964, Stephen Spender wrote: 'In the long run poems survive not merely because they receive critical approval, but because people fall in love with them. They live because phrases, imagery, music, echoes, the idea of all the poems coalescing into a world single with the poet, hang about our hearts, become part of our lives. The tremendous impact, on both sides of the Atlantic, of the poems which Edith Sitwell wrote during the forties, was due to that quality in them that made people fall deeply in love with them; as, in entirely different circumstances, where other needs of the spirit were unsatisfied, they fell deeply in love with *Façade*.'

At the beginning of the war, Edith Sitwell spent most of her time at Renishaw with Osbert, sometimes visiting Weston Hall near Towcester, a house which had for a long time been in the family, and had been given to Sacheverell and his wife Georgia by Sir George. Sacheverell had become adjutant to the local Home Guard when it was formed at the time invasion was expected in 1940. As late as January 1942 she wrote to Rée Gorer, who had gone to America, 'Here I have stayed, for a whole year, with the exception of one week spent at Sachie's — without moving. For what is there to move for? . . . One tries to go on with one's daily life, and regard the whole time — excepting for the unspeakable disaster and horror of it — as a railway journey which has to be undertaken. But when one thinks of the thousands of millions of wrecked lives, it is a little difficult to think of any life as continuing at all.

'I have sent, or rather, Macmillans have sent, my new book of poems to you, and to Geoffrey. I hope they all arrive safely. . . .'

It was the publication of this new book — *Street Songs* — and the acclaim it received, that in the event brought Edith and Osbert down to London, on far more frequent visits to that 'almost stable society' that was created in the capital between the end of the blitz and the renewed raids, mainly by V1s and V2s, that heralded the final phase of the war against Nazi Germany. The success of *Street Songs* brought many new admirers and friends to Edith, and the parties she began to give at the Sesame Club in Grosvenor Street were thronged with great celebrities, lesser celebrities, celebrities-to-be, soldiers and airmen on leave, relations, fervent fans and eccentric hangers-on. At the same time she began to be invited to give readings of her new poetry, either by herself or with other famous contemporary poets, or on the B.B.C.

There were two especially memorable public poetry occasions during the war, in which Edith Sitwell's contribution was outstanding. In the spring of 1943 a poetry reading was organised, in aid of a charity connected with the Allied cause — the first of several similar readings. They were social occasions as well, patronised by Royalty, and crowded with celebrities who would normally only be seen in the boxes at Covent Garden. To this first reading the Queen had agreed to come, and brought with her the young Princesses Elizabeth (now H.M. the Queen) and Margaret. As well as Edith and Osbert, T. S. Eliot, Walter de la

Mare, W. J. Turner, Gordon Bottomley, Vita Sackville-West and Lady Gerald Wellesley (later the Duchess of Wellington) were billed to read. Edith was one of the chief organisers; and Lady Gerald was the chief thorn in her flesh. 'The shades of — less the prison house than the lunatic asylum — are drawing ever nearer to me,' she exclaimed in a letter a few days before. When the day came, the excitement proved too much for Lady Gerald. The poets had arranged to read in alphabetical order; Edith read magnificently; but when the turn of W. came after W. J. Turner had performed (vastly exceeding his agreed space of time, in spite of repeated bursts of applause from the audience that were intended to cut him short but taken as encouragement to go on), there was no Lady Gerald Wellesley on the stage. A few minutes before, an extremely agitated Vita Sackville-West had slipped out to search for her, and found her in no fit state to go on. On the way out, Lady Gerald was found sitting in a dejected heap at the head of the stairs, and Edith, who had just managed to prevent an encounter with the Queen, standing in tears beside her.

The second famous occasion was at the Churchill Club during the autumn of 1944, while the doodle-bug raids were on. 'I do not imagine that anyone who was present will ever forget it. The three Sitwells were reading from their poetry. This attraction had drawn the whole of the smarter artistic and literary world . . . there seemed very little room indeed in the hall for the ordinary members of the allied forces for whom the Club was supposed to be run. As Edith got up to read, and began with her poem about the air-raids in 1940, *Still Falls the Rain*, the warning whistle was sounded in the Club. She had, I believe, never experi-

Osbert Sitwell with one of his staff on the Renishaw estate

Above: *Renishaw Ironworks* Below: *Renishaw Hall, part of the south fa*

enced a doodle-bug raid before; but she seemed quite un-
perturbed. As she recited the passage:

Still falls the Rain —
Still falls the blood from the Starved Man's wounded Side:
He bears in His Heart all wounds —

the rattle grew to ominous proportions, and it was impossible not to think that the monstrous engine of destruction
was poised directly overhead. . . . Edith merely lifted her
eyes to the ceiling for a moment, and, giving her voice a
little more volume to counter the racket in the sky, read
on. . . . She held the whole audience in the grip of her discipline, the morale of her unspoken asseveration that poetry
was more important than all the terrors that Hitler could
launch against us. Not a soul moved, and at the end, when
the doodle-bug had exploded far away, the applause was
deafening.'

Some years later, when I published *I am my Brother*,
E. M. Forster wrote to me that he had been reading my
'account of that immortal evening at the Churchill Club.
I am so glad it should have been caught by you. The lower-
ing of the voice, after the bug had passed, was, in my recollection, even more moving than its heightening for the
approach. You are right, no one will forget it.'

All this occupied a great deal of her time and nervous
energy. She was constantly falling ill: with neuralgia, headaches, neuritis, 'flu, sprained ankles and broken toes; but
her indomitable vitality carried her through. There were
constant minor, serio-comic irritations. In November 1943
she writes from Renishaw: 'It is almost impossible to do any
work today. Someone seems to be dictating a book on
Philosophy and Meteorology, through a megaphone, to

Robins, Osbert's old soldier-servant, who is now butler. This has set off the fox-terrier (belonging to R) who is carrying on like Cerberus. Really, how *one* dog can make so much noise is a miracle to me!' In May of the following year, she writes, again from Renishaw: 'Oh, the Cows! *The Cows!!* Poor girls, whatever their trouble is, I wish they would tell somebody else about it. This *cri de cœur* is really torn from me. They seem to have started a mothers' meeting just under my window.' And so on. What is remarkable is not that these irritations should occur, for they occur to almost every creative artist in search of concentration, but that she should so constantly mention them and so constantly make them funny.

What was peculiar to Edith, however, was a kind of self-punishing magnetism for attracting cranks, bores and sheer lunatics. One cannot escape the impression, in reading her letters, that this persecution continued throughout her life. It started early. A short while before the publication of *Troy Park* in 1925 she wrote from Paris to Harold Acton: 'I have received from a doctor at Ipswych (I can't spell) the photograph of fourteen children (presumably his) who have been brought up on my poetry. They are dressed in Highland costume, and above them is printed *Scots wha hae*. Imagine my unbounded horror and disgust.' When her fame revived during the war, the persecution appears to have reached even greater heights. In January 1944 she wrote to me from Renishaw: 'I am having a most awful time with lunatics. Is this *your* time of year for them? It is mine. But they have begun rather early. Generally February is the month.' In August of the same year she wrote: 'Did I tell you that a woman I know in America has written to say that her autobiography has just been accepted by publishers. There are to be *800 pages about her life before she went to school.* She is sending this masterpiece over to *me* in order that I may "read it, criticise it, make suggestions, and cross out in red pencil anything that won't do". She adds "The poor censors. It will take them 6 weeks to read it," and continues that she has *not* shown it to her husband, "because I am afraid it might bore him. He reads Dante and Aeschylus in the original."!!!!'

In 1945 she and her brothers were anxiously trying to find out what had happened to Sir George's money, after his death in Switzerland. In August she writes: 'Just as we were waiting to hear about my father's money, a woman whom we had never seen in our lives, but who is the wife of a schoolmaster near here, arrived on a bicycle (time 9.15 p.m.) and said we had to build her a house — cost £3,000. And if we *didn't* build it, she and her husband *and their five small children* would come and live here, in *this* house. "Mr Eliot is a great admirer of my husband's poems!" she told Osbert. Oh-ow!' On another occasion in her Club in London, 'a large pink woman blooming in the midst of a lot of imitation pink roses, stopped and said to me, "We were so *amused* by your luncheon party yesterday." I said, "I am so glad. We put on the Act to give you a good laugh, and I'm glad it did." She said, "*We* are *never* allowed a party of more than *eight*." (She evidently thinks I go in for black magic.) She then said, peering at me: "Are you ill? You are so pale." I said, "I always go as white as a sheet when I am bored" (which is true). She then went away.'

Sometimes Osbert suffered from these inexplicable strangers as well. In July 1944 Osbert and she went to Leeds, because she was doing a recording for the B.B.C. During the visit, she relates, 'a very drunken gentleman asked Osbert if he was a Norwegian. Osbert replied in the negative. "Oh, but you are not English, are you?" enquired the gentleman. "Yes, I *am* English. Why do you ask?" "Because, if you will forgive my saying so," said the gentleman, "you have such a funny accent. It doesn't sound like English." Osbert was *perfectly furious*. He answered coldly, "I speak *proper* English. Very [few] people do, nowadays."'

After a particularly severe period of trials from bores, she once wrote: 'You know there are moments when I feel that in some past life I must have *A* imprisoned, and martyrised an old lady *B* driven somebody to suicide through *sheer boredom* and *C* committed the most horrible aesthetic crimes. No other theory will meet the case.'

Not all the attacks, however, to which she was subjected were unpleasant. In the same summer she wrote: 'I've just been violently slapped on the face by two butterflies. They were exceedingly drunk, poor boys, and couldn't steer properly. Eventually they went back to the budleia (if that is how one spells it) which had been the cause of their moral downfall and had some more. They were peacocks — and too lovely for words. There were about fifty of them there, simply carousing as if the Government didn't exist, or care, or anything excepting honey and the sun and their own lovely wings.'

12

BY the time Edith had begun to make her wartime visits to London, and to entertain at the Sesame Club, the activity of the metropolitan literary world had settled into a fairly well-defined pattern which it kept until the fighting was over.

Two of the great figures of the English literary scene who had survived to the outbreak of war, W. B. Yeats and Virginia Woolf, were now dead. T. S. Eliot was completing what is perhaps his greatest masterpiece in poetry, *Four Quartets*, but his critical presence was diminished by the final folding of his quarterly review, *The Criterion*, which by 1939 had fallen to an extremely low point of circulation.

Of the other literary magazines which had lasted through from the twenties to the thirties, the *London Mercury* was no more. *Life and Letters* continued to exist, in an attenuated form, under the editorship of Robert Herring, whose friendship with the Sitwells continued to gain their contributions. There were three newcomers to the scene: *Horizon*, *Penguin New Writing* and *Poetry London*, the first a regular monthly, the other two making occasional appearances, as printing facilities under wartime restrictions and difficulties allowed. *Horizon* had been founded in the first autumn of the war* by Cyril Connolly, with Peter Watson as patron and co-editor and Stephen Spender as third co-editor. Its aim, quite simply, was to keep literature, and the sensibility

* Vol. I, No. 1 is dated January 1940.

that responds to art, alive against the pressures that total war would inevitably bring with it. Cyril Connolly's attitude is best expressed in the observation that 'art occupies in society the equivalent of one of those glands the size of a pea on which the proper functioning of the body depends, and whose removal is as easy as it is fatal'.

Penguin New Writing was, in essence, an adapted paperback version of the book-magazine *New Writing* which had been launched in 1936, and continued in fact to exist, first of all as *Folios of New Writing* and then as *New Writing & Daylight*, throughout the war. The Penguin version, which Allen Lane invited me to edit in the spring of 1940, began as an anthology of the best contributions which had appeared in the book-magazine series; but its success encouraged us to develop it as an independent literary magazine, part of it consisting of *New Writing* reprints as before, part of entirely new material, with the proportion of the latter gradually increasing.

Poetry London was founded early in 1939 by the eccentric Sinhalese poet Tambimuttu, with Anthony Dickens as general editor. In its pages were published in particular the new young poets in uniform, who seemed to increase in immense proliferation year by year. The Sitwells never appeared in Tambimuttu's magazine, but they were very soon involved with *New Writing* and *Horizon*. Many of Edith's wartime odes appeared in the former, and her *Eurydice* outstandingly in the latter, with Osbert's *Letter to My Son* in its original version.

One of the more curious side-results of the war was that it became a great feast of reading. Civilians were largely immobilised, soldiers and sailors, as in all wars, had little to do most of the time, and all were anxious to immerse in art and philosophy rather than in hate, killing and destruction. These, and others that followed them, were the magazines that were read in the long black-outs and in the boredom of training camps, that were sent to soldiers, sailors and airmen wherever high strategy assembled them. They were read with a fierce love and enthusiasm such as perhaps no magazines in our century have been read before or since.

Their contributions to these magazines brought many new friends to the Sitwells, and the social gatherings that developed out of them facilitated meetings with the admirers of *Street Songs* and *Green Song*. A new literary world emerged in wartime London, in which the Sitwells played an important part, strikingly different from the part they had played two decades before. Then they had been the *enfants terribles*, the last word in far-out modernism; now they — or rather, supremely, Edith — represented an attitude of deep imaginative, human response to inhuman happenings.

The remarkably named 'Sesame Imperial and Pioneer Club' is in Grosvenor Street, the haunt mainly of elderly ladies of impeccable respectability and well-to-do middle-class origins, among whom Edith, though undoubtedly imperial in mien and a famous pioneer at least in the arts, seemed as out of place as a hoopoe in a flock of starlings. It had, however, the advantage, priceless during the years of austerity, of an excellent chef and an extremely able and intelligent manager; so that Edith's parties, in spite of the war during which they began, were in their amenities as different as could be from the bun-sessions of Pembridge Mansions twenty years before. They were not the ideal occasions for getting to know Edith, or indeed her brothers who were in attendance whenever their presence in London coincided with hers, for she was engrossed by the desire to be especially attentive to young writers or musicians — unknown and unintroduced to most of the company — who had just introduced themselves to her, and distracted by the need to keep control of the latest 'lunatics' who managed to be present whether invited or not. Nevertheless, for those who were on her habitual invitation list, there was always the lottery excitement of getting to know some brilliant and distinguished poet, critic, philosopher or composer on whom the sun of Sitwell favour had suddenly begun to shine.

One of the most welcome new guests at the gatherings in the Sesame Club, as the war went on, was Dr Maurice Bowra (now Sir Maurice Bowra), the Warden of Wadham College, Oxford. Edith had been delighted and deeply moved when she read the articles, full of praise and perceptive understanding, which he had been publishing about her wartime poetry. They started a long correspondence which continued to her death. In one of her earliest letters to him, she writes: 'I wish I could express what it means to me to have my poetry so understood — understood so richly and completely. It is a great happiness to me.

'There is so much to say, and so much to be grateful for, that I scarcely know where to begin. What you say about my technique fills me with gratitude. It must surely now enter the heads of your readers that perhaps someone who could work so hard — work with such endurance and patience — may have something to say. I am very glad that you chose my poem "Poor Young Simpleton" to speak about in that connection. It was extremely difficult to manage — or would have been if I hadn't got my technical muscular system under control.'

It was characteristic of Edith that she had little admiration or respect for the work of other women poets, whether dead or alive. In the same letter she makes a frank and unashamed confession of her attitudes. 'Women's poetry, with the exception of Sappho (I have no Greek and speak with great humility on that subject) and with the exceptions of *Goblin Market* and a few deep, and concentrated, but fearfully incompetent poems of Emily Dickinson, are *simply awful* — incompetent, floppy, whining, arch, trivial, self-pitying — and any woman learning to write, if she is going to be any good at all, would, until she had made a technique for herself (and one has to forge it for oneself, there is no help to be got) — write in as hard and glittering a manner as possible, and with as strange images as possible — (strange, but believed in). Anything to avoid that ghastly wallowing.'

His criticism of 'Street Song' above all delighted her, and she gives a most interesting description of what the poem meant to her — she felt that it had been widely misunderstood. 'It is a poem that for some reason gives me a pang — again, as though I had just written it. I think it is one of the saddest of all the poems, in spite of the ending. It is a dangerous thing to say, but I can say it to you. Sometimes, when I begin a poem, it is almost like automatic writing. Then I use my mind on it afterwards. It was so here. For that reason, partly, it means several things to me, whilst being deeply experienced. Sometimes I think a barrel-organ was playing in the street, and a young woman passing it, hears through it the voice of her dead love, killed in battle, and buried — a little hopeless sound. Or else she hears it just in the sounds of the streets, of the children playing, and the people selling and buying. In any case, it is meant to be a love song from a dead man to a living woman, or from a man who is about to die — but I think dead — and seeing the world as it is now, and seeing the woman who had been his peace and his night of rest. Then he sinks back into his deeper night, and she realises that the counsel of despair, sounding through the words of love, was perhaps only that of the ruined world speaking. As you so finely say: "It is possible that the cry is really from the depths of the human heart as some brutal tyranny pursues its relentless way; but it is no less possible that the present agony is some little understood process of change in the world."'

She was also grateful for his articles, which he sent her, about the Symbolist poets and their successors (collected in his two books *The Heritage of Symbolism* and *The Creative Experiment*). Throughout these years she showed a remarkably youthful keenness to learn about writers she had failed, for one reason or another, to study before.

She maintained that Maurice Bowra had made her understand, and appreciate at last, the poetry of Paul Valéry and Guillaume Apollinaire. About the latter, she wrote a long letter to Bowra in March 1945: 'I have inhabited Apollinaire's poetry, ever since you sent me the book, and now I am beginning to feel at home in it. They are curiously vitalising, and at the same time, one can see in them many living roots, from which later poetry, painting, and even music, has sprung. As soon as I began to know his poetry at all, the images made an impact on my mind — almost like a blow, perhaps because of the hard sharpness of the best of them — their sharpness and poignance is such that they make one relive an experience as a scent does, although, in a way, they are so material.

'I think it is the poetry of a man who has sprung from an uncertain and unhappy past. Even when his poetry seems to arise from triumph, or to speak of triumph, one knows that first there is something to overcome, — and that in spite of the great vitality and driving force of his images. What an amazing life of the senses he lived — (I had put "led" but I don't mean "led"). What a passionate vitality!'

In another letter to Maurice Bowra, in May of the same year, she laments her lack of a classical education, apropos his book *From Virgil to Milton*, which she says is 'opening another new universe to me'. She goes on: 'It happens with each book of yours. I cannot forgive my father for having given me no education. Latin and Greek poetry should have been a part of my life, and it is a crippling [disadvantage] for a poet to be deprived of these. Sometimes I think I can guess at the grandeur of sound in Latin: I *think* I hear it, and hope I don't hear it wrong.'

During the war years she also made two other important discoveries, very different from one another. The Hogarth Press had brought out a selection of Hölderlin's poems, in a translation by J. B. Leishman. I sent her a copy, and she wrote back: 'I cannot tell you how grateful I am to you for sending me the poems of Hölderlin. It is a great and wonderful experience to read such a poet for the first time. What nobility, and how ennobling! They have a deep effect on one, of making the horizon wider, and of removing noise and littleness. The poems only arrived on Thursday afternoon, and I do not nearly *know* them yet, although I have read them all. But at first sight I think "Descend, descend, fair sun", "Diotima" and "Often while still a boy" are among the most wonderful. But I am deeply moved and impressed by all.' She continued: 'The wind has started one of its non-stop rages — howling like a universe of wild beasts. We are near the *Wuthering Heights* country, and that is the

atmosphere at the moment. Sachie has lent me a book called
London Labour and the London Poor by Henry Mayhew
(published 1851) that has nearly reduced me to committing
suicide. But I have turned from him (Mayhew) to Hölderlin, and he has calmed me. All the same, the Mayhew book
makes me want to go and hit the Archbishop of Canterbury
very hard in the face. I know it isn't *quite* fair, because this
book was published over ninety years ago, but still he
ought to be hit because of his predecessor's smugness. Mel-
ville's *Redburn* made me feel the same way when I read it.'

Edith Sitwell was always deeply affected by stories of
human poverty and suffering, as one can see by her reactions not only to *London Labour and the London Poor* and
Redburn but also to the George Orwell novels to which
Geoffrey Gorer had introduced her. She deeply resented
the false picture, to which some critics enjoyed giving currency, of her as a rich aristocrat who had always had it easy.
Sometimes she could laugh about it. 'When I am told by
the left-wing boys,' she once wrote, 'that I can't write
poetry because I have no proletarian experiences — I often
wonder how many of them, at the age of 17, have been sent
out to pawn false teeth — parental false teeth!!!!! You get
10s. on them. And whiskey was then 12/6. My handwriting
at that point became wobbly from an attack of *fou rire*.
Mind you, I couldn't sympathise more with the owner of the
false teeth, as regards that. The life would have driven anyone to it. But I did not lead exactly a "sheltered life" as a
child and young girl.'

Another of the new guests at her parties during this
period was the young Greek philosopher and poet, Demetrios Capetanakis, who had come over to England just before the war on a British Council scholarship. He had been

introduced to her through Beryl de Zoete, who had come to know him at Cambridge, and when they met he found in her the same mixture of passionate devotion to her art and eccentric, sharply outlined personality that delighted him in Gertrude Stein. She, on her side, was fascinated by the ardour of his temperament, his immense knowledge of European poetry, and his rather impish gaiety. When he began to write poetry in English, I sent her his first poem to be published, *Detective Story*, and she wrote back at once that it seemed to her 'really astounding. It has a force and concentration of tragedy, and a real fire and passion which must prove to anyone that he has the life of a poet behind him. I am going to write to him about the poem which has moved me greatly.'

Towards the end of the year, he succumbed again to the leukaemia from which he had so miraculously revived the year before. He was admitted to Westminster Hospital, and by the end of January it was quite clear that he was getting steadily worse. On 8 February 1944 Edith wrote: 'How distressed I am about poor Demetrios: so is Osbert. Will you please let us know if there is any earthly thing we can do to help? And another thing, I do not know what effect his illness has, I mean, if he *can* read, and *wishes* to read, or if it tires him unutterably. If the former, do you think he would like me to send him books? If so, please send me a postcard. One can't send flowers, one can't send fruit (I suppose).' On 9 March, the day on which he in fact died, though she did not know it when she posted her letter, she wrote to me again: 'I am distressed beyond any words about poor Demetrios. I simply cannot *bear* to think what he is enduring, and that there seems to be no hope. . . . I helped nurse poor Helen Rootham who had brought me up from a child, and who was like my mother, through cancer of the spine, in a tiny flat. She used to watch one's face closely for any sign. So I know just what you are going through.'

In the article on his poetry which she wrote for the memorial volume, she said: 'The poems of Capetanakis are extremely strange, and the realization of their great strangeness grows upon one, instead of diminishing. The concentration of meaning is so amazing that it conveys, now a feeling of a blinding light (as I have said already), now that of a powerful and terrible darkness, a quintessence of force, almost like a physical presence. . . . Of the loss of those poems, that will never be written I cannot trust myself to speak.'

In a letter to me just before the first anniversary of his death, she wrote: 'One will miss him *always*. Beautiful, strange, silent creature who understood everything.' And again: 'he altered my *whole* life for me.'

Among the poets of my generation (to whose work she was now far more reconciled), and younger, frequent visitors were Stephen Spender and his wife Natasha, Cecil Day Lewis, Henry Reed who had written an enthusiastic article about her in *Penguin New Writing*, George Barker, David Gascoyne and Louis MacNeice with his wife Hedli Andersen. Originally, as I have described, she had been entirely out of sympathy with MacNeice's poetry, but when she read *Brother Fire* and *Whit Monday* in *Penguin New Writing* she changed round completely, finding them 'superb'.

She had also renewed her friendship with Roy Campbell, which had begun when he was an undergraduate at Oxford in the twenties. Remarkable poet though he was, he had such violent political and literary prejudices that the problem of mixing him with her other guests caused endless headaches.

Edith admired him for his poetry, in particular his translations from St John of the Cross, for his extravagant character — she thought he would have been more at home in the Tudor age — and for his love of her poetry. Characteristically, this enthusiasm blinded her to his intolerance, malice towards many who had befriended him in the past, and advocacy of what amounted to cruelty to animals.

The most beloved poet of all was Dylan Thomas, who attended, with his wife Caitlin, whenever he could be got to London. Edith had been largely responsible for his becoming widely known, and breaking through the small circle which had admired his *Eighteen Poems* (published in December 1934) to a national audience. In February 1936 she had been captivated by his poem *A Grief Ago* and wrote in the *London Mercury*: 'I know of no young poet of our time whose poetic gifts are on such great lines.' He was twenty-two at the time. And to Dylan Thomas himself she wrote: 'I know now, without any possibility of doubting it, that in you we have a poet from whom real greatness may be expected.' In September of the same year, his second book, *Twenty-Five Poems*, was published by Dent, and Edith wrote an enthusiastic review in the *Sunday Times*.

From that moment she took him to her heart, and though he was always a little shy of her *milieu*, they became the closest friends. *Twenty-Five Poems* shocked a great many poetic conservatives and Philistines, and a controversy developed in the press, in defence of him, which Edith entered with her usual zest. 'It was my privilege and pride,' she wrote later, 'to give the attackers, during two months, more than as good as they gave. The air still seems to reverberate with the wooden sound of numskulls soundly hit.'

When they first met, she was immensely struck by his

look of 'archangelic power'. She was even more struck by his human qualities. 'I have never known anyone more capable of endearing himself to others. And this was not only the result of his great warmth, charm, and touching funniness. I have never known anyone with a more holy and childlike innocence of mind. The exuberance of his strong physique, of his strong physical life, never marred or blurred that. He loved humanity, and had contempt only for the cruel, the unkind (these are not always identical), and the mean.'

She once said, on the B.B.C., that she had 'never seen him behave anything but beautifully' with her, 'like a son with his mother'. Nevertheless, Dylan's increasingly Dionysiac impulses caused awkward moments, and she became more and more aware of the dangers he was running unless the fatal circle of habit could be broken. At one of the last of the great poetry readings, of which I have already written, Dylan was asked to recite Blake's 'Tiger, tiger, burning bright'. The Queen (now Queen Elizabeth the Queen Mother) was again in front. Dylan appeared on the stage in a brilliant red muffler instead of tie, and read the famous poem in a more extraordinary fashion than it can ever have been read before or since. The sombre pace, the sudden long pauses between words, as if Dylan was himself wrestling with an invisible tiger, were electrifying; but it was clear that they were more due to the Dutch courage with which he had primed himself than studied artistry. After the reading, Edith Sitwell, who had been one of the organisers, gave a large dinner party, to which Dylan and Caitlin came. Edith was in a state of considerable tension and anxiety, but Dylan managed to get a grip on himself, and no sensational incidents occurred.

Edith decided that Dylan must be helped to go abroad for a complete change of scene. A few years earlier, in 1943, a rich friend of Edith's, who preferred to remain anonymous, had given a considerable sum of money to provide a yearly 'travelling scholarship' after the war, for an author, either young or old, who might benefit from the experience. The fund was administered by the Society of Authors, and the choice was made by a special committee appointed by the Committée of Management.* Edith made up her mind that the award for 1947 should go to Dylan.

'In re *Dylan and the Fund,*' she wrote to me in December, '*A.* I think, in fact I am sure, John, that Dylan ought to be the sole beneficiary. We are not likely to get another man of such genius — such *great* genius — (between ourselves George Barker, the one other runner-up, has just got a Bursary Fund — Osbert has something to do with it, only that is private to you and me). The Anonymous Donor does *not* wish *journalists* or people of minor talent to get it. She wants the greatest artist in poetry or prose who can be found.

'*B. The danger of the use of the money doing harm to his creative work.* I worry about a certain habit, terribly. But that is because I am terrified of it harming him *physically*. It obviously does *not* harm his work, because his latest book of poems is infinitely greater than anything else he has done. We don't want what happened to Swinburne to happen to him.

'*And* I think he has a fabulous physique. That does not mean that I do not wish to God that he would stop it. —

* The first chairman of this special committee was Sir Harold Nicolson. Edith herself became chairman in 1947, but asked me very soon afterwards to take her place.

Only, he would have (for that to be any good) to stop it of his own accord — not *be* stopped. I need hardly say I know the moral point of view is not what you are considering — but I'd rather give the fund to Coleridge than to Southey.

'*C. America.* I was aghast when I heard he was going there. I've tried *everything* — imploring, owl-like prognostications of disaster — saying that Caitlin will have a rotten time because she isn't rich. *Nothing* sways him. And his hostess at Oxford, Mrs Taylor, the wife of a don, says it is like measles — you have to have it and get over it — I mean this mania to go to America.

'I am terrified of the family going there with *no* money, and that is why I am so anxious Dylan should have the whole of the Fund. If he will go — (and it is certainly necessary the eldest child should be taken out of this climate) then I feel we must do our best for him. And he has real nobility. I know he will try not to let us down.'

There was a scheme that the men members of the Committee should try to persuade him to go to Switzerland rather than to America. In the end, however, having been awarded the whole of the sum then available, he went, with his family, to Italy. He worked at several of his most remarkable last poems there; but from the therapeutic point of view, the visit was not the success Edith and others among his closest friends had hoped.

Another young writer whom she befriended during these years, and who felt himself deeply indebted to her for her encouragement and public enthusiasm for his work, was Denton Welch. His illness prevented him moving from his country home very often, but his *Journals* are full of references to her letters, and he has left a characteristically detailed account of their first meeting at the Sesame Club.

In 1942 *Horizon* published a witty and maliciously observant article he had written about a visit to the painter
Walter Sickert. This so delighted Osbert and Edith, that
she wrote him a four-page letter of praise. 'It was such a
beautiful, generous, deliriously exciting letter,' he records
in his *Journal*, 'I was childish with vanity, and still am, from
its effects. . . . It is so thrilling to have such warm-hearted
praise from a great genius. It was so utterly unexpected.' He
added that he had 'fed on her letter all day', and that he
could 'never hope again to get quite such a generous dose of
appreciation, sent straight from the blue sky'.

They began to write to one another, and each time her
letter filled him with joy and a feeling that it was almost too
good to be true that she should praise him. He was only in
his middle twenties. 'Another precious letter from Edith
Sitwell,' he wrote in his *Journal* on 31 October 1942. 'I
realize that I almost begin to live for these. It is so funny, so
winey, so toxic, always to be hearing fine things about one's
attempts from someone famous. How much she says with
no fear of using words full of feeling.' She agreed to contribute a foreword to his first book, *Maiden Voyage*, in which
she wrote: 'This is a very moving and remarkable first book,
and the author appears to be that very rare being, a born
writer. I have not seen a first book that produces this impression more strongly. . . . He never fumbles.'

At last, in the spring of 1943, she invited him to come
and visit her and Osbert at the Sesame Club. 'Now I am
home and will not write about it till the morning, for I have
too much to say and I must think,' he wrote afterwards in
his *Journal*, and the next day he followed this by several
pages of minute recording of the event, what they drank,
what they ate, etc., the dreary impression the Sesame Club

made on him, what Edith and he said to one another, and how Osbert and he shared a taxi afterwards, and Osbert invited him to come and see him. 'As if I were ever likely to, unless properly asked. Still it was nice, the idle sentence.' He finished the long entry: 'Remember the atmosphere in that drawing-room again: dark, aqueous, cold, with figures passing, repassing; the glistening door opening and shutting; Edith's head turning, her white hand lying on her breast so that the huge ring sparkled like ice on fire in the gloom.' He did not see her again before he died in 1948.

During these years of the forties Edith Sitwell produced a continuous stream of books in the midst of her increasing social and public activities. *A Poet's Notebook* appeared in 1943, and was complemented five years later by her *Notebook on William Shakespeare*. *A Poet's Notebook* throws the most remarkable light on the width of her reading, and her favourite authors. There are quotations from St Augustine, Bede and Aquinas; repeatedly from Blake, Coleridge, Emerson, Baudelaire, Wagner (particularly on Beethoven), Rimbaud and Cocteau; there are other quotations from Traherne and St John of the Cross to Van Gogh and Gauguin; and special chapters devoted to Chaucer, Herrick, Smart, Wordsworth and Shakespeare. In her *Foreword* she wrote: 'The aphorisms on Poetry, or applicable to Poetry, with which this book begins were noted down by me, originally, for my private use. All — or nearly all — poets have made examinations into the necessities of Poetry, and I, for one, would rather read by the light of the sun than by lamplight.' She was already an addicted anthology-maker: *The Pleasures of Poetry* (in three volumes) had appeared between 1930 and 1932, *Edith Sitwell's Anthology* in 1940, and *Look! the Sun*, a poetry anthology that purported to be for children, in 1941. Now she produced a small, happily inspired anthology, *Planet and Glow-worm*, which she sub-titled 'A Book for the Sleepless', and began work on a more ambitious anthology on which I had encouraged her to embark for my own publishing firm, *The American Genius* — eventually published in 1951.

All her life she had been fascinated by the Tudor era and the life of Queen Elizabeth I, and in 1946 she produced her story of the Queen's childhood against the background of Henry VIII's six marriages, *Fanfare for Elizabeth*. Like its successor, *The Queens and the Hive*, which she wrote in the last years of her life, this was no scholarly study and broke no new grounds in research. It was rather a dramatic re-creation of Elizabeth's early history as seen through her powerful, identifying imagination. At the same time it was in no sense a 'popular' biography: its value derived purely from the fact that a poet with an exceptional gift for studding her prose with glittering images had written it.

In 1945 (before the appearance of *The Shadow of Cain*) she published her third volume of wartime poetry, *The Song of the Cold*. This was, in effect, a reissue, rearranged, of her first two volumes *Street Songs* and *Green Song*, together with a number of poems which had been printed in periodicals since then, and a small selection of her earlier poems. She was continually rearranging and rewriting her poems: a habit that makes the task of the bibliographer especially difficult. Each time she was convinced that she had brought out the meaning of her work more completely. On this occasion, she wrote: '*You simply wouldn't know them* again — arranged this way. For some reason the poems all assume their real and proper aspect, an aspect they did not really wear before.'

In 1947–8 she was very much occupied with William Blake, always one of her favourite poets. In September 1947, she wrote to Maurice Bowra from Bournemouth: 'Everything is almost unbearably dreary at present, excepting for a really wonderful new book on Blake (I don't think it is out yet, I was sent it by the *Spectator* for review), *Fearful Symmetry*, by Northrop Frye. . . . Do, when you have a moment, read it when it appears. I say a moment, but one can only read a few pages a day. It is that sort of book.' Her review had a comical-disastrous result. In January she told Maurice Bowra that she had had 'a wonderful letter from a gentleman who seems to be a lecturer at Strasbourg University. He says that he has written a long book on Blake, to bring forward his discoveries that *A* Blake was *serious*, and not simply pulling people's legs, and *B* that he was interested in, and influenced by, Swedenborg. He says my way is now clear. I am to spend the rest of my life in getting this book published, and before I do that, I am to get it translated.'

Edith Sitwell's review encouraged me to suggest that she should prepare an anthology of Blake for me to publish. She was keen to do it, but was daunted by what seemed to her the magnitude of the undertaking. She wrote to me: 'John, will you please believe I am doing my very best with it. But I think it will be perfect ages before it is finished. I *must*, for all our sakes, do the best I can, and it is a labour of love, as I have a special personal love for Blake. There is an enormous amount to assimilate, *and* I have to read all kinds of works associated with Blake, and about him. After the great Northrop Frye book, especially, I have to be damned careful (it really is a terrific book: have you read it?) so I don't hope to have the book ready yet — unless you would like one *without* a preface, but I imagine that isn't so.'

Unfortunately, the projected Blake anthology never materialised. Edith Sitwell's mind was more and more pre-occupied with the forthcoming, long-planned, lecture-tour of America, for which she and Osbert set sail in October 1948.

13

As I have already suggested, the outbreak of war in 1939 presented Osbert, checked in his passion for travel and the exploration of the art and civilisation of remote countries and obscure times, with an opportunity which he very soon understood and grasped. He set to work to explore his own past, and the civilisation in which he and his brother and sister had grown up and been shaped to become a trio of artists, in one generation, from one family, that had caught the surprised attention of the English-speaking world between the wars.

The result, as everyone knows, was the five-volume autobiography, *Left Hand, Right Hand!*, one of the most extraordinary and original works of our time. If one excludes the appendices, this work consists of nearly 1,500 pages and approximately 600,000 words. The first volume — which has come to be known by the title of the whole series, though the author intended it to be called *The Cruel Month* — was published in March 1945: this, under the conditions of wartime publishing, means that it must have been finished about a year before. The subsequent volumes followed with remarkable speed: *The Scarlet Tree* was published in July 1946, *Great Morning* in April 1948, *Laughter in the Next Room* (finished in February 1948 before *Great Morning* appeared) in May 1949, and the coda, *Noble Essences*, in September 1950. *Tales My Father Taught Me*, essentially an afterthought and not belonging to the design of *Left Hand, Right Hand!*, was not published as a volume until 1962.

In the introduction to the first volume, as also in the Envoy to *Laughter in the Next Room*, Osbert Sitwell has been at pains to describe his intentions and his grand design. 'In this cruel and meaningless epoch,' he writes, 'behind the bars of which I now write, neither past nor future seems to have any existence; only the present which contains the dead ashes of the past. Since the whole of life and its background is being dissolved to chaos before our eyes, it is impossible — because our balance from day to day remains too precarious —to wrest a book from the future. In consequence, I have resolved to start the story of my life, to describe some of it, and some of those who have figured in it.'

'I want my biography,' he continues a little later, 'no less than a novel or a book of travel — and, indeed, it must partake of the essence of both — to be a work of art, upon which I can expend not only such gifts as I possess, but the skill acquired through many years of labour at my task. I plan, if I am allowed to finish it, a book of several volumes to cover a longer span of time than is usual. The first portion will deal with many people who died before I was born, but who still influence me, perhaps, in ways I do not know as well as in ways to be recognised, for past and future both work upon the present; but the chief interest of the earlier chapters must derive from the circumstances surrounding, and the events befalling, a family which has produced three writers in a single generation. . . .'

Osbert appears, in this prefatory explanation, explicitly to exclude any deep self-analysis. 'I will not,' he says, 'concern the reader with those parts from which I want, myself, to escape, for the aim of this book is to beguile, and not to improve, the mind. I do not pretend to tell the reader everything, only to paint for him in a setting, a portrait, of which, as in a surrealist picture, many diverse incidents compose the features. I leave the skeletons in their cupboards. . . . I *want* this to be gothic, complicated in surface and crowned with turrets and pinnacles, for that is its nature. I mean it to be full of others besides myself and my brother and sister, giving scenes and *divertissements* crowded with people of every sort. . . .'

To this advertised intention, Osbert Sitwell remained remarkably faithful; but when he had completed the central structure of four volumes, he was aware of having created rather more than he had proposed. 'Since I began to write this autobiography, in 1940,' he wrote in the Envoy, 'the world has again changed out of recognition. . . . For myself, I had never expected the world I knew to endure, and this, perhaps, gave a sharper edge to my vision, to my living. From my earliest youth, I had, I believe, an unusual sense of time, of the recession of the present into the past, and its emergence into the future. Even as a child, I had tried to fix in my mind scenes that I wished to stay with me, so that I could enact them again in memory. And so it was that later I set myself to record them, and to fuse with them into a work of art the story of the development of three artists — for, whatever the future may bring, the temperament of poet and painter, volatile though it may be, will remain true to type and, in such manner, stable.'

He concludes with a rhetorical appeal to the future, in a manner which, as in the finale to *England Reclaimed*, seems a little overwrought in relation to the shrewd observation and sensibility, the unforced sense of historical evolution which precedes it: 'I, a citizen of the Sunset Age, an Englishman, who saw the world's great darkness gathering, salute you, Stranger, across the Chasm. I strain toward the dawn of a new age, and offer you the story of events and persons in a day when the light flared up before it failed. I have tried, by such art as I could capture in my sum of days, to transmit to you almost the physical sensations, the feeling of our hours of warmth and cold, I have summoned to my aid every power I possess of evocation, to paint for you the life of which I was part, the places I saw, the people, the absurdities, cruelties, immensities, virtues and comic lapses of man's character, the incomparable capacity for joy and sorrow of that paragon of animals.'

It is difficult to define the structure of this five-volume work, for though the time-sequence advances throughout from ancestors to childhood, from boyhood to manhood and eventually the outbreak of the second World War, there are so many doublings-back in time, so many portraits introduced discursively — and not only in the final volume devoted to portraits, *Noble Essences* — that really belong to the whole work and not merely to one particular moment of it, that though it is continuously readable and continuously fascinating to mind and imagination, it is not easy, when one closes the fourth volume, *Laughter in the Next Room*, to remember where any particular episode or portrait occurs.

Take the third volume, *Great Morning*. This contains two 'books', 'Mars Victoryall' (a quotation from William Dunbar), and 'The Rose and the Thorn'. The first book opens with a description of the Tower of London and Osbert as a young Grenadier Guards officer of twenty, in 1912, mounting guard there. It is one of the most evocative and beautifully finished passages in the whole work.

Very soon, however, he interrupts it to describe the progress
of his father's eccentricities from an earlier period, and to
introduce admirably vivid portraits of Sir Edwin Lutyens,
Lady Colvin, wife of the Keeper of Prints and Drawings at
the British Museum and a distant family connection, and the
gamekeeper at Renishaw, Mark Kirkby, which gives him
the opportunity to revel again in the Derbyshire countryside of his youth and its traditional life. In the middle of this
comes the account of his father's purchase of the Castle of
Montegufoni, which took place in 1909, and his early delight in the new family acquisition. Taking up the thread of
his own story, he then records his incapacity as a young man
to pass examinations or decide on a career, and the sudden
discovery that he had — through family influence — been
granted a commission in the Yeomanry. A macabre-comic
description of life at Aldershot in 1911 follows, and his first
visit to the Russian Ballet in a brief escape to London. The
next book, 'The Rose and the Thorn', opens with his de-
cision that he could no longer stand Aldershot, his flight to
Italy, and a poignant account of how his mother became
entangled in the toils of the money-lender, Julian Field,
how his father, characteristically, misjudged the situation,
and his mother's involvements went from bad to worse.
From this he leaps to a rhapsodic description of the estate of
Montegufoni and of Florence; and then, in the next chapter,
is back again in 1912, transferred as if by a miracle (he gives
us no clear explanation) from the Yeomanry to the Brigade
of Guards. This new incarnation he obviously enjoyed, and
has only the warmest words of praise for the spirit of the
regiment, the highly disciplined yet civilised way its affairs
were conducted, and the officers of his own generation
whose friendship he made there (most of whom, he reminds

us with ominous reiteration, were to be killed within two years). The rest of the book consists of a description of the life that opened itself for an intelligent young Guards officer of means and many important social connections in a London at the height of its pre-1914 brilliance and extravagance, the great houses and great hostesses, including Lady Asquith, Lady Brougham, Mrs Keppel and Lady Cunard, and the excitement he derived from meeting many stars of opera and ballet, including Diaghilew, Massine and Chaliapin. In the last chapter, he is back with his family and his father at Renishaw; the book ends with the outbreak of war and his return to his regiment, which he had abandoned for a brief period to equip himself, at his father's inexplicable insistence, to become 'Town Clerk of Scarborough'.

This method of procedure—which is characteristic of all the four volumes of the biography proper — is bound, as related above, to sound more than a little confusing and disorganised. And yet, if one has already fallen under the author's spell in the earlier volumes (and it is difficult to conceive that one should not), one goes on reading with delight, eager to discover, not the next turn in the story but the next turn in Osbert's recollections. I have already stressed my belief that his power of descriptive writing, of conveying atmosphere, whether here of a foggy night at the Tower or an October morning in the Renishaw woods, is one of his most remarkable gifts as a writer. And in the autobiography, as so rarely in the short stories and novels, it is allied with an affectionate humour as well as a mischievous wit when he introduces his characters. He becomes, perhaps, a little too urbane in describing some of the great hostesses, but nearly all the other characters are made to live by his capacity for observing the quirks and quiddities that

give them flavour and individuality; and at the same time he
penetrates through to the inner nature, responding at once
to generosity of heart, disinterested love of the beautiful,
the roots of melancholy, the spark of creative fire, or simple-
minded ambition, even when the surface most conceals
them. He can be extremely poetic, inviting the reader to
experience a spring morning in Tuscany or a stormy night
in Scarborough at one moment; and the next produce a
passage of pure comedy (especially in the gradual filling in
of his father's portrait) or of rhapsodic yet soundly based
and detailed artistic appreciation. And his strength as a
'beguiler' — for one should never forget his stated intention in embarking on the work — lies in his capacity
cunningly to mix and vary these ingredients, so that the
reader is continually refreshed by changes of mood and
pace.

I have, I think, sufficiently illustrated the style of the
work by the many quotations I have of necessity made
throughout this book. Taken individually, his idiosyn-
crasies as a writer, his fondness for instance for long sentences of involved construction, or for using the rather self-
conscious punctuation of three dots, may seem in these
quotations sometimes to be irritating flaws. These flaws,
however (if flaws they be), are, I believe, swallowed up in
the broad and scintillating flow of the total work. A more
damaging criticism may be that throughout the five volumes
there is an almost complete absence of any examination of
passion. The work, it may be said, lacks one of the essential
and most *beguiling* ingredients of life: a love story. Here
again, one should beware of taking it for what it is not.
Some thoughtless comparisons have been made with
Proust's masterpiece *A la Recherche du Temps Perdu*, where

passion in all its manifestations is one of the chief and most absorbing themes. Proust's work, however, is first of all a *novel*, even though it partakes of some of the qualities of a disguised memoir; while *Left Hand, Right Hand!* is the reverse, a memoir that has some of the liberties of fiction in it. This Osbert Sitwell clearly states as his aim, and he is indeed justified (for who could believe all his stories to be exactly true without artistic embellishment?). And even though he goes at some length into the sorry affair of his mother's entanglement with money-lenders (devoting a whole appendix to the detail), he warns us at the very beginning that he intends to 'leave the skeletons in their cupboards'. One may regret the absence of anything more, in the author's account of his own adult emotional life, than the few paragraphs in which he tells us that he fell in love, during his pre-war years in London, with a girl who remained his constant companion through five years; but such dramas, it seems fairly clear, were not on the programme as drawn up.

Many admirers of the autobiography have taken the view that its chief triumph, if not its *raison d'être*, is the portrait of Sir George Sitwell that extends over the first four volumes (and is taken up again in *Tales My Father Taught Me*). It is indeed *one* of the triumphs; as L. P. Hartley wrote in a long appreciation which appeared in 1954. Sir George in these pages has been turned into 'a comic character as unforgettable as Don Quixote or the White Knight,* both of whom he in some ways resembles. . . . But as a personality he was more formidable than either; as Sir Osbert observes, "being

---

* The comparison with Lewis Carroll's White Knight appears earlier in a letter from Hamilton Temple Smith quoted in Appendix D to *Great Morning*.

his son was an occupation in itself".' When, however, Mr Hartley goes on to say that it is the conflict between these two 'that gives the work its most dramatic and consecutive interest', I think one should be cautious of agreeing. The overriding triumph is, I cannot help feeling, the grand sweep of the whole work, by which the author brings to life an epoch of unparalleled wealth and power in English social history, to see it shaken by terrible and long-prepared catastrophe — and survive, deeply scarred and with many illusions gone. Coming, as he did, from 'the stalls', he is able to depict *from the inside* (though with a constant undertone of mocking criticism) the social life of the English upper classes, who controlled the destiny of a world-wide Empire at its apogee, in all the extravagant splendour of their London setting and in their vast country estates; to see a way of life changing even before the catastrophe of the war, and good things disappearing with the bad; and at the same time, as he grows up, to add more and more facets of intellectual and artistic life. It is not, of course, a complete picture, because no man could experience an epoch at every level; but it is Osbert Sitwell's achievement to have presented with such skill and artistry a pageant so much more diverse than that of any other memorialist (or indeed novelist) of our time.

Again, a further implicit triumph is the portrait of the author himself, as it gradually emerges, with a rare absence of egotistical insistence, in the complex development of the work. One side of him is revealed in his loving descriptions of the countryside in the many homes in which he passed his boyhood and youth, and of country characters such as Mark Kirkby; another, especially his impish and irreverent humour, in his relations with his father; another in his devoted admiration for his sister and brother, fellow-explorers as he sees them, on an expedition where enemies lurk at every turning; and yet another in his relations with other writers, with artists, dancers and singers, his passionate readiness to discover beauty and accomplishment in every new manifestation of the creative spirit, and to assist in its flowering. There is, finally, one quality which includes but goes beyond this. It has been admirably defined by L. P. Hartley in the article from which I have already quoted, as a 'power of understanding people, of seeing them as they are, and of wanting them to be what they are'. 'More than once,' Mr Hartley continues, 'he speaks of his delight in watching people unobserved; he enjoys taking them, as he enjoys taking the reader, by surprise. But though an acute he is not altogether a realistic observer. Fantasy and poetry enter in. His Dickensian eye delights in the absurd, and he is unexpectedly tender towards anyone who manifests it — which partly explains his father's fascination for him.' Only about his deeper emotional life beyond his attachments to his home and his family, as I have already said, are we left, to a large extent, guessing.

In earlier chapters I have already quoted from some of Osbert's descriptions of, and anecdotes about his father. He emerges from the autobiography, one cannot help thinking, as a rather more comic figure than he actually was. Osbert enjoyed teasing him, and knew exactly how to provoke some of his most extraordinary observations. The two brothers were increasingly on the defensive as they grew up, because Sir George had the profound conviction that he knew better than anyone else and could give useful hints to everyone — whether gardener, politician, general, painter or poet. This led to an atmosphere of unceasing interference when the brothers were trying to write at Renishaw — or in London — after the war, and they decided to go abroad for at least half the year to avoid Sir George's continual visits and letters of advice. To make their escape watertight they invented a yacht, on which they were constant guests, and from which they could write to their father — though he could not write to them. 'We ordered a supply of special writing-paper,' Osbert writes, 'of which for many years we made frequent use. Engraved on it at the right-hand corner was the name of an imaginary yacht, *S.Y. Rover*, and opposite this it carried a burgee, showing a skull and crossbones, in white, on a black ground. By this means we could always reach my father by post, if so we wished, for we could write to him from where we were staying for the autumn and winter months, explaining that our friend Jonah's yacht had "just put in" at Ostend or Naples or Athens, or wherever it might be — and that we had "come here for a few days' rest, while the craft is being overhauled". We would add, "In the meantime, dearest father, do not trouble to answer until we can give you an address. Our next stopping place is uncertain, and the letter will only be lost."'

It should, I think, be admitted, that Sir George took his sons' teasing, when their devices were discovered, in very good part, and appears seldom, if ever, to have lost his temper or complained; though Osbert records that he was once moved to exclaim, after one of his elder son's sallies, 'Rude to me in my own motor car!' The chief trouble was Osbert's allowance. He admits that he was extravagant, and his father had frequently to stump up; but perhaps he would not have had to do so so often if he had not insisted on Osbert joining an expensive regiment, and had not calculated the allowance, according to Osbert, as something between what a Lord of the Manor would have given his heir at the time of the Black Death and what some of his more elderly friends considered appropriate for a young man about town. Sir George, like many very rich men, was close with the pennies but lavish with the pounds — for his own purposes. He suffered from the building craze — which has ruined so many dynasties and nations — and never stopped making extravagant alterations, improvements and additions to Renishaw and Montefugoni. Thousands of pounds were spent in this way almost every year; but at the same time he would dispute an item of 4s 10d in a chemist's bill — and almost every item in Osbert's bills. It was not till many years of wrangling had passed that a friend of the family, who had studied Sir George with shrewd understanding, told Osbert that all his father's irritatingly petty 'tricks, all his deductions and small charges, arose from a childlike desire to play', and that he could find no one willing to join him in the game. Osbert took the hint, and on the next occasion challenged his father's complaints, and produced a counter-list of his own to Sir George's revision of the expenses he had presented, adding 1½d here and deducting 2d there. 'He was,' writes Osbert, 'absolutely delighted.'

Edith came in for a far worse time. 'Once, though her whole allowance was only fifty pounds a year, he had caught her giving five shillings to a beggar. "Such a mistake!" And, after all, it was really his money. He should have been consulted. She seemed unable to pass a tramp or a beggar without giving him something, whereas the correct thing to do was not to *see* a person of that kind.'

One point is rarely emphasised in studies of the autobiography: that though Osbert brilliantly illuminates his father's character (and his own) by describing their constant differences, arguments and clashes, he also uses another foil: Henry Moat, his father's butler and personal servant. Henry Moat was devoted to Osbert, and his letters to the son about the father make some of the funniest passages in the work.

As an example of Osbert's writing at its most impishly satirical and at the same time most poetic, a passage which at the same time beautifully reveals his deep sympathy and love for his sister, I will quote in conclusion his description of an 'unfortunate episode' of her youth: 'My sister had been paying a lengthy visit to my grandmother Sitwell, to whom she was much attracted, at Bournemouth; in which camping-ground of godly invalids, everywhere breathing heavily in red-tiled shelters, pitched *à la japonaise* under pine trees, or reclining on beds and sofas under turrets and pepper-pots of red brick and rough-cast, behind luxuriant hedges of arbutus and fuchsia, over which they can distinguish the spires, rain-grey, of many churches, my grandmother had taken a house. The prevailing atmosphere of religion and old age may at times have been a little uncongenial: but the life to which my sister was exposed at home made her eager to pay as many visits to my grandmother as possible; at least she was always treated with kindness and consideration, and allowed that dignity which is so precious to a young human being. At first, therefore, my sister was very happy, for she was away from home, and the tormenting which in her case the word spelt. But the circles of visiting clergy that, wherever my grandmother might be, at once sprang up round the old lady like a circle of plainly inedible fungi, took soon to wrestling daily with my sister over the poems of Algernon Charles Swinburne, with whose works she was at the time intoxicated. They were immoral, the toadstools pronounced, and she should not be permitted to read them. Canon Groucher urged on my grandmother that they should be impounded and burnt. Any reasonable girl should be content, so far as poetry was concerned, with the works of T. E. Brown and Elizabeth Barrett Browning. In the course of time, my sister became so much enraged by the continual attacks made upon her favourite poet that she determined to show her feeling for him in a manner that could not be mistaken.

'Very early then, one lovely September morning, she had flitted, having given no previous notice to my grandmother of her going, and, accompanied by her maid, had boarded the small boat that plied from Bournemouth to Ventnor, Isle of Wight. There, a few hours later, under the bright pennons of the summer weather, with its fleecy white clouds and high-flung seas, a singular spectacle must have greeted the curious eyes of any passers-by. A tall, fair, rather thin young lady, paler than usual after her rough journey, yet with colour coming and going from the love and defiance in her heart, disembarked, bearing a large sheaf of red roses: after her, the second figure in this frieze of two, came with faltering steps a woman of about thirty, with all her lady's-maid trimmings dishevelled by the crossing, her face a sour green, and wearing this morning an expression of the plainest condemnation of the whole enterprise in which she found herself engaged, and of dislike (if the spectator could discern that much) both for poetry and the sea; she carried a jug of milk, a honeycomb, a wreath of bay-leaves, and the young lady's coat. After a few moments my sister found an open cab, drawn by a horse so old that Swinburne himself as a boy might have ridden behind it, and drove, with her maid still disapproving, through lanes just tinged with autumn's first fine gold, to Bonchurch: where, alighting, the procession entered the churchyard. After a furious battle with a sexton, who objected to such foreign ways, Edith triumphed and, bending low under an enormous fuchsia, its tasselled flowers of scarlet and purple trailing over a headstone, in the Grecian mode poured the milk, and placed the wreath of bay-leaves, the honeycomb and the red roses, upon the grave of Swinburne. . . . This safely accomplished, she drove back with her maid to Ventnor, and returned to Bournemouth and my grandmother. An appalling storm broke and long raged round her head, alternating with calm patches of religious resignation.'

14

ALREADY in March 1948 Edith and Osbert Sitwell were making their plans for their first joint lecture tour of America. A tour had been planned for Edith before the war. Negotiations were carried on by her trusted agent, David Higham, with the American tour agents Colston Leigh and Lee Keedick between 1936 and 1938. Edith wrote sardonically to Rée Gorer in 1937 that, as far as she could make out, the American agency wanted her 'to bicycle round and round the platform on the tip of my nose, with my feet in the air, intoning at the same time on the effect that texture has on the caesura — in other words is making everything as difficult for me as possible by insisting that I must not *read* my lectures. As I have no memory, and as the lectures on poetry are highly technical, and any slip would be fatal, I have said that I am *going* to read them.' These negotiations, however, chiefly owing to the increasing gravity of Helen Rootham's illness, never came to anything.

Osbert had visited the U.S.A. before the war, in 1927, and had come back with warm feelings about the Americans — and some characteristically amusing comments. He wrote, in a newspaper article, that he was particularly impressed by 'the extraordinary intelligence, kindness and courtesy of the American newspaper reporters. Why and where have the English formed their ideas as to their crudity and brutality? In no journal in New York would you find adopted that tone of silly rudeness towards modern art and artists, which is so marked a feature of the "chit-chat" columns of the more uninteresting English papers. But then the average American approaches intelligence with an instinctive respect, rather like that with which we approach games in England. He has, too, an almost German reverence for expert opinion, and would never consider himself free, as the Englishman would, in the presence of an expert, first of all to admit his entire ignorance of the subject, and then to lay down the law about it.'

He remarked that 'America is overwhelmingly foreign. The difference between Europe and America is as great as that between Europe and China.' And he concluded: 'The kindness, lavishness and extent of American hospitality are incredible. Nowhere else will people, out of simplicity and kindness, take so much trouble. They even allow their guests to express opinions — except for certain subjects on which they are touchy. Steam-heating is one fetish of this sort: the Englishman may, if he is uncivilised enough, abuse every major institution in the States, but directly he mentions steam-heating, a shiver of horror at his blasphemy passes round his audience. . . .'

In 1948 Edith was delighted to find that Maurice Bowra was going to be at Harvard at the same time. Alice Pleydell-Bouverie (who had been in England during most of the war) and her sister-in-law Mrs Vincent Astor were planning a great social welcome; James Laughlin and other publishers and authors a great literary welcome. There were moments when Edith thought of it not only as an opportunity to let the Americans hear her wartime poetry but also as a golden chance to get her own back on some of her detractors — whose criticisms continued to cause her far too much shock and dismay, though rousing her own pugnacious instincts at the same time. 'Nobody realises what a tough old demon they've got to deal with,' she cried in a letter to me in June. 'You wait till I get to America!'

In the midst of her many engagements and movements that summer, which included travelling to Durham to receive her Hon. D.Litt. there, and taking Evelyn Wiel, Helen Rootham's sister, to Bournemouth for a holiday, she was finding the preparations exhausting. 'I truly am nearly dead with fatigue,' she wrote at the beginning of August. 'I have to get 2 more lectures (with all the reading up for them) done by the end of this month, have just finished 2 lectures and one broadcast, and have another broadcast on my poetry to write. Tom Eliot wants me to send a poem to an American friend of his before the 15th (no hope). And my Good Man Friday, José Garcia Villa, wants the symposium* on my poetry to come out after all. (Mr Laughlin is publishing it.) *But* Charles Ford, who is exceedingly determined and forceful, took it away from José when the thing went kaput before. And for some time the *whole* MSS was lost — José saying Charles had it, and Charles saying Laughlin had it, and Laughlin saying *where* was it. Then they all telegraphed it was lost, and *I* must find it. Now, finally, most of it — but not all (however, thank heaven your essay is there) — has turned up, where Charles said it was, in Mr Laughlin's office.'

At the same time, the bores and the lunatics were keeping it up. A young American fan, who had been extremely persistent in her not entirely balanced attentions, and for whom Edith felt unnecessarily responsible, had 'taken to making scenes at Westminster Abbey — shouting the Lord's

* *A Celebration for Edith Sitwell*, edited by José Garcia Villa, was published in the spring of 1948 by New Directions.

Prayer very slowly, when the Dean is taking it fast, — and "just falling down, several times, *quite quietly*, after Holy Communion".' There were renewed rows with Geoffrey Grigson. While she was working against time at Renishaw 'a woman got into the house, stayed for three hours, and asked me if I realised how wonderful Time is. "It goes on and on, Miss Sitwell. I do *wonder* for what reason it was made, don't you? And what the world would be like without Time."'

They arrived in New York at the end of the third week in October. A few days after they disembarked, Edith wrote to me from the St Regis Hotel: 'A thousand thanks for your telegram to the boat — which made us feel slightly less like convicts bound for a Penal Settlement. Oh dear! Well, here we are, after two bad days at sea, twelve hours delay, and four and a half days — no I mean hours (that wasn't a bad joke, but a slip) — in the station because all our large luggage had been lost. Eventually we recovered it, and arrived here at 11 in the evening, having had nothing to eat since 1. Osbert and I sat up till nearly 2 arranging the most lovely flowers — but bending over them has given me lumbago. . . . I miss you very much, and do wish you were here. I feel very melancholy, and the boat is still swirling under my feet.'

In *Taken Care of* Edith wrote: 'My first impression of New York was overwhelming. Everybody appeared to be young. It was not possible to imagine that people so alive could be old. And the immense blocks of houses lit up by different colours at night like jewels was a sight that has lived in my memory like the burnt gold of the Mexican soil and the strange, touching union of beggars outside the massive churches of this neighbour country.'

The arrival in New York was also the scene of the tragi-comic episode of Edith's reunion with Pavel Tchelitchew. He was overwrought, perhaps ill; perhaps also in some corner of his heart he was jealous of the fame and honour that had come to his old friend since they parted. They fell into one another's arms on the Pier when the ship docked; but immediately tension developed. When Edith went to see his famous picture, *Hide and Seek*, in the Museum of Modern Art, he bitterly resented her silence — a resentment which, one cannot help feeling, her subsequent letter of enthusiastic admiration did not entirely remove. In fact, the undertone of resentment and criticism continued throughout the visit, and caused much unhappiness to Edith. Peace was only restored a few years later, when Tchelitchew came on a visit to Europe with his friend Charles Henri Ford, and spent a few days at Montegufoni.

The American lectures and readings were very soon under way, and were proving a triumphant success. Edith's lecture was on 'Modern English Poetry', and Osbert's on 'Personal Adventures' and 'The Modern Novel, its Cause and Cure'. In addition they had agreed to appear together, to read from their own poems. At the beginning of December, Edith wrote: 'I like the Americans more than I can say — finding them courteous, charming and kind. And I enjoy myself, most of the time, very much. And we *seem* to be having a great success, if I may say so. 10,000 tried to get into the Town Hall, where we read poems. I lectured to 1,400 people at Yale, and read, the same evening, to the Elizabethan Club, to which only two other women have ever been admitted. Have you been there? They have wonderful Shakespeare Quartos. It is also said that we are the only two people to whom the magazine *Life* has ever been polite.'

Christmas was spent in Boston: 'It was deep in snow, and everything we touched gave us an electric shock. Flames, blue and livid, sprang from keyholes when keys were put into them. . . . We read poems at the Cambridge School, and I had a short sharp row with a psychiatrist. He said to me, "I don't like to find you writing so much about Christ, as if you had to rely on Him." "Oh, isn't He good enough for you?" I enquired. "What do you want me to substitute for Him — the goodness of the Atomic Bomb? Is *that* what I ought to urge people to rely on?" "I would like to see you writing about the Dignity of Man," he replied pompously. I don't know what he thinks I am writing about, *inter alia*, when I write about Christ, if *not* that. And apart from Christ, I don't think the Dignity of Man is on a very high level at this moment. And I said so. We parted with no feeling of friendliness.'

She had just given a lecture to 'crowds of people' at the Colony Club, and had lunched with her old friend, Jean Cocteau, who happened to be in America. She found him kind and charming as ever, but felt herself unequal to 'the hustle and crackle of French', as she had had no sleep the night before, owing to the reappearance of her young American fan and persecutor, who suddenly arrived at the St Regis Hotel and took a room there, and began writing a flood of notes to her. Nowhere, and never, was Edith free from these obsessed camp-followers with bees in their bonnets. She had also had an attack of influenza at the beginning of November, the aftermath of which was still troubling her. In spite of all this, her favourable impression of the Americans in their homeland continued. 'How much I *do* like the Americans. Anyone who doesn't, must really be mad.'

In February she wrote again from New York: 'I must

admit that the Americans seem to have taken to us almost with violence. *Façade* was a wild success, and at the dress rehearsal, to which all the poets, artists and pressmen were invited, the whole audience rose to their feet when I came into the hall after the performance.' She made new gramophone records of *Façade* for Columbia which she thought much better than the old set. At the same time, on the tide of this popular success, she began to write poetry again.

Edith and Osbert returned to England in the middle of March. They knew now that they had conquered the American public, and established themselves not only as artists but also as outstanding English personalities. The impact they made on the rather tattered post-war image of Britain on the other side of the Atlantic, was almost as great, in their own field, as the impact of the Sadler's Wells Ballet which was to follow in the autumn of 1949. In some way, this country, since the Battle of Britain, had become legendary in America. The Americans watched with dismay the immediate post-war years of austerity, the impoverishment, the rationing, the drabness, the envious egalitarianism, the break-down of industrial activity, and asked themselves whether Britain was finished. Yet, I believe, they longed *not* to come to that conclusion; and suddenly among them appeared two famous English literary figures, who belonged at the same time to the past and to the present, and whose flamboyant personalities seemed to deny in themselves the prevailing idea of the queue-forming prisoners of a war-exhausted, war-battered, even if victorious country. As one journalist observed of the Sitwells at the time, 'their roles are as remote from the Century of the Common Man as the Aztecs'. And *Life*, in a huge illustrated feature celebrating their tour, called Edith and Osbert 'the senior members of England's most celebrated living literary family', and claimed that their appearance had given 'the New York literary set its biggest thrill in years'.

The immense dignity, punctiliousness and charm of their manners appear deeply to have impressed their audience and their fellow-guests at the innumerable luncheons, cocktail parties and dinners given in their honour. 'In the process of being lionized along the Eastern seaboard,' *Life* continued, 'the Sitwells have behaved more like lambs than lions. They gave a joint reading of their poetry at Town Hall, where the largely female audience bustled rudely in and out during the program, but the Sitwells patiently read on. At big cocktail parties they surprised everyone by their polite habit of shaking hands with and saying goodbye to everybody. At appointments they were punctual to the second. While Edith had the flu Osbert dashed off to give lectures at Montreal and Buffalo. . . . Edith swept round New York looking like a mediaeval sorcerer, in flowing capes and gowns topped off by a vermilion turban.'

In spite of the extreme courtesy of their manners, which attracted the Americans so much, the old bite remained. At one of their lectures Osbert was asked: 'How can you tell good poetry from bad?' and replied: 'In the same way as you can tell fish. If it's fresh it's good, if it's stale it's bad, and if you're not certain try it on the cat.' At the same lecture someone in the audience cried: 'We can't hear.' To which Osbert sharply replied: 'Then pay attention and you will.'

On one occasion an unknown lady ran up to Edith after a reading and said gushingly how much she had longed to attend the reading but just couldn't get a ticket. Edith, who knew that the ticket office had opened several weeks before, replied: 'We all missed you so much.' On another occasion an ardent guest at a literary party rushed up to her and exclaimed: 'I have read one of your books!' Edith replied like a flash: 'Now don't spoil me!'

Of all the welcoming receptions given for them, the cocktail party at New York's famous bookstore, the Gotham Book Mart, was the most impressive from the literary point of view, assembling as it did so many young admirers with famous figures of an older generation. Marianne Moore was there, with William Rose Benet and Horace Gregory; Richard Eberhart, Randall Jarrell, Elizabeth Bishop, Charles Henri Ford; the young novelist Gore Vidal and the young playwright Tennessee Williams who had so recently made their names; and the English poets Wystan Auden and Stephen Spender.

The success of this first tour, in popular acclaim, and — what was particularly important to Edith — financial results, encouraged them to agree to a second, wider-ranging tour at the end of summer in 1950.

On this second tour, after some weeks in New York, they visited Chicago, Columbus (Ohio), Cleveland, Kansas, Austin and Houston in Texas, and crossed over the border to Mexico City in the middle of December. Early in the new year of 1951 they were back in the U.S.A., with engagements in San Francisco and Hollywood. In February they were touring the southern states, with stops at New Orleans, Jacksonville and Sarasota; in March, after six months of exhausting but exciting work, they were back in England again.

On the way over, in the *Queen Elizabeth*, Edith had a frightening experience. Her porthole blew open in the middle of the night during a gale, and the sea came into her cabin. The gale threw her about, and she could not get hold of a steward for half an hour.

Some idea of the further rigours of the tour can be formed from Edith's letters. On 2 December, she wrote to me from Columbus: 'As soon as we had recovered from the initial rushing and tearing about that happens as soon as one gets to New York, somebody kindly gave me acute bronchitis. I was in such pain with my right lung that I couldn't lie down, and it was supposed I was in for pleurisy. However, that was headed off. As soon as I recovered from that, I had to have three inoculations against typhoid, which made me feel like *hell*, and I had to rehearse every day the reading of Lady Macbeth's part, that I did at the Museum of Modern Art. During all this time it was impossible to settle anything. . . . I have just made records for Columbia of the invocation to darkness and the sleep-walking scene from *Macbeth*, Cleopatra's death-scene, and Desdemona's willow-scene, and when I get back to New York on the 2nd of March I am going to record some of my own poems. I think I must play them all over to Carlotta,* to see if she recognises who is speaking.

'The next four days are going to be blue hell, as I shall be whirling to Chicago (this afternoon), Cleveland, Ohio, on Sunday night, arriving there at 6.30 a.m. Then I am going to have a nice morning being badgered by the Museum, and some of the employees who are trying to *sing* me four songs (poems of mine which were set and performed without my permission having been asked!) Then I lunch with the head of the biggest book-shop, sign books all the afternoon, lecture at 8.30 for 1½ hours. Then there is a reception. Then I dash to the train which leaves at 12.30 (night) change

* My spaniel, to whom Edith and Osbert had taken a great liking.

Edith and Osbert at Renishaw

The Castle of Montegufoni

at Chicago, and arrive at Kansas City next afternoon at 4.30!'

Edith's fundamental constitutional strength, her resilience and will-power were never more clearly in evidence than on this tour. After the acute bronchitis in New York, she caught amoebic dysentery in Mexico, and was so ill that she was convinced she was going to die. As soon as she was up again, she had to spend three days and three nights in the train to Los Angeles, and caught bronchitis again. In spite of this, racked by a violent cough, she gave three readings before leaving for San Francisco.

Hollywood turned out in force to greet her. At her *Macbeth* reading the audience included Harpo Marx, much to her delight, among a large number of film-stars. During the sleep-walking scene a member of the audience began to utter the most piercing shrieks: he was carried out by four men, foaming at the mouth in a fit. One of the spectators said to her afterwards: 'You ought to be awfully pleased. It was one of the most flattering things I have ever seen.'* They saw much of their old friend Aldous Huxley and his wife Maria, visits which, for Edith, 'recaptured the fun, the liveliness and happiness' of her lost youth. They met Mary Pickford, who discoursed to them of her performance as Little Lord Fauntleroy, Ethel Barrymore, 'a superb statue endowed with life and with wit', and Merle Oberon 'like a dark and lovely swan'. Edith also met Marilyn Monroe through the machinations of a 'certain American magazine with a huge circulation', since this magazine considered that they were born to hate each other, and that their insults to each other 'would cause a commotion when reported'.

* I take this description from a letter E. S. wrote to me, but in *Taken Care of* she ascribes the remark to Miss Barrymore.

Edith remarked drily: 'They were mistaken.' In fact, Marilyn Monroe became a warm friend and admirer. 'In repose,' Edith wrote, 'her face was at moments strangely, prophetically, tragic, like the face of a beautiful ghost — a little Spring-ghost, an innocent fertility-daemon, the vegetation spirit that was Ophelia.'

Temperature and cough notwithstanding, Edith's verdict was enthusiastic: 'I must say I couldn't have enjoyed Hollywood more.'

It was during this tour that Edith heard that she was going to be made an Honorary Doctor of Letters by Oxford University. Writing to express her gratitude to Maurice Bowra from Sarasota, in Florida, she described, with a macabre humour that was characteristic of her when recounting accidents that befell her, how she had nearly been killed two days before: 'Swerving to avoid a motor, I went hurtling with a speed remarkable in a woman of my age and size, right across the road, eventually falling with a crash with my head under a motor that was moving backwards. Strangely enough, the motor didn't hit my head — if it had, I suppose I would have been killed — but my knees are cut to ribbons. So infuriating!' The fates seem to have done their best to finish her off on this tour: there was not only the accident on the *Queen Elizabeth* and this incident in Sarasota, but also on the way to New Orleans, the train in which she and Osbert were travelling crashed into and completely wrecked a train ahead, and then caught fire. One has almost the impression that the 'tough old demon' revelled in these hair's-breadth escapes.*

* When, on her return, in June 1951, her Honorary Degree was given her at Oxford, she described the occasion as the greatest day of her life. She was particularly delighted with the Address delivered in

It was on these two first tours that the reputation of Edith and Osbert Sitwell in America was established. They were back again in Hollywood in the winter of 1952–3, during which trip the project, which the director George Cukor had proposed, of making a film of *Fanfare for Elizabeth*, was set going, and Edith made two more visits for the preparatory work on the film — which was, in fact, never made in her lifetime — leaving the U.S.A. for the last time in April 1955.

Edith's reactions to Hollywood on the last three visits were not so enthusiastic as on the first. This is not particularly surprising, as she was working hard, and, it seems, for much of the time against the grain. 'I worked like a slave in Hollywood,' she wrote from Renishaw in May 1953, 'had a journey from there to New York of three days and three nights, followed by fresh incessant work at the film and making records. . . .' Only a week or two later she wrote: '*I have got the whole of my film treatment to rewrite —* and I am almost demented *A* with worry — *B* with a fatigue so frightful that I have never felt *anything* to touch it. In addition I have both sciatica and fibrositis in their most acute forms, and the masseur says I will have to spend the whole of every afternoon with him.'

In the midst of her labours and invitations in Hollywood, she was, as always, alive to the humorous side. She has described her first encounter with a scriptwriter who had been assigned to help her: 'He is a man with a great sense of fun,

Latin by the Public Orator, T. F. Higham, Fellow of Trinity College, which described her as 'a votaress of Apollo and Companion of the Muses, the sea-nymphs and the gods of the countryside' (*Praesento vobis Phoebi antistatam, Musarum, Nereidum, deorum agrestium comitem*, Edith Sitwell).

but looks very serious. We went over the list of scenes together. "And now we come," said Mr ——, "to that scene where you have those Cardinal guys threaten the King" (Henry the Eighth) "with everlasting damnation. And you have the King say to them: 'That's o.k. by me, boys, you go right ahead! And you boyos can go tell your boss the Pope that *I am the* King of England. And to *Hell* with his everlasting damnation!'"" And in a letter to me she revealed that 'as soon as my back was turned, "they" gave King Henry VIII napkin rings. . . . I have thrown them out.'

The struggles continued on her next visit and her high-spirited comments as well. 'I've been feeling deathly ill,' she wrote to me early in 1954, 'and have to work 8 hours a day, including Sundays.' One of her collaborators 'was determined from the beginning that the atmosphere of Henry's Court should be a cross between that of "Le Nid" and "Mon Repos" in Surbiton, and that of the sixth-form dormitory at St Winifred's. Anne Boleyn eats chocs behind a pillar, and pinches Jane Seymour's bottom behind Cardinal Wolsey's back. She is frequently addressed by her brothers as "sister mine" or "little sister".' She complained that if contradicted 'he shrieks so piercingly that, although I am on the tenth floor, he can be heard on the fourth. It is exactly like a battle picture by Géricault transformed into sound (a cavalry regiment, complete with horses, mowed down by cannon, and uttering their death shrieks). "Dr Sidwell," said Mrs Pastor, the sweet elderly Hungarian who cooks for me "dose shrieks dey heard down de lift shaft on de fourth floor, and doze people dey crowd round de lift wid their eyes raised to heaven."

'George [Cukor] says he won't have the atmosphere of

"Le Nid" and "Mon Repos" — but *he* will have to do the fighting as I want my voice for reciting, and my iron will has got very badly dented.'

She found the attentions of the gossip columnists exasperating. On one, who had been persecuting her for weeks, she got her own back with one of her most elaborately crushing retorts. She wrote to tell her that she intended to punish her in one way or another, sooner or later, and concluded: 'I do not know how to address you. I cannot call you a goose, as geese saved the capitol of Rome, and no amount of cackling on your part would awaken anybody! Nor can I call you an ass, since Balaam's constant companion saw an angel, and recognised it. I can only imagine that you belong to the vegetable tribe, and that all the fizzing and spurting of yours is the result of a vegetable decaying.'

These three later visits were little more than footnotes to the great impact that had been made in the earlier years. Sacheverell went on a lecture tour by himself in the autumn of 1951, visiting the main centres of the East Coast, as well as Houston in Texas, Chicago, Palm Beach and Montreal. From that time the Sitwells considered the Americans as their established friends and admirers; perhaps more loyally so than their own countrymen.

15

IN 1952 Osbert Sitwell celebrated his sixtieth birthday. His massive autobiographical work had put him in the top rank of English contemporary authors, and he was still continuing to write. His volume of 'balnearics', *Wrack at Tidesend*, appeared in that year, and during the next ten years volumes of poetry, his collection of travel essays, *The Four Continents*, and his postscript to the autobiography, *Tales My Father Taught Me*, also appeared. He had made an impressive reputation as a speaker, writer and personality in the United States.

On the day after his birthday, Evelyn Waugh wrote a glowing appreciation in the *Sunday Times*. 'The physical profile is familiar,' he wrote. 'The bland, patrician features have been cast in brass by Mr Frank Dobson and exquisitely limned by Sir Max Beerbohm; they have been photographed by a host of cameramen. The tall, well-dressed figure, the courteous manner, might at first glance belong to any well-to-do cultivated English bachelor of a passing generation. Closer scrutiny reveals a hint of alertness and menace, as though a rattlesnake may be expected round the next corner and the nice conduct of the clouded cane might any minute require a good whack. There is little to indicate the transition that has occurred in the last fifteen years between the *enfant terrible* and the Grand Old Man of English Letters. . . . His natural growth has continued into late middle age so that his latest book has always been his best.

He acquired his reputation first, then seriously settled down to earn it.'

Evelyn Waugh went on, speaking for his post-1914 generation, to make the significant confession that in his youth, in the days when Osbert Sitwell made his first bow to the public, the English literary scene appeared to be dominated by a number of august and overwhelming figures — Hardy, Yeats, Bridges — and yet it was not these *chers maîtres* he and his young friends who were on the threshold of their writing careers wanted above all to know, but rather the Sitwells, 'for they radiated an aura of high spirits, elegance, impudence, unpredictability, above all of sheer enjoyment. Most writers are best known in their work. They are dull dogs to meet and come alive only at their desks, pen in hand. Sir Osbert is a full, rich singular personality first, and a shelf of books second.'

He then pointed out the singular paradox that though the Sitwells had made such an impression, they had scarcely any imitators. 'There is no identifiable School of Sitwell. Three of them was enough.' He and his generation, he maintained, had not found their models in their escapades or in their mannerisms, but had, quite simply, received immense stimulus from the enjoyment and the excitement they generated. 'They declared war on dullness. The British *bourgeoisie* was no longer fair game. Their self-complacency had gone with their power during the war. The Sitwells attacked from within that still depressing section of the upper class that devoted itself solely to sport and politics. By 1939 English society had been revolutionised, lightened and brightened, very largely through the Sitwell influence. They taught the grandees to enjoy their possessions while

they still had them. They made the bore recognised and ab-
horred as the prime social sinner.'

Evelyn Waugh put his finger on another peculiar characteristic of the Sitwells: they had the disdain of aristocrats
for middle-class conventions of behaviour, a contempt that
showed itself nowhere more outrageously than in their frank
enthusiasm for publicity. If most English people are em-
barrassed by it, while a minority guiltily hide the fact that
they long for it, 'the Sitwells left their press-cuttings in
bowls on the drawing-room table. Popular newspapers with
all their absurd vulgarity were just a part of the exciting
contemporary world in which the Sitwells romped. They
were weapons in the total war against dullness.'

This did not of course mean, as Evelyn Waugh was quick
to remind his readers, that they accepted offensives mounted
against them without any counter-offensive. (I hope I have
made it clear in these pages that the very reverse was true.)
Most writers eventually learn, in the course of their careers,
to accept ignorant or ill-mannered abuse in public comment
with the same stoic silence with which they pass over praise
they know to be exaggerated. 'Not so the Sitwells. If those
bowlfuls of press-cuttings survive they will make a rich
store of material for future biographers: controversies on
every conceivable subject, appalling snubs, sledge-hammer
blows on thick skulls and frail insects alike. At one time,
indeed, these ferocious campaigns threatened to undo their
own work of publicity, for editors and critics alike became
timid of mentioning Sir Osbert at all for fear of consequences. . . .'

In his concluding paragraphs, Evelyn Waugh underlines
the other side of Osbert Sitwell's character, all too often
forgotten because so much less public and lending itself so

little to witty anecdote: his 'continuous kindness to other artists'. If one remembers all the vigorously proclaimed antipathies and tirelessly pursued vendettas, one may feel that Evelyn Waugh is a little too sweeping when he goes on to claim that 'there can be few painters or writers or musicians of his period who are not bound to him with gratitude'. Nevertheless the instances he gives are known by Osbert's friends to be chosen out of a multitude. 'A penniless undergraduate, thought at the time a promising poet, was sent down from Oxford. He was immediately invited to make Renishaw his home until he had found his feet. Another young man, now a fine novelist, then unknown, worked in the publishing office which produced Sir Osbert's earlier books. He seemed lonely and dispirited. Sir Osbert invited him to give a dinner party for his friends at his own London house.'

Evelyn Waugh's final judgment on the autobiography was to place it among the masterpieces of our age: 'These calm, leisurely pages were written during the stresses of the second World War. Sir Osbert refused to be hurried: refused to modify his idiosyncratic attitude to life in deference to the debased standards of the time. He knew he had a valuable message to deliver — one of urbane enjoyment. He knew he had an artistic creation to perfect — his portrait of his own father. He knew he had an uniquely rich experience to develop — a lifetime lived in and for the arts. Those five volumes have given him a secure place in English literature.'

During the years that followed, Osbert Sitwell's health began to fail, making him increasingly an invalid, and he eventually left England to live more permanently in Italy, at the Castello di Montegufoni. It is unlikely, however, that his illness has deprived us of any greater achievement than the autobiography, or indeed of the record, as Evelyn Waugh says, of 'a lifetime lived in and for the arts'.

In the early summer of 1966 I paid a visit to him at Montegufoni. Of the fifty or so rooms in the Castle he had only kept open about a dozen, though all were maintained in good repair. It was his habit to settle in his chair every morning at the south-western corner of the little formal garden, known as the Cardinal's Garden, opposite the windows of the great gallery which he uses as his general sitting- and writing-room. There, with a view of vine-covered slopes of the Val di Pesa outside the Castle grounds on one side and a huge deep-pink oleander in the centre of the garden on the other, he would read his papers and letters and be read to by his secretary and constant companion Frank Magro. Behind the little patio begins the wistaria-covered pergola which partly hides the village church, with lizards suddenly darting in and out like flashes of green lightning.

In the east frame of the garden is the entrance to what used to be Lady Ida's bedroom, and is now used as a small dining-room: a prettily decorated double room, the two halves divided by a rather theatrical grotto-work arch, and the ceilings and walls covered with seventeenth-century paintings of an overall tone of subaqueous grey-green. They appear to represent a kind of sky school for extremely mischievous *amorini*, with all the appurtenances of discipline amusingly represented. I could not help thinking of some of the illustrations in Bentley's edition of Gray's *Poems*.

Osbert, who, in his chair piloted by his secretary, conducted a tour of the seemingly endless ground-floor rooms, informed me that all the furniture and pictures, some of great beauty, had been collected by his father or by himself, and that nothing was original to the Castle at the time his father bought it except a handsome dark-glassed mirror in the gallery, and several huge antique terracotta jars intended for olive oil.

Pottering around the lower garden, I met the old gardener, Guido Masti, in his straw hat and apron, and bowed to him. As Osbert has related in his autobiography, he was responsible for saving the Uffizi pictures, which had been stored in the Castle during the war, from the destructive rage of the Nazis when forced to retreat. He had recently been made a 'Cavaliere' by the Italian President — an honour that came to him late, but not too late. I thought to myself, as I saw him bending over the lemon trees in their great tubs, that he was a hero and one of the unsung benefactors of humanity in our age. He smiled in shy and silent embarrassment, when I asked Frank Magro to convey to him my profound respect and admiration.

On the Sunday evening there was a Corpus Christi celebration at the Castle for the villagers. Elia, the widow of Luigi Pestelli, who had for so many years been Osbert's agent and personal servant until he died of cancer, had prepared an altar in the great courtyard of the Castle and arranged tubs of hortensias around it. Osbert stationed himself in his chair in the opening of the French windows facing the altar, with myself and his secretary on either side, while the village procession wound its way up from the church to the courtyard. It was a feudal scene, yet heartfelt; deeply touching was the pleasure the villagers showed in seeing Osbert there to welcome them, in spite of his invalid state.

In *Journey to the Ends of Time* Sacheverell Sitwell records an extraordinary dream he had about his brother, at the time when they were living under the same roof: 'I woke up on a summer morning in my room in Carlyle Square,

Oh! a long time ago! and opening my eyes I saw my brother sitting in a chair beside my bed, sitting there quietly with his hands upon his knees. We were both young, and he was a young man in my dream. I can see his straight hair and long thin face. I thought I had overslept, and that he had come upstairs from his room below, had come upstairs to tease me for being still asleep; and turning on my other side, I shut my eyes and went to sleep again. I heard no noise, no movement in the room, but looking again, after a moment, I saw him close beside me, sitting in the same attitude in a chair upon the right side of my bed. His eyes were shut, as though he was pretending to be asleep, but as I raised myself to look at him, he was not there, and when I turned, gone, too, and as I realized it was a dream I heard him talking in the room below. What did it mean? What was the meaning of my dream? That he was sitting there, so woodenly, at both sides of my bed, first on one side, and then on the other, with his eyes shut, and his hand upon his knees? Was it, I wonder, that he was to write his life, and in large part my life, and call it *Left Hand, Right Hand!*? Was it prophecy of his illness? I have never had another dream like it, and I remember nothing else about that day.'

Since the war, Sacheverell and his wife have continued to live at Weston Hall in Northamptonshire, the family house which has descended to the present generation of Sitwells, almost always through the female line, since the eighteenth century. Georgia Sitwell, in an admirable preface to a collection of family letters found there, says that 'its essential character is a happy conglomeration of every date from 1690 to 1910'. It was handed over to Sacheverell by Sir George in the twenties, and they have lived there ever since 1929. Among many striking portraits in oils it contains one of especial interest in the main living-room, representing that ancestor on his father's side — whose career could not be more completely in contrast with that of his descendant in possession — General Hely-Hutchinson, who defeated Napoleon's armies at the battle of Alexandria in 1801 and so drove the French out of Egypt. For this exploit he was created Lord Hutchinson of Alexandria and Knocklofty. Later, in 1825, he succeeded his brother as Earl of Donoughmore. There is a portrait of this brother also at Weston, and Sir George was wont to point to it and say: 'Any brains there may be in the family come from that man.'

Of Weston, Osbert has written that he has never known a place 'in which you could hear more clearly the heart-beat of other centuries than our own'. The house is not large by the standards of the eighteenth-century landed gentry, and modest indeed by comparison with Renishaw. The main rooms are, however, handsome and give an impression of ample space. It may therefore seem almost perverse that Sacheverell has chosen a small room on the first floor, looking out on the driveway and the beds of old-fashioned roses of which he has made a speciality, as his own lair. Here he has made emergency sleeping quarters, almost in the austerity of a *wagon-lit*, with a neatly enclosed wash-cabinet in one corner equally reminiscent of the *Grands Express Européens*, and works at a small desk amid piles of books that have gathered higgledy-piggledy on the floor. No more assiduous writer can be imagined: when not briefly visiting London or on his travels, he works all day at his imaginative fantasies and the books on art and travel that have continued to pour from his pen since 1945. An idea of his energy of authorship can be glimpsed from the record of the travels he has undertaken with books in view during the last twenty years or so. Apart from the habitual visits to Italy, he and Georgia have journeyed to Holland, Spain, Portugal, Austria, Bavaria, Denmark, Sweden, Turkey, Lebanon, Syria, Persia, Egypt, Jordan, Malta, Madeira, Japan, the Latin American states of Mexico, Guatemala, Ecuador, Peru, Bolivia, Brazil, also Curaçao and the West Indies. In the winter of 1952-3 he made the visit to North America already mentioned, which included lectures (on art) at New York, Boston, Washington, Chicago, Montreal, Louisville, Houston, Charleston, Shreveport (Louisiana) and Palm Beach. In 1961, directly after his Latin American tour, he went to the Far East, visiting India, Ceylon, Thailand, Cambodia and Nepal.

At the luncheon organised by the *Sunday Times* to celebrate his sister Edith's seventieth birthday, Raymond Mortimer remarked at one point: 'I think Sacheverell Sitwell's first poems were perhaps the most *promising* poems written in our lifetime,' and added: 'It seems to me a great tragedy that he has deserted poetry for prose.' Sacheverell, the traditional younger son, might well have replied that one can't keep up a family estate that comes to one in trust and bring up two sons on poetry alone.

During these years Edith Sitwell continued to entertain her friends on a lavish scale at the Sesame Club while visiting London. She had gathered a circle of new, younger friends around her, including the Australian pianist Gordon Watson, the Portuguese poet Alberto de Lacerda, Humphrey Searle who set *Gold Coast Customs* and *The Shadow of Cain* to music, Malcolm Williamson who had been commissioned to make *The English Eccentrics* into an opera,*

---

* This was presented at the Aldeburgh Festival in 1964, and afterwards at the City Temple in London.

the dancer and choreographer Robert Helpmann, and Colin Wilson of *The Outsider* fame. On a famous occasion the American 'Beat' poets, Corso and Ginsberg, conspicuous by their jeans, turtle-neck sweaters and sandals, took luncheon with her at the Sesame: two young poets who did not, for once, need her in any sense for their success, but of whose work she spoke with generous sympathy. Allen Ginsberg's *Howl* in particular impressed her, and she wrote in *Lilliput*: 'I think there is no more important young poet, no young poet of greater gifts writing at this time.' At the same time she conceived a great admiration for the poems of Robert Lowell, and thought his *The Ghost* the greatest poem produced by his generation since the death of Dylan Thomas, on either side of the Atlantic. She discovered, and wrote with the utmost enthusiasm about the young American novelist James Purdy. The new friends she had made in America were always eager to visit her whenever they came to London: it was like paying homage to a Head of State — in this of Poetry. And Mrs Whitney, the wife of the American Ambassador, had become a devoted friend.

She also found new English friends in an older generation: in particular Sir Charles and Lady Snow (Pamela Hansford Johnson), 'Henry Cecil' (Judge Leon) and his wife, Jeanne Stonor, a fellow-Catholic, for the restoration of whose private chapel she gave a reading at the Dorchester in 1957, and Lancelot Law Whyte, physicist and philosopher of science; not to mention Father D'Arcy and Father Caraman, her confessor. Her friendship with Graham Greene, which had begun in 1923 when he was an undergraduate at Oxford, was revived and cemented by her conversion to Catholicism. She had become attached to Jack Lindsay, Australian-born critic and translator, owing to an enthusiastic review

he wrote of *The Shadow of Cain*, though his desire to interest her in certain Communist poems he admired caused
exacerbation at times. Edith always maintained that she
didn't know what was what in politics; but she *did* know
what a thoroughly bad poem was.

In the fifties, Edith found herself out of sympathy with
the new 'Movement', and crossed swords with several of
the leading figures, maintaining that their poetry was trivial,
flat and derivative. The only young poets she confessed
admiration for were Charles Causley and Ted Hughes. Of
Thom Gunn's poems about boys on (motor) bicycles, she
remarked mischievously that Canon Beeching (1859–1919)
had done it all before.

Since her first tour of America in 1948–9, she had continued, in the ever more elusive intervals between public
appearances and the increasing attentions of her 'lunatics'
and those who pestered her to sign manifestoes of protest
against this or that, to write poetry. She also produced her
great anthology, *The Atlantic Book of British and American
Poetry*, which was completed in the spring of 1958, and
what is almost certainly her most remarkable prose work,
The Queens and the Hive, a sequel to *Fanfare for Elizabeth*,
which was published in 1962, the year of her seventy-fifth
birthday and its celebration with a concert in her honour at
the Festival Hall.

Writing of the *Atlantic Book* to her old friend Malcolm
Bullock just before its publication, she said: 'About the
9th of November, I shall be sending you (you will be one
of the only six people I shall be sending it to) my gigantic
anthology in two volumes, the work of my life. It has the
most heavenly early religious poems — some quite unknown outside specialist anthologies, wonderful early love

Montegufoni: a mediaeval courtyard with Signor Masti

Montegufoni: the Cardinal's garden

Jean Cocteau to Edith Sitwell, September 1957

1ᵉ Septembre
1957

'SANTO
St JEAN

Ma très
chère
et si grande
Edith   to the
livre
Collected poems
est un cadeau royal
dans une époque
sordide
Je t'oy Salue

Jean Cocteau
x
(1957)

Jean
x

Edith Sitwell reading her prize-winning poem at the presentation of the Guinness Poetry Awards, 1959 poems, Tudor poems, and Elizabethan and 17th-century poems. Also I claim that I am the first anthologist to represent Clare and Yeats properly. And as for the country ballads and light songs . . . .'

In writing of *Fanfare for Elizabeth*, I stressed the fact that it would be a mistake to judge it as a work of historical research and scholarship. This is just as true of *The Queens and the Hive*, the central theme of which is the clash between Queen Elizabeth I and Mary Queen of Scots. It has as little, and as much, to do with history as *The Duchess of Malfi* or *Richard III*. It is a work of sustained imaginative force, which should be appreciated and judged as the creation of a poet, whose concern is not with such prosaic matters as the inflation of the currency, or inventions in the technique of war, or shifting class-relationships, but with the human soul. The qualities which made *Fanfare for Elizabeth* remarkable are displayed in an even higher degree in this sequel. Edith Sitwell *lives into* the period, its macabre horrors and cruelties no less than its public triumphs and aesthetic splendours, with their endless devious undertones of ruthless political and religious intrigue, almost as if she had been through it all herself. She shows an empathy that continually astonishes for the individual dramas of love, ambition and despair, illuminating them with a penetrating compassion and an unfailing sense of bitter dramatic irony. The impression that the book leaves is more of darkness than of light, the darkness of a heavily thunder-clouded day in which the skies are blotted out, filled now with bursts of music and now with hideous cries, out of which phosphorescent figures emerge, such as Leicester, Essex and Darnley, and vanish again into the darkness. Sometimes a shudder seems to run through a whole scene as she describes it, using quotations from contemporary letters, despatches and reports to heighten her dramatic effects, her agonised immediacy. It is Jacobean rather than Elizabethan in tone, and the poet it most frequently recalls is Webster.

It is perhaps worth commenting here that crimes of violence always had a peculiar fascination for her. Long before she was confined to a chair, she had ceased to go out — even at Renishaw she never took a walk in the garden; but she liked to be taken out in her car, and one of her favourite drives was to 10 Rillington Place.

Before that, in the Queen's Birthday Honours of 1954, Edith had been made a Dame Commander of the Order of the British Empire, an honour that gave her immense pleasure and satisfaction. She wrote to Sir John Gielgud: 'I was so happy to get your most kind telegram of congratulations. I think it gave me more pleasure than all the others coming from a great artist whom I so much admire.' There is a story that, on one of her later visits to America, a guest at a party said: 'Why do you call yourself Dame Edith?' Without hesitation Edith replied: 'I don't. The Queen of England does.'

In 1957, as I have already observed, her seventieth birthday had been celebrated by the *Sunday Times*, with a luncheon at which she was interviewed by a number of friends and admirers. The taped interview, in a condensed form, was then published in the newspaper on Sunday, 1 September.

Those present were Raymond Mortimer, Frederick Ashton and William Plomer, with myself in the chair. Several more who had been asked were unable, for one reason or another, to come, including Sir William Walton. Leonard Russell and Jack Lambert of the *Sunday Times* were also there, in the capacity (as they described it) of 'bottle-holders'. Raymond Mortimer's introductory flourish set the tone: 'When I was a young man,' he said, 'Edith Sitwell was considered the most dangerous Bolshevik, the terror of Colonels, the horror of golf clubs, causing panic among dog-lovers . . . .'

Edith herself, for some reason or other, seemed not entirely at ease; but as the discussion warmed up she produced some extremely interesting information about her life and career, and the influences which had meant most to her. She insisted that she was essentially a *country* poet, that the springs of her poetry came from her childhood and youth in country scenes, while T. S. Eliot, she felt, had always been a *town* poet. She spoke of the great influence that painters had had on her development as an artist, especially Picasso, Tchelitchew and Severini. Greater, however, she maintained, had been the influence of music, especially of Debussy and Ravel. From music, she claimed, she had learned about phrasing in poetry: nearly all the great musicians had used long phrases in their compositions, and from them she had understood the importance of long lines, especially in her later work. She also mentioned that she found Benjamin Britten's setting of *Still Falls the Rain* 'so moving that when I hear it I relive the awful experience of having written it'. She discussed various poets, remarking that George Peele — introduced to her by Sacheverell — had meant a great deal to her in her early career; that 'I always think I am not going to like Wordsworth when I read him, and then I adore him when I do read him'; on the Sitwell *bête noir*, Matthew Arnold, she was unrelenting. She also commented on the fact that some poets lend themselves marvellously to reciting in public, and others scarcely at all — instancing Hopkins as an example of the latter. William Plomer, at this point, re-marked on her own beautiful and original way of speaking poetry, and Raymond Mortimer added that American friends of his who had heard her read the sleep-walking scene from *Macbeth* said the blood froze in their arteries at the very thought of it.

Edith was now entering a new phase in her career: as a bizarrely impressive, sibylline public figure, especially in more and more frequent television appearances, in which her opinion was asked on almost every subject under the sun, and her pungent, idiosyncratic replies treasured. She was awarded the Foyle Poetry Prize in 1958, and in 1959 she gave a recitation at the Edinburgh Festival. In spite of care-ful rehearsal, she had trouble with the audience at first, seve-ral members of which shouted that they could not hear her. 'There was a rumpus at Edinburgh — but I won. *Always*, no matter who recites, there are two deaf old women who say they can't hear! On the occasions when I recited with Dylan, as soon as we met in the artists' room, Dylan would say to me "What side of the house do you think the Afflicted Pair have got themselves to?' And he would draw his thumbnail across his throat as one cutting it, and would utter a loud snarl. Oddly enough, the Edinburgh rumpus ended in the audience taking a fancy to me, and I was told the largest crowd that had waited for any artist at all, waited for me, outside, for three quarters of an hour. There must have been at least 500 people.'

In the same year she had a famous interview with John Freeman in his 'Face to Face' television series. In this inter-view she began by observing: 'I can't wear fashionable clothes. I'm a throw-back to remote ancestors of mine, and I really would look so extraordinary if I wore coats and skirts. I would be followed for miles, and people would doubt the existence of the Almighty.' A little later on she remarked: 'I was a changeling, you see. When I was born my mother would have liked to turn me into a doll. It was a great disappointment to them that I was not a boy. If I'd been Chinese I should have been exposed on the mountain with my feet bound.' She followed this rather telescoped view of the disadvantages of being born female, with the declaration that: 'To be an artist is a terribly painful thing. I mean, the great leaves break out of me — you see, one has a perpetual resurrection in one's life, as the art returns to one, after long deadness.'

Later that year, in an interview with Robert Muller, she said: 'When I appeared on "Face to Face" I received 200 fan letters. I'm a shy person, but I feel no shyness in front of cameras. . . . The reason that I'm thought an eccentric is that I won't be taught my job by a lot of little pipsqueaks. . . . I am simply alive, and *they* don't like people to be alive. Nobody has ever been more alive than I! I am like an unpopular electric eel in a pond full of flatfish.'

In May 1960 she was the guest of honour in the television programme 'This is Your Life', with T. Leslie Jackson as producer and Eamonn Andrews as master of ceremonies. In theory, in this programme the person to be honoured was not supposed to know that just that was going to happen; but in view of her age and the state of her health it was decided to let Dame Edith into the secret and obtain her consent. Her brother Sacheverell was one of those who spoke, summing her up as a person who had always been absolutely fearless, and who had determined at an early age to be remarkable and had succeeded; with her cousin Veronica Gilliatt who recalled the twenty-first birthday treat given for Edith at Doncaster racecourse, during which she kept her back to the races the whole time; Geoffrey Gorer, who described the occasion in the late twenties when she had been mistaken by the crowds outside the Finsbury Empire for Nellie Wallace; Cecil Beaton, who paid a tribute to Edith's marvellous patience when he was taking his eccentric photographs of her as a young woman; Marjorie Proops from the *Daily Mirror* (where her first poem had appeared); Professor Anthony Bernard of the London Chamber Orchestra, who had been in the audience at the second private performance of *Façade*, in February 1922, at the house of Mrs Robert Matthias; Diana Matthias, whose duty it had been to look after Edith at that performance; Tom Driberg, who painted an amusing picture of the parties at Pembridge Mansions with their gallons of strong tea and 'mountains of penny buns'; and John Robins, Osbert's former batman and personal valet, who remembered how Edith, when at Renishaw, had spent much of every day in bed, working at her poems with books strewn all round her and logs blazing in the fireplace even in August. A special surprise for Edith was the appearance of Velma Roy, the coloured maid who had looked after her in her Los Angeles hotel and formed a deep attachment to her, flown over by the B.B.C. for the occasion. At the end, Osbert, with Edith's two nephews Reresby and Francis, made their bow.

This programme was an event which stirred deep emotions.

During and since her American tours, Edith had continued, as I have said, to write poetry. Some of this seemed, even to her fondest admirers, merely to repeat what she had already achieved in that supreme period which produced *The Shadow of Cain* and *Eurydice*. She was, I think, looking for a new way, which did not come easily to her, exhausted as she was by travel, illness and her still unceasing battles with the Philistines and her bores and 'lunatics'. Nevertheless, it is difficult not to feel, reading her two last published volumes of poetry, *Gardeners and Astronomers* (1953) and *The Outcasts* (1962),* that some new impulses were stirring, that she was beginning to move beyond her previous work. In such poems as *The Death of Prometheus* and *At the Crossroads*, there is a savage bitterness of contempt for what is mean and petty in life in its struggle against what is generous and noble, that reminds one of the mood of *Gold Coast Customs*. And in several of the songs, such as *La Bella Bona Roba* and *The Yellow Girl*, a lyrical purity re-emerges, allied with a now absolutely effortless seeming mastery of music and texture, making discoveries of astonishing freshness and resonance.

When her *Collected Poems*, a volume which contained more than 400 pages of poetry, came out in 1957, many critics were struck by the range and variety of her work in its four main phases. Cyril Connolly wrote: 'I read *The Sleeping Beauty* when it first appeared. . . . There is nothing so moving as when we absorb in youth a contemporary work of art hot from the press, and so I put off re-reading *The Sleeping Beauty* for fear of being disappointed. Yet now it overwhelms me as an astonishing *tour de force*.' And he concluded: 'When we come to compare the collected poems of Dame Edith Sitwell with those of Yeats, or Mr Eliot or Professor Auden it will be found that hers have the purest poetical content of them all.'

The story of Edith's last years has been written with

* Published in America as *Music and Ceremonies* in 1963, with the addition of several poems not included in the English edition.

touching affection and sympathy by her secretary Elizabeth Salter. Her health gradually deteriorated, though her courage and her capacity to make comic incidents out of her frequent falls did not. Her morale was worn down in particular by the almost incessant noise of banging and hammering in the building next door to the Sesame Club, which was being reconditioned. Eventually, she was persuaded to move to a flat in Hampstead, where she was surrounded by cats, some of them strays who had come to her as if by instinct, knowing they would find a good home with her. After Elizabeth Salter had made several trips of exploration to Paris, to Helen and Evelyn Rootham's flat, and had made the astonishing discovery of an enormous cache of Edith's early manuscript books and many of Pavel Tchelitchew's drawings and paintings, the miraculous portrait, in profile, of Edith as a young woman hung in the flat where she could see it from her bed. It was one of the few works by Tchelitchew which she kept. She lived constantly above her income, and in 1962 had a collection of thirty-nine works by Tchelitchew auctioned at Sotheby's — a sale which brought in just over £10,000. She had begun to write *Taken Care of*, an autobiography she had long delayed embarking on owing to her profound anxiety not to compete in any way with Osbert's *Left Hand, Right Hand!* It soon became clear she had left it too late: the book as it eventually appeared cannot be considered as anything more than a rough sketch of what she would have liked to write if her health and her powers of mind had lasted a few more years.

Edith's pleasure in inviting large groups of her friends to luncheon or tea or drinks continued; but these occasions exhausted her, and she was obliged to spend much of her time in bed. Attacks of bronchitis and other ills frequently assailed her; each time she recovered it seemed a miracle. On one occasion, in 1963, she told me that through her semi-conscious state she heard the doctor say to the nurse: 'Well, if she gets through tonight she has a fifty-fifty chance' — and thought they must be talking about someone else.

Even in this weakened state, like an old war-horse she responded with awakened zest when she heard from afar the trumpets of a literary controversy. Her darts of repartee often, now, fell wide of the mark, but nevertheless retained an unmistakable and unique flavour. She had for long held persons (however dear) who sneezed or coughed in her presence as personally, almost criminally responsible for any cold or chill she caught. In the serious illness I refer to above, she was convinced that the trouble had started when her neighbour in the flat above had left the bath-tap on and water had started to drip through her ceiling. She observed to me: 'I wrote to him and said I had always had sympathy with the working-classes, but now I felt more like the mother of Lord Berners, who had remarked about daddy-long-legs: "I always feel sorry for them, such long legs and so clumsy."' This was written with her tongue in her cheek, and she would, I think, have been horrified if the recipient had taken it *au pied de la lettre*. Nevertheless, for those who did not know Edith, such ripostes could be baffling.

After her disastrous trip to Australia, from which she returned seriously ill in the spring of 1963, she moved to a little house in Keats Grove, far more suitable and more homely, where Elizabeth Salter and her devoted Irish nurse, Sister Farquhar, looked after her in her last months. She named it Bryher House, after her great friend and patroness of many years' standing, reputed millionairess and author of historical novels. Her courage was as extraordinary as her sense of humour, and she bore mean and cruel attacks on her literary reputation, which were made with incredible bad taste when everyone knew she was at death's door, with bitter dignity. She knew that she had many champions who would reply for her, even though she could not herself. She also knew she had accomplished her life's work, in sixty years devoted to poetry.

I have left to the last the climax of Edith Sitwell's career, which came with the Celebration Concert that was given in honour of her seventy-fifth birthday at the Royal Festival Hall on Tuesday, 9 October 1962; because it was a triumph not only for her but in a sense also for the whole 'delightful but deleterious trio' of so long ago who shared in the acclaim, and the last time all three appeared in public together. What was especially remarkable was the enthusiasm of a younger generation, who formed a high proportion of the audience in the packed Festival Hall. All the seats had been sold.

The Concert, which was organised by the Park Lane Group — a society which had made a name for presenting talented young artists in contemporary or rarely heard music — in association with Edith's nephew Francis, consisted of a first part in which Edith read seven of her post-1939 poems, *Her Blood Colours My Cheeks*, *The Queen Bee Sighed*, *Most Lovely Shade*, *Choric Song*, *Prothalamium*, *A Young Girl's Song in Winter* and *Praise We Great Men*. This was followed by Benjamin Britten's setting of *Still Falls the Rain*, with Peter Pears as the tenor, Neill Sanders at the horn, and Stephen Bishop (replacing Benjamin Britten himself who was ill) at the piano. The first part ended with Rossini's 'Sonata No. 1 in G' and Mozart's 'Divertimento in D', played by the English Chamber Orchestra under the direction of Emanuel Hurwitz. The second part, after the interval, was entirely devoted to *Façade*, in its complete version of twenty-one pieces, with Sir William Walton conducting the English Chamber Orchestra and Irene Worth and Sebastian Shaw as speakers.

The audience seemed absolutely determined from the very start to give Edith Sitwell a tremendous ovation. She was wheeled in, in her bathchair, by her nephew, as the lights went down and two spotlights fell upon the frail yet still commanding figure in her scarlet and gold accoutrements. Her voice was clear, assured, musical in a contralto way, the loudspeaker arrangements conveying it without fault to every part of the auditorium. The reception was overwhelming: she had to be wheeled back several times to take her calls, and gave little gestures each time like shy blessings. When, a few minutes later, she reached the box where the family was assembled, the audience spotted her and broke into furious applause once more.

The *pièce de résistance* of the evening was, of course, the complete performance of *Façade* after the interval. The tense audience waited, like a lion at the approach of its keeper with food, for the first bars of the first poem, *Hornpipe*: one could almost feel a savage excitement mounting. They responded to every turn of wit, every fantastic image and rhyme, with a kind of low growl of laughter and delight. No one who was there will ever forget the occasion, the last time Edith Sitwell was able to take part in her immortal creation, nor the way the younger part of the audience lapped up the free-wheeling fancy, the impudent gaiety and wit, and the perfectly matched music. *Façade* ought, by all the rules, to have died with the twenties; instead, there it was, the original outrage it created a matter of ridiculous history, delighting a different England after the passage of nearly forty years, perhaps even more than at its original performances, because a quality it radiated had become so much rarer and more precious in the interval.

At the end, when the performers had taken many rapturous calls, the audience spontaneously rose and turned towards the Sitwell box, and started clapping. A spotlight was thrown on Edith and her brothers, and the applause became deafening.

Over twenty years before, in connection with a question about advertising of her books, Edith had written to Rache Lovat Dickson at Macmillan's: 'Osbert, Sachie and I are extremely displeased when we are treated as if our works are a mass production. We do not like to be treated as if we were an aggregate Indian god, with three sets of legs and arms, but otherwise indivisible.'

The years, of course, had shown that the differences between the three as writers were far greater than the similarities that originally bound them together. Nevertheless, it cannot be denied that the conviction in the minds of the public that they were a kind of 'aggregate Indian god' persisted: more, perhaps, due to their attitudes than to their actual productions. Aristocrats who defected to the arts were more common in the sixties than forty years before, but the Sitwells still appeared as the pioneers. The words that Arnold Bennett had written at the very beginning of the story still hovered in the air above their heads: 'They exult in a scrap. Battle is in the curve of their nostrils. They issue forth from their bright pavilions and demand trouble. And few spectacles are more touching than their gentle, quiet, surprised, ruthless demeanour when they get it, as they generally do.' And whatever the more academic critics might say, the point that Evelyn Waugh so shrewdly defined in his article remained valid. They had declared war on dullness, and a whole generation had received 'immense stimulus from the enjoyment and excitement they generated'.

SELECT BIBLIOGRAPHY

The abbreviations are those used in the References below, where the page-numbers given are those of the British editions.

EDITH SITWELL

The Mother, B. H. Blackwell, Oxford, 1915

Twentieth Century Harlequinade (with Osbert Sitwell), B. H. Blackwell, Oxford, 1915

Wheels (First cycle, 1916; Second cycle, 1917; Third and Fourth cycles, 1919; Fifth cycle, 1920; Sixth cycle, 1921)

Façade, Favil Press, 1922

Bucolic Comedies, Duckworth, 1923

The Sleeping Beauty, Duckworth, 1924; New York: Alfred A. Knopf, 1924

Troy Park, Duckworth, 1925; New York: Alfred A. Knopf, 1925

Elegy on Dead Fashion, Duckworth, 1926

Rustic Elegies, Duckworth, 1927; New York: Alfred A. Knopf, 1927

Gold Coast Customs, Duckworth, 1929; Boston: Houghton Mifflin, 1929

AP   *Alexander Pope*, Faber, 1930; New York: W. W. Norton, 1962

The Pleasures of Poetry, Duckworth (First series, 1930; Second series, 1931; Third series, 1932)

EE   *The English Eccentrics*, Faber, 1933; Boston: Houghton Mifflin, 1933

AMP   *Aspects of Modern Poetry*, Duckworth, 1934

VE   *Victoria of England*, Faber, 1936; Boston: Houghton Mifflin, 1936

SPE   *Selected Poems*, Duckworth, 1936; Boston: Houghton Mifflin, 1937

ILUBS   *I Live Under a Black Sun*, Gollancz, 1937; New York: Doubleday, Doran & Co., 1938

Trio   *Trio* (with Osbert and Sacheverell Sitwell), Macmillan, 1938
        Edith Sitwell's Anthology, Gollancz, 1940
        Look! The Sun, Gollancz, 1941
        Street Songs, Macmillan, 1942
PN   *A Poet's Notebook*, Macmillan, 1943; Boston: Atlantic–Little,
            Brown, 1950
        Planet and Glow-worm, Macmillan, 1944
        Green Song, Macmillan, 1944; New York: Vanguard Press,
            1946
        The Song of the Cold, Macmillan, 1945; New York, Vanguard
            Press, 1948
        Fanfare for Elizabeth, Macmillan, 1946; New York: Mac-
            millan, 1962
        The Shadow of Cain, Lehmann, 1947
        A Notebook on William Shakespeare, Macmillan, 1948; Boston:
            Beacon Press, 1961
Cel   *A Celebration for Edith Sitwell*, ed. José Garcia Villa, New
            Directions, New York, 1948
        The American Genius, Lehmann, 1951
        Gardeners and Astronomers, Macmillan, 1953; New York:
            Vanguard Press, 1953
CPE   *Collected Poems*, Macmillan, 1957; New York: Vanguard
            Press, 1954
        The Atlantic Book of British and American Poetry, Gollancz,
            1958; Boston: Atlantic–Little, Brown, 1958
        The Outcasts, Macmillan, 1962
        The Queens and the Hive, Macmillan, 1962; Boston: Atlantic–
            Little, Brown, 1962
TCO   *Taken Care of*, Hutchinson, 1965; New York; Atheneum, 1965

                        OSBERT SITWELL

        Twentieth Century Harlequinade (with Edith Sitwell), B. H.
            Blackwell, Oxford, 1915
        The Winstonburg Line, Hendersons, 1919
TF   *Triple Fugue*, Grant Richards, 1924; New York: George H.
            Doran, 1925
        Discursions, Grant Richards, 1925; New York: George H.
            Doran, 1925
BB   *Before the Bombardment*, Duckworth, 1926; New York: G. H.
            Doran, 1926

England Reclaimed, Duckworth, 1927; Boston: Atlantic–Little, Brown

A A S   *All at Sea* (with Sacheverell Sitwell), Duckworth, 1927; New York: Doubleday, Doran & Co., 1928

The Man who Lost Himself, Duckworth, 1929; New York: Coward–McCann, 1930

w c   *Winters of Content*, Duckworth, 1932; Philadelphia: J. B. Lippincott, 1932

M S   *Miracle on Sinai*, Duckworth, 1933; New York: Henry Holt, 1934

B   *Brighton*, Faber, 1935; Boston: Houghton Mifflin, 1935

E W M   *Escape With Me!*, Macmillan, 1939; New York; Harrison–Hilton Books, 1940

A Place of One's Own, Macmillan, 1941

S P O   *Selected Poems, Old and New*, Duckworth, 1943

L H R H   *Left Hand, Right Hand!*, Macmillan, 1945; Boston: Atlantic–Little, Brown, 1944

L M S   *A Letter to My Son*, Home & Van Thal, 1944

S T   *The Scarlet Tree*, Macmillan, 1946; Boston: Atlantic–Little, Brown, 1946

G M   *Great Morning*, Macmillan, 1948; Boston: Atlantic–Little, Brown, 1947

L N R   *Laughter in the Next Room*, Macmillan, 1949; Boston: Atlantic–Little, Brown, 1948

N E   *Noble Essences*, Macmillan, 1950; Boston: Atlantic–Little, Brown, 1950

Wrack at Tidesend, Macmillan, 1952; New York: Caedmon, 1953

F C   *The Four Continents*, Macmillan, 1954; New York: Harper & Row, 1954

On the Continent, Macmillan, 1958

Tales My Father Taught Me, Hutchinson, 1962; Boston: Atlantic–Little, Brown, 1962

SACHEVERELL SITWELL

Dr Donne and Gargantua, first canto, Favil Press, 1921 (Canto the second, Favil Press, 1923; Canto the third, Shakespeare Head Press, 1926; The first six cantos, Duckworth, 1930)

Southern Baroque Art, Grant Richards, 1924; New York: Alfred A. Knopf, 1924

ASD *All Summer in a Day*, Duckworth, 1926; New York; George H. Doran, 1926

CF *The Cyder Feast*, Duckworth, 1927; New York: George H. Doran, 1927

The Gothick North, Duckworth, 2 vols 1929–30; Boston: Houghton Mifflin, 1929

Mozart, Peter Davies, 1932; New York: Appleton & Co., 1932

CGA *Canons of Giant Art*, Faber, 1933

Touching the Orient, Duckworth, 1934

M *Mauretania*, Duckworth, 1940

SPL *Sacred and Profane Love*, Faber, 1940

SM *Splendours and Miseries*, Faber, 1943

SPS *Selected Poems*, Duckworth, 1948

JET *Journey to the Ends of Time*, vol. 1, Cassell, 1959; New York: Random House, 1959

REFERENCES

1 magnified: LNR 184
1 music: LNR 192
2 drivel: LNR 192
2 stopped: LNR 193–4
2 mad: TCO 122
3 cockade: CPE 120
3 weep: CPE 137
5 aviary: Harold Acton, *Memoirs of an Aesthete* 128 (Methuen, 1948)
6 poesia: LNR 198
7 preceding us: TCO 123
7 patterns: Decca Mono LXT 2977
7 leg-pulling: TCO 123
7 folk: *Journals of Arnold Bennett 1921–1928* 130 (Cassell, 1933)
9 gaiety: LNR 188–9
9 discovery: LNR 191
12 encouragement: E.S. to A.B. 14 Nov 1922
12 reviewers: Frank Swinnerton, *The Georgian Literary Scene* 349 (Heinemann, 1935)
16 hedges: ASD 15–16
17 part of me: LHRH 104
17 Crown: TCO 32
17 mice: TCO 33
18 round us: LHRH 10–11
19 orchards: LHRH 124
20 peril: TCO 64
21 silence: TCO 64–5

22 death: TCO 26–7
23 inhabitant: ILUBS 49–51 (TCO 23–4)
24 hedges: LHRH 3–4
25 enough: ST 85–6
26 sands; TCO 18
26 blood: SPE 10
26 stone: ST 85
27 over it: ST 85
28 everything: ST 85
28 edges: LHRH 82
29 icicles: LHRH 82
30 put to sea: LHRH 115–17
30 light: LHRH 117
32 left over: TF 44–6
33 describes: BB 66
34 attack: BB 260
36 mass: ASD 227–8
37 imagine: ASD 207–8
38 balanced: ASD 235
38 comedy: ASD 237
39 within her: LHRH 98
40 deserted them: LHRH 90
41 world: TCO 40
42 else: TCO 39
42 over it: TCO 43
43 texture: TCO 43
43 from him: E.S. to. J.L. undated
43 childhood: ST 157
43 friend: ST 146
45 gold: TCO 79
45 masters: ST 257

46 beauty: GM 237
46 *Khovanshchina*: GM 237
47 expense: Virginia Woolf, *Roger Fry: A Biography* 153–4 (Hogarth Press, 1940)
47 movement: GM 235
48 Nijinsky: GM 241
49 century: GM 140
49 wives: GM 208
50 scene: GM 256–7
50 extinction: GM 227
51 quarter: GM 245–6
52 easily: ST 228
52 Marches: ST 248
53 people in it: LHRH 179
55 experienced: LNR 115
55 fantasy: LNR 115
56 mouth: LNR 116
56 own: LNR 117
57 to us: LNR 118–19
58 sticks: ST 175–6
60 teased: LHRH 221
60 ribbons: LHRH 223
61 hat: TCO 50
61 sittings: TCO 51
61 nowhere: Cecil Beaton, *Photobiography* 42–3 (Odhams, 1951)
65 syncopation: LNR 17–18
65 sufferance: TCO 86
66 gentleness: LNR 19–20
67 thoughtfully: TCO 85–6
67 pelican: LNR 22
68 discomfort: TCO 83
68 June: TCO 89
68 candle: TCO 89
69 monologue: TCO 89–90
69 Siamese cat: TCO 90
70 disinfectants: LNR 38–9
72 newspapers: LNR 147–8
73 close: David Garnett, *The Familiar Faces* 22–4 (Chatto & Windus, 1962)
75 stage: LNR 148–9
75 prostitution: LNR 155
76 despair: LNR 156
77 public: LNR 157–9
77 shilling: LNR 154
79 elders: LNR 172
79 unusual: LNR 172
79 myself: LNR 172
79 consideration: LNR 176
80 learning: LRN 178
80 music: LNR 170
80 asked: LNR 253
81 birthright: LNR 349
82 screen: LNR 257–8
82 alleges: LNR 260–1
83 aren't any GM 75–6
83 made: GM 155
84 dream: GM 155
84 music: GM 172
85 horizon: GM 174–5
86 house: LNR 276
86 home: LNR 296
86 much: E.G. to S.S. quoted in LNR 296
87 details: TCO 44, 49
88 preceding us: CPE xv
89 seraphim: CPE 78
89 Apollo: CPE 19
90 night: CPE 23
90 freedom: Edwin Muir, *Transition* 157 (Hogarth Press, 1926)
90 give us: ibid. 151
91 sank he: CPE 139
92 land: CPE 144–5
93 lair: Edward Lear, *Nonsense*

Songs and Stories 81–2 (Warne, 9th edn n.d.)

94 die: CPE 178–80
95 dies: CPE 229
96 last: ASD 61
96 simplicity: ASD 56
97 answer: ASD 42
97 rage: CPE 174–7
97 lost: CPE 174
98 comfort me: CPE 176
101 heard of them: E.S. to T.D. 27 Jan 1927
104 melted: E.S. to C.A. 2 Apr 1941
104 painters: Acton 130
105 men: Acton 130
105 encounters: Acton 131
106 development: E.S. to H.A. undated
108 life: Peter Quennell, *The Sign of the Fish* 29 (Collins, 1960)
108 habitat: Quennell 31
109 produced: NE 238–9
111 starved: CPE xxxv–xxxvi
112 cones: CPE 237–8
113 die: CPE 245–6
113 history: *The Letters of W. B. Yeats* ed. Allan Wade 776 (Hart-Davis, 1954)
114 marching on: CPE 253
114 birth: SPE 47
115 lost: Dilys Powell, *Descent from Parnassus* 130 (Cresset Press, 1934)
116 hell: TCO 135
118 against them: AP 16
119 leaves: AP 265
121 rock: ILUBS 41–3
121 rain: ILUBS 204–5

122 firmament: ILUBS 77
122 leaves: ILUBS 88
122 crowd: EE 285
124 St Giles: VE 162
124 writing it: E.S. to V.G. 23 Nov 1934
124 talker: LNR 31
125 nest: TCO 100
125 appreciation: Wyndham Lewis, *The Apes of God* 123 (Nash & Grayson, 1931)
126 War: Lewis 565
127 contemplating him: AMP 31
127 majesty: AMP 68
128 pools: AMP 101–2
128 movement: AMP 179
128 labelled: AMP 181
130 letter: E.S. to C.A. undated
132 Grigson: E.S. to R.B. 16 Mar 1935
132 years: *Trio* 121
133 jaguar: *Trio* 106
133 cricket: *Trio* 131
134 used: *Trio* 144
135 must have: Gertrude Stein, *The Autobiography of Alice B. Toklas* 250 (John Lane, 1933)
136 ferocity: TCO 139
136 others: TCO 138
137 head: TCO 139
137 vistas: E.S. to V.G. 23 Nov 1934
138 Michelangelo: see Parker Tyler, *The Divine Comedy of Pavel Tchelitchew* 338 (Fleet Publishing Corporation, New York, 1967)
138 began: TCO 141

146 smoke: MS 252–3
147 upon it: 349
147 never met: AAS 37
148 Cant: AAS 41
151 bull: AAS 13
152 rose: LMS 6
152 thrift: LMS 28
152 musician: LMS 20
153 starve: LMS 21
153 paradise: LMS 16
153 victories: LMS 9
156 vanished: SPE 7
157 itself: SPO 148–9
157 hand: SPO 11
158 war: NE 108
158 to take: NE 108–9
159 replaced them: SPO 8
160 men: SPO 59–60
160 shades: SPO 60–1
162 flowers: SPO 79
162 hill: SPO 113
163 been away: SPO 95–6
165 shadow: CF 37
168 death: CGA 102
168 peace: CGA 106
169 bees: CGA 108–9
169 only dead: CGA 109
170 manifests: SPS v–vi
173 type: WC 133–4
174 vulgar: WC 136–7
175 triumphs: WC 226–7
176 half-wits: B 105
176 next: B 105–6
177 militant: EWM vii
177 weapons: FC 237–8
178 amusement: EWM vii
179 home: EWM 196
179 conquerors: EWM 202
182 recall: M 27, 35
184 nuns: SPL 146

184 blue sea: SM 17
185 ever done: SM 225
186 morning: SM 76
186 rules: SM 257
190 disaster: LMS 10
191 war: *Cel* 64
191 intensity: *Cel* 21–2
192 sun: CPE 274
192 sky: CPE 276
192 Cross: CPE 272
193 hymns: *Cel* 16
194 man: *Cel* 114–15
195 stages: TCO 153–4
195 door: CPE 372
195 philosophic poem: *Cel* 66
195 being: *Demetrios Capetanakis: A Greek Poet in England* 91 (Lehmann, 1947)
195 existence: *Capetanakis*, 92
198 nearer to me: E.S. to J.L. 6 Apr 1943
199 deafening: John Lehmann, *I am my Brother* 280–1 (Longmans, 1960)
199 forget it: E.M.F. to J.L. undated
200 miracle to me: E.S. to J.L. 8 Nov 1943
200 window: E.S. to J.L. 10 May 1944
200 disgust: E.S. to H.A. undated
200 month: E.S. to J.L. 25 Jan 1944
201 original: E.S. to J.L. 28 Aug 1944
201 Oh-ow: E.S. to J.L. 24 Aug 1945
201 went away: E.S. to J.L. 15 Jun 1948

202 nowadays: E.S. to J.L. 7 Jul 1944
202 case: E.S. to J.L. Aug 1947
202 wings: E.S. to J.L. 13 Aug 1947
204 fatal: Cyril Connolly, *The Condemned Playground* 267 (Routledge, 1945)
208 world: E.S. to M.B. 24 Jan 1944
209 vitality: E.S. to M.B. 17 Mar 1945
209 wrong: E.S. to M.B. May 1945
210 read it: E.S. to J.L. 2 Sep 1944
210 girl: E.S. to J.L. 29 Aug 1945
211 greatly: E.S. to J.L. 28 May 1943
211 suppose: E.S. to J.L. 8 Feb 1944
212 going through: E.S. to J.L. 9 Mar 1944
212 speak: *Capetanakis* 37, 41
212 life for me: E.S. to J.L. undated
213 expected: TCO 167
213 soundly hit: TCO 168
214 mean: TCO 168–9
216 let us down: E.S. to J.L. 11 Dec 1946
217 blue sky: *The Journals of Denton Welch* 8–9 (Hamish Hamilton, 1952)
217 feeling: Welch, *Journals* 16
217 fumbles: Denton Welch, *Maiden Voyage* v (Routledge, 1943)
217 must think: Welch, *Journals* 54
218 sentence: Welch, *Journals* 65
218 gloom: Welch, *Journals* 66
218 lamplight: PN v
219 wear before: E.S. to J.L. 12 Dec 1944
220 sort of book: E.S. to J.L. 15 Sep 1947
220 translated: E.S. to M.B. 27 Jan 1948
221 isn't so: E.S. to J.L. 11 Jan 1948
223 figured in it: LHRH v
223 generation: LHRH ix
224 every sort: LHRH ix–x
224 stable: LHRH 323–4
225 animals: LNR 328
230 in itself: L. P. Hartley in *The Times Literary Supplement* 6 Aug 1954
231 fascination for him: ibid.
232 only be lost: LNR 137
233 desire to play: GM 151
233 of that kind: GM 44
236 resignation: GM 45–6
237 read them: E.S. to R.G. undated
238 law about it: 'How America "got" me', *Daily Express* 24 Feb 1927
239 America: E.S. to J.L. 23 Jun 1948
239 office: E.S. to J.L. Aug 1948
240 Communion: E.S. to J.L. 29 Jul 1948
240 Time: E.S. to J.L. 12 Aug 1948
240 under my feet: E.S. to J.L. 23 Oct 1948
240 country: TCO 174

241 Montegufoni: see Tyler, *Tchelitchew* 460–70

241 polite: E.S. to J.L. 12 Dec 1948

242 friendliness: E.S. to J.L. 6 Jan 1949

243 performance: E.S. to J.L. Feb 1949

244 turban: *Life* 6 Dec 1948 165–6

244 and you will: TCO 176

247 4.30: E.S. to J.L. 2 Dec 1950

247 happiness: TCO 181

247 swan: TCO 181

248 Ophelia: TCO 183

248 infuriating: E.S. to M.B. 19 Feb 1951

249 records: E.S. to J.L. May 1953

249 with him: E.S. to J.L. 23 May 1953

250 damnation: TCO 181

251 dented: E.S. to J.L. 5 Feb 1954

251 decaying: TCO 180

255 literature: Evelyn Waugh in the *Sunday Times* 7 Dec 1952

258 about that day: JET 6

258 1690 to 1910: *Dear Miss Heber* ed. Francis Bamford with introductions by Georgia and Sacheverell Sitwell xvii (Constable, 1936)

259 our own: LHRH 40

261 this time: 'Of Wrath and Writers', *Lilliput* Nov 1959

263 songs: E.S. to Capt. Sir M.B. 13 Oct 1959

264 admire: E.S. to Sir J.G. 14 Jun 1954

266 500 people: E.S. to J.L. Sep 1959

269 them all: Cyril Connolly in the *Sunday Times* 29 Jul 1957

274 indivisible: E.S. to R.L.D. 14 Jul 1949 in *Letters to Macmillan* ed. Simon Nowell-Smith 355 (Macmillan, 1967)

274 generally do: *Adelphi* Aug 1923

275 generated: Waugh, *Sunday Times* 7 Dec 1952

INDEX

In this index E = Edith, O = Osbert and S = Sacheverell